ALUMNI

ONLINE ENGAGEMENT

101

Strategies to Manage Alumni Engagement from Cradle to Grave!

Don Philabaum

ALUMNI
ONLINE ENGAGEMENT

**101 Strategies
to Manage Alumni Engagement
from Cradle to Grave!**

Don Philabaum
dphilabaum@gmail.com

Alumni Online Engagement, "101 Strategies to Manage Alumni Engagement from Cradle to Grave!"

First Printing: January 2007

The author and Internet Strategies Group have attempted throughout this book to distinguish proprietary trademarks and service marks by following the capitalization style used by the owner.

The author and Internet Strategies Group can not attest to the accuracy of this information. Use of a term in this book should not be regarded as affecting the validity of any trademark or service mark.

Every effort has been made to make this book as complete and accurate as possible. However, because of the possibility of human or mechanical error, the author and publisher do not guarantee the accuracy, adequacy, or completeness of any information, and are not responsible for any errors or omissions, or the results obtained from such information.

Managing Editor: Tracy Leigh Ritts
Graphics: Jonnie Kalmbach
Cover, Interior Book Design & Production: Studio 6 Sense • info@6sense.net

ISBN: 978-1-60037-298-8

Published by:

Morgan James Publishing, LLC
1225 Franklin Ave. Ste 325
Garden City, NY 11530-1693
Toll Free 800-485-4943
www.MorganJamesPublishing.com

Celebrating Success
211 Harcourt Drive
Akron, Ohio 44313
330-990-0788
info@yourbusinesscoach.net

CONTENTS

The Index is linked to each chapter for faster navigation.

THIS BOOK IS DEDICATED TO...

Ron Finklestein founder of AKRIS LLC, business coach, author, speaker and one of the most creative persons I know!

Ron and I were introduced in 2002 by a business associate. We both shared a passion for helping local business leaders get recognition for the great things they were doing. That introduction led us to found the Northeast Ohio Business Conference.

Ron later became my business coach. In our weekly hour coaching sessions which many times extended to 90 minutes, Ron challenged me to following up on my goals. During one of our meetings, Ron suggested that I send a weekly email outlining how alumni and advancement professionals could use Internet technology to help them achieve their goals. He suggested that I develop 101 ways that could be done. No small task but after I started it, I realized I had enough to say to write a book – the book you are reading!

Later, when I shared with Ron that over a 1,500 people attended our free online webinars, he suggested that I consider developing a consulting division within IAC. So while writing the book, I started working on developing a division that would focus on helping organizations implement the 101 strategies I was writing about in the book. On December 7th, 2006 we officially opened the Internet

Strategies Group.

If you don't have a business coach, I urge you to consider finding one. I will even share Ron if you want to hire him (info@yourbusinesscoach.net). Not only has Ron made me more productive, but he's been able to help me see the forest for the trees and craft a direction I've always wanted to go. Check out his website at www.yourbusinesscoach.net

INTRODUCTION

In the last decade, nearly 50 percent of all alumni associations have adopted password protected online directories and communities.

Using Internet technology, these organizations have been able to welcome thousands of alumni to their websites each month. Their online communities are helping them:

1. Communicate more frequently.

2. Reduce paper, printing and postage costs.

3. Increase the amount of personal data collected.

4. Increase contributions.

Most are seeing a significant amount of unsolicited online contributions prior to reunions, homecoming, and year end. In fact, one private college has received over $1,000,000 in online contributions in just five years.

However, none of this is happening without a commitment to increase staffing and funding. Organizations that have been the most successful in increasing participation in online communities are those that are developing written Internet strategies that include planned additions of new services, promotion, and marketing procedures. They are also aggressively developing Email Acquisition Campaigns with a goal of getting nearly all their alumni email addresses.

The organizations that are most successful recognize that simply creating an online community for their alumni represents only ten percent of their Internet strategy. The other 90 percent of their success comes from the creation and execution of their written Internet strategy. To many, developing an Internet strategy for their organization may feel like an overwhelming responsibility and challenge. It doesn't have to be.

I'm hopeful this book will provide you the framework in which you can develop your own procedures that will include an ever-increasing commitment of staff, money, and time. Some of the Internet strategies offered are easy and cheap and can be done immediately. Others will require more time and discussion. I've included in the back of the book a form you can fill in to identify which strategies you'd like to adopt.

This book is designed for organizations like yours who are looking to take their online community to the next level. You have 101 proven ideas you can pick from to create a comprehensive Internet strategy for your organization. I guarantee the time and effort you invest in building your strategy will provide a huge payoff in achieving the above four points for your organization. It's worth it!

WIREDCOMMUNITIES.COM & THE INTERNET STRATEGIES GROUP

Throughout this book, you will find references to www.wiredcommunities .com and www.internetstrategiesgroup.com I want to make sure you understand why I am referring to both of them.

After working with alumni and development officers for many years, I realized the alumni and advancement industry in general was struggling to develop their web presence. With limited staffing and budget, they were having a difficult time figuring out what services they should offer to alumni. This created two situations. An alumni association either:

- Did nothing because they didn't know what they should do.

- Spent hours in meetings discussing things of which they had little expertise and knowledge.

That's not to say some good ideas weren't being introduced; they were. However, with 4,500 alumni associations in the United States, it was difficult for others to find out what was working and what wasn't.

That's when I created Wiredcommunies.com. My goal was to find individuals and organizations that were developing practical Internet technologies and concepts, interview them, and then promote their idea by publishing it in my free Wiredcommunities.com blog. Frankly, all I was doing was carrying the concept of CASE (Copy And Steal Everything) to the Internet!

Experience had shown me that organizations who were adopting best practices were realizing a significant return on their investment, resulting in higher participation in events, registrations in their online communities, and increased contributions. Since I established www.wiredcommunities.com in 2004, I've found hundreds of really great ideas and concepts. The website consistently receives a large number of visitors who are looking for proven ideas they can adopt.

After alumni associations started paying attention to what they needed to do to benefit their alumni, they realized they needed to develop a written strategy so they would know not only where they were going, but what they needed to do to get there.

When I looked around the advancement industry, I found consultants who played a pivotal role in assisting annual giving professionals develop their strategies and goals. I discovered that capital campaigns did not even get off the ground without the expertise of consultants and advisors who help in identifying the opportunity, assisting in setting goals, targeting the prospects, developing the five- to ten-year plan, and guiding the execution of that plan.

But when I looked at the alumni and advancement industry, there were few consultants who focused exclusively in helping organizations to develop their Internet strategy.

That led me to create the Internet Strategies Group. www.internetstrategiesgroup.com

The Internet Strategies Group is dedicated to assisting organizations in creating and executing a comprehensive Internet strategy. Members sign up for a series of distance learning courses that focus on:

- Increasing Registrations

- Engaging Young Alumni

- Handling Bad Addresses

- Internet Marketing

- Using Video, Audio & Multimedia

- Developing Blogs, Podcasts, RSS

- Identifying Staffing Needs

- Developing an Internet Strategy

- Website Design

- Acquiring More Email Addresses

- Using Volunteers Effectively

- Increasing Communication

In addition to the "take-at-any-time distance learning courses," members have access to live Webinars, reports, podcasts, blogs, relevant resource materials, and contact with peers who have the same challenges.

The reason I have mentioned Wiredcommunities.com and the Internet Strategies Group is to give you additional resources for locating more of the information you're interested in.

At the end of selected chapters you'll find a WIRE-Tip logo that will encourage you to see examples of that chapter in www.wiredcommunities.com. Or you may see a NET-Tips logo, which provides you an opportunity to get additional information, reports, white papers, statistics, and guides on how you can implement specific strategies at the www.theinternetstratgiesgroup.com website.

My hope is this information will save you time and money and assist you in better serving your increasingly savvy Internet-oriented alumni.

TIPS TO GAIN THE MOST OUT OF READING THIS BOOK

This book is designed so you can start virtually anywhere.

However, I think you will find it beneficial to read the first four chapters in order to:

- Gain an understanding of the importance of online communities.

- Learn how to explain to your management the ROI online communities provide.

- Understand how to create your own comprehensive written Internet strategy.

- Get a quick overview on my top ten strategies you should consider adopting.

Once you've read those, feel free to skip around and read any of the 101 strategies that interest you. I purposely did not give them to you in any particular order.

In evaluating each of the 101 strategies, I've found all can fit into one or more of the following categories:

1. Fun

2. Registration

3. Participation

4. Career Networking

5. Data Collection

6. Content

7. Communication

8. Networking

9. Young Alumni

10. Strategy

For those who are interested in locating all of the ideas to help in any one specific area — for example, engaging Young Alumni — you will find a list at the end of the book that details each of the suggestions in this topic. You will find this useful in assisting in the development of multiple strategies to accomplish individual goals.

I've designed a special form you can use to keep track of
the strategies you are most interested in.
Visit www.internetstrategiesgroup.com
and type in "101" in the Net-Tips search box.

IT'S ONLINE COMMUNITY - STUPID!

Your future relationship with your alumni is online

Online community found its roots in The Well

When Bill Clinton was running for the presidency in 1992 against George Bush, he had a simple slogan – It's the economy – Stupid! This slogan was a reminder of the negative effects President George Bush's policies had on the economy and how it affected each American, their family and neighbors. Clinton and his campaign team focused on the simple message and kept delivering it in every event and sound bite they could.

This chapter is titled, "It's Online Community – Stupid!" to remind you and me where our focus will be throughout this entire book. This book will focus on how you can develop an engaging, active online community that benefits your alumni. We'll also show in many different ways how your alumni online community will benefit your alumni, advancement, admissions, and other departments on campus. In fact, I'll prove how – 101 different ways.

Along the way, we'll help you understand and determine:

- What the components of an online community are.

- What your return on your investment is.

- How to get more staffing and funding for your community.

Besides giving you 101 strategies to build your online community around, one of my goals is to help you develop a written Internet strategy. I'll show you how a written Internet strategy will enable you to gain the staffing and budget you will need to execute it properly.

Before we get started, allow me to take you back in time to the roots of online community. After all, you can't really understand where you are about to take your organization until you know where the concept you are adopting began.

The early roots of online community

Online Community would never had happened if Steve Jobs and Steve Wozniak did not start Apple Computer on April Fools day in 1976. Nor could it have happened without IBM introducing their personal computer in 1981. While business was excited about the efficiencies offered by word processing and spreadsheets, others were discovering that computers could be used to connect people in a different way. While the phone was in many ways an easier and more efficient way to connect with friends, the computer led to the development of online bulletin boards. Online bulletin boards were programs that enabled people to post comments and others to respond to them.

To participate, your computer modem would dial the bulletin board's number and you would connect to a world teaming with conversation.

One of the more popular early online bulletin boards was created by Stewart Brand and Larry Brilliant in 1985. They called their online community the Whole Earth 'Lectronic Link (Well). The Well was actually an electronic bulletin board where people were able to connect, discuss, and expand their relationships. Members would access the service via phone dial up.

While coffeehouses were the place that intellectual discussions occurred in the late 50's and early 60's, The Well became the place of intellectual discussion and dialogue in the mid 1980's. This was a time when many in America were dressing in polyester shirts and pants at disco clubs around the country. Dressed in a fashion the current generation (or for that matter those who participated) might regard as humorous today, the majority of young America danced until dawn. As they wandered into their homes around the country a small server in Sausalito, California, continued to log in and out a new generation of individuals who were becoming addicted to the ability to anonymously communicate with hundreds of people simultaneously. They were participating in a bold new experiment that enabled them to communicate across space and time 24/7 without ever meeting each other. They used their fingers to share their thoughts and expressed their commitment, passion, intellect and wit in rapid-fire digital signals.

The early pioneers in online communities were addicted to this new technology. Bulletin Boards offered a new way to engage and involve others. All found it exciting to expand their circle of friends through electronic dialogue. Nearly all were drawn by the fact that their thoughts and positions on issues were out there for everyone to react to. Some of the more focused members' lives began to change as the online community began to look to them for leadership on ideas and in discussions. Many found liberation in being able to develop strong relationships across gender lines. Men became more understanding, women became more intellectual, and all were equal. Most importantly, participants began to realize that regardless **of their size, shape, color and/or looks, none of it mattered, because the members only knew each other by the words they shared together**.

This truly was an experiment that proved that all men and women were created equal. Howard Rheingold later coined the phrase that began to define this phenomenon as a virtual community in his book *The Virtual Community*. The book examines his participation in this emerging communication and socializing tool.

Online communities were proving to be "gold mines"

GeoCities was founded in 1994 by David Bohnett in Los Angles as an online community that provided different virtual neighborhoods you could settle in. Originally starting with six neighborhoods, it eventually expanded to include 41 different neighborhoods. Users had the choice of locating their home page in a high rent neighborhood or in putting their page in a rougher neighborhood.

The company went public in 1998 and was acquired in 1999 by Yahoo for over three billion dollars when GeoCities had ONLY 4.2 million users. Needless to say, the dot-com boom had officially taken off! Fast forward and look at some of the acquisition costs for today's online communities. In 2005 MySpace with 40 million users was acquired by News Corporation for a mere $585 million and YouTube with 72 million users was acquired by Google for a mere $1.65 billion dollars. (OK, you are right, these are still BIG numbers!)

Another very popular online community in the early days, prior to the dot-net crash, was Tripod. Tripod was formed by three Williams College students to help college students transition from college to the workplace. The tool they originally created was an HTML résumé builder that would enable students to post résumé information online. As with any new tool, the public saw a different use and they shifted their focus to providing a home page builder to college students. In 1998 a privately held firm, Lycos, purchased the organization and still operates it today.

My introduction to Online Communities

During the early 1990's I was experimenting with bulletin board communities like The Well. In today's standards, online communities then were very crude, but it didn't stop people like me from participating.

I loved technology and was drawn into the possibilities online communication could provide. At the time the company I founded while in college, Aardvark Studios, photographed graduates as they received their diploma on graduation day. We pioneered the concept of photographing the graduates as they received their diploma and then sending a free proof to their parents to give them an opportunity to purchase enlargements. By 1995, my teams of photographers were photographing nearly 200,000 graduates, within 60 days, at 550 graduation ceremonies. In order to track these orders we had 30-plus computers that like FedEx tracked the graduates' photo orders at multiple points in the production process.

By 1994, I realized I wanted to use my photography firm's knowledge and technology expertise to create online communities. I started reading every book I could find on the subject. In order to gain an understanding of communities and their value, I got up early in the morning and surfed websites, joined communities, read prodigiously, and began narrowing down what I wanted to do.

During the summer of 1995, my family and I moved to Telluride, Colorado. My love for the mountains was a perfect backdrop to give me the time and inspiration to determine what kind of Internet business I could start. While my family and I waited for a home to become available, we lived

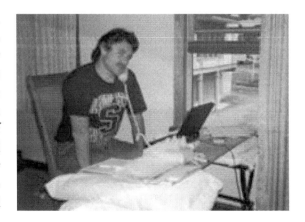

in a loft above a store in downtown Telluride. My office desk was made out of the door to the bedroom I considered my office.

Within the month, I had developed a 40-page business plan that outlined a path of establishing online communities for businesses, students, parents, grocery stores, corporations, membership organizations, and newspapers. Without much fanfare on a Saturday morning, we officially declared the start of the Internet Association Corporation.

Actually, there wasn't any organization that I didn't honestly believe would benefit from an online community. In the early spring of 1996, I was flying back from our corporate office of my photography firm in Akron when I met the owner of three funeral homes in Charleston, South Carolina. He was on his way to Telluride to go fly fishing with a supplier. After listening to him talk about his industry and his kids possibly taking over his business, I couldn't resist suggesting that he offer his clients an online community where they could remember those who passed on.

As our 19-passenger jet began to slowly descend just west of Mt. Wilson, I could tell he was becoming disinterested in the idea and concept. I followed up later with a letter to him and a general outline of how he could better serve his clients and generate more revenue. Then I followed up on his advice to contact the largest funeral home company in the world, located in Texas. It didn't take long for me to realize that this idea was way ahead of its time so I didn't put any additional effort into it.

I hadn't thought about Pornography Online Communities!

When I founded IAC we didn't have any customers, we didn't have a product. All I knew is that we were going to use Internet technology to bring people together via online communities.

One of the first Internet services we offered was an open online community for anyone interested. The goal was to offer a more graphical community than The Well and a more personalized community than AOL. We called our community Toptown.com. Anyone who was interested could create their own home page and connect with others. At the time, we had an old reconditioned computer as the host of Toptown.com and we had a very small connection to the Internet. Within a couple of months of going live, we were receiving 500,000 hits a day.

Our server was choking from the phenomenal hits we were getting, but we were ecstatic. We thought we had hit on something big!

After examining our traffic patterns, we discovered that our huge numbers of visitors were coming to view three home pages that were posted by individuals from users in different parts of the world. These users had placed pornographic photographs on their free home pages, and each was getting thousands of visitors! Our balloon popped! Our first Internet tool that appeared as if it was going to be successful really had a false start. It put us in a line of business we had no intention of being a part of. Instead of becoming one of the first pornographic online communities, we notified the creators of the home pages that we did not allow pornographic photographs on our website and deleted their information. The number of hits dropped to less than 50,000 per day, and our server was sitting quietly waiting to be challenged. We were all disappointed!

Given a little more time, we ended up building a community of 40,000 users, which for 1996 was significant, but didn't get us enough traffic to generate sufficient revenue to support an ongoing operation.

After Toptown.com – came Topresume.com, Toplooks.com Toplinks.com, Topmalls.com and Topmail.com

In early 1997 and 1998 it seemed like everyone was registering domain names (Internet web address names) like day traders trade stocks. Everyone was registering domain names in anticipation of the next big website. It was the new "gold rush." Anyone could register for them and they were. Myself included! The domain naming business hit a feverish pitch in 1999 when the domain name Business.com was sold for five million dollars. (If you still want to get into this line of work register a name you are interested in and register it at www.afternic. com. Sex.com sold in 2006 for 12 million dollars!)

I envisioned a series of websites built around the "top" theme. Toptown.com, as you know, was a site where anyone could get a free home page.

While we were developing online community tools, we began experimenting with other Internet products and services. We created online games and contests designed to engage and involve customers, but again found we were introducing the idea before the market was ready. In toying with an idea of using the web for résumé posting and job listings, we created a site called Topresume.com. The idea of this site was for people to be able to post their resumes online. We envisioned a day when job hunters would post a video of themselves to share their achievements and successes with prospective employers. With no experience in that market, and no apparent way to put money in the bank in the next six months, we decided to move on.

Toplooks.com was to be a site where people could rate others' looks. We spent a little time attempting to get national glamour photographers to promote the site to their customers but failed to gain any interest. After failing to see a need, market, and revenue stream, we put this project on the back burner.

Another project we started was Toplinks.com. The site catalogued educational websites and provided them as a study resource tool for students. In 1995, search engines were not as sophisticated as they are today. Our website identified the best sites within specific categories and offered a paragraph summary for each.

The site offered categories like activism, career corner, creative impulse, educational focus, chats, explore, and discover. It was labor intensive but a valuable resource for students. We paid editors to provide a brief description of each site. In our business model, we were to generate enough traffic to sell advertising. After landing a few high profile advertisers like *USA Today*, we continued promoting the site but ultimately were unable to gain enough "eyeballs" to justify the continued investment.

Topmail.com was initially designed to become a free email site; however, it never made it to production. Soon after I had registered the domain name, I received an email from a firm in Barcelona, Spain, that wanted to buy it to use for a project they were developing. I told them the web address was a part of a family of web addresses that we couldn't break up. After we went back and forth in a number of email interchanges and faxes I ended up selling them the web address Topmail.com for nearly six figures!

Our version of Facebook.com was 7 years too early

With our experience at creating online communities for the general public and experience at developing a series of online study and resource websites for students, we decided to focus on creating an online community just for college students, modifying the technology we created for Toptown. We called the community StudentAccess.com, provided college students a free profile page, email address and community building tools. Students were able to enter content, upload photographs and link to other websites. In the fall of 1996, we launched the website.

Soon after we launched, I received a letter from lawyers representing Princeton Review, who indicated that we were infringing on their copyright by using the name StudentAccess, and they wanted us to cease and desist. It appeared that the attorneys for Princeton Review were trying to protect the intellectual rights and copyright for a series of books they had called *Student Access to Law School, Student Access to Medical School*, etc. In addition, they wanted us to give them our domain www.studentaccess.com. We were floored! Not only did we have hundreds of thousands of ads showing up on college campuses around the country at the moment I received the letter, but we had spent a great deal of time and money developing the concept. We started a legal fight with them, and each day I received an update from my attorney. I began to question if it was going to be worth long protracted litigation for something that the ongoing success had not yet been determined. If it had been financially successful, we could have afforded a prolonged debate and discussion on who had the rights to the domain www.studentaccess.com. But the reality was, it was not.

While the idea seemed sound, students were not as web savvy in 1996 as they are today, or for that matter in 2003 when Facebook was introduced to the market. When marketing efforts failed to attract a large enough audience to support our student online community with advertising, we decided to throw in the towel. We gave the domain to Princeton Review and began to look for another place to use our emerging Internet expertise and technology.

Yearbooks online?

In the summer of 1996, I had an opportunity to make a presentation to Morris Drake, then President of Taylor Publishing in Dallas, Texas, one of the largest yearbook printing companies in the world. I created a PowerPoint presentation that showed that the future of the yearbook would be online. Morris was late for the meeting and looked a bit disheveled as he entered the conference room. He explained that he recently had made a million-dollar investment in digital printing to print yearbooks faster, in color, and at less cost, but he was having numerous production issues that were putting them behind their promised delivery schedules. Clients were complaining, sales representatives were taking a lot of heat, and it all rolled up to his office. It wasn't exactly the right time to make a presentation to him that focused on a theme that printed yearbooks were on their way out.

My presentation focused on providing each high school student, each athletic team and group, their own home page. Throughout the year, students, administrators and others would update the online community. (Our programming team felt they could modify the StudentAccess.com code to create this product).

When the presentation was complete, and the lights were turned back on, Morris looked me in the eye and said, "Don, how am I going to make money with this?" I told him each student would pay a yearly subscription fee and he could develop alternative revenue sources from sponsorship and advertising. It didn't resonate with him, and I realized when I left that his head was focused on getting his million-dollar investment in digital printing working, not in the future of where yearbooks were going.

It only took that meeting for me to realize I needed to find another market for the Internet tools we were developing. We'd introduced and tried to enter a number of different markets to no avail. At this time, AOL was sending a CD every month to every home in America and growing by hundreds of thousands daily. It became apparent that AOL and others were bringing people together through online communities centered on their interests and hobbies. If the future of online communities rested in local, niche, private labeled communities, why not offer online communities to alumni associations?

Alumni Associations had print directories

Excited about the success that AOL had as a "super online community," I envisioned that schools, nonprofits, and associations would also want to use Internet technology to better serve their constituents.

Having taken a couple of stabs at creating commercial online communities based on advertising and sponsorship, and facing a growing number of employees with no venture capital to support us and no revenue coming in, we decided we needed to find organizations who would pay us to provide our services. That led us to schools and alumni associations.

Providing online communities to alumni associations seemed to be a natural move for us. For one thing, the software code we had developed for StudentAccess.com could be modified to provide private password communities for each alumni association. For another, we already knew quite a few alumni directors because many were in charge of their graduation ceremonies.

Excited about the possibilities within this market, we started making phone calls, visiting alumni professionals, and sending out mountains of letters and flyers. At our first alumni conference, we received enough favorable responses that we decided educational associations would be a great niche to offer the online community tools we created for the student market.

The existing competitor to the online directory at that time was the alumni print directory, a book that contained the names of all alumni. In the early 1960's, college alumni associations started offering their alumni this print directory, which contained the contact and some personal information of everyone the college considered an alumni. Third-party companies handled the gathering of new address information from alumni, as well as selling and fulfilling orders for the alumni print directory. The alumni association not only benefited from new data gathered, but they also received a share of the revenue generated.

In 1995 there were mixed reactions to providing alumni online directories:

- Some administrators were concerned that the online directory would compete with the print directory.

- Some saw no need to have an online directory.

- Others were excited to think they may never have to produce a print directory again!

This last group believed, as many still do today, that a printed alumni directory was not worth all of the work and effort as it was out of date by the time it was printed. In some cases it consumed staff time, resulted in customer service issues and miffed a few alumni who felt they were getting oversold.

Having no background and experience in print directories, my team was excited about the opportunities and benefits that an online directory/community could provide alumni.

For example:

- Print directories only provided a ¼ inch listing of an alum's personal information. However, with online directories and communities, alumni could put as much personal information as they wanted on their private and public profile pages.

- Alumni would have the ability to post photographs, update others via class notes, register for events and contribute online.

- It would be easier for alumni to find each other using online search tools.

My interactions and meetings with alumni administrators helped give me a better understanding of their goals, strategies, and overall mission. As I saw it, my job at the time was to help them see how adopting an alumni online community would help them:

- Communicate more frequently at less cost.

- Decrease the time it took to get young alumni involved.

- Increase contributions.

- Increase participation in events and activities.

- Gather more data and address updates from alumni.

- Reduce mundane jobs like building lists, depositing checks, etc.

For those who adopted the program the first year, it didn't take long for alumni associations to prove that a relatively small investment in technology would provide these benefits and more!

Online Directory OR Online Community?

As we looked at how others were developing communities within their niche, we began to shift our product from simply being an online directory tool that allowed individuals to search for others, to an online community where they could interact with others, post content, and search on a variety of characteristics.

The new Pinball Online Directory we developed allowed alumni to find others based on hobbies, interests and location, and virtually any data field could be searched. I could effortlessly find alumni in Akron, Ohio, who liked to play golf, were interested in photography or who had read the latest big novel. Our programmers followed by creating dozens of online community tools and services.

It was during this time period that we began to share the benefits and the opportunities that existed for alumni associations in the arena of online communities. We wanted them to understand the amazing differences that would exist if they moved from offering a simple online directory to a complete and engaging online community.

Our focus groups and discussions with users led us to introduce:

- Viral marketing tools to increase participation on the website.

- PUSH/Pull techniques to drive information to alumni and drive them back to the website.

- Social networking tools to connect alumni with each other.

As the alumni online directory became more of an online community, alumni not only visited the community more frequently, but they expanded their relationships with each other and with the college.

We introduced our online community in late 1995 at the Chicago CASE conference for only $995. Within a few years, we moved our online directory toward more of a social networking directory built around our Pinball Directory product, and the cost increased to $4,995. Shortly we partnered with our 100th client and continued to increase the functionality as we climbed to 200 clients worldwide. We were thrilled when we picked up our first European client, Open University, and later the London School of Economics. Within the next year we were working with two of the top five business schools in Europe – HEC School of Business in Paris, France, and Bocconi School of Management in Barcelona, Spain.

After testing products for a couple of years and doing a great deal of research and development, we had finally found a market to fulfill my dream of building online communities!

The cost of online communities still represented an issue to many colleges as it does still today. To help offset those costs, we continued to look for ways that the community would pay for itself.

Shopping Online Communities were next!

In 1999 at the height of the dot com boom, we introduced online community shopping malls for alumni associations. We created private label shopping malls where alumni could shop online at websites like Amazon, J.Crew, CDNow, and nearly 200 other online merchants. Depending on the merchant the alumni association received an average of five to ten percent of every dollar spent at their stores. This looked like the ultimate revenue generator.

We developed a number of innovations in our product, like allowing alumni to shop and browse with a friend. We installed about 30 malls in our clients' websites and encouraged them to spend a great deal of money marketing and promoting their alumni online communities. We shared with clients that the average consumer that shopped online in 1998 spent $535. We suggested if 1,000 of their alumni shopped online spending the same amount, their shopping mall at seven percent commission would generate $37,000! Two things worked against this idea at the time. First, even though there was a prospect of generating revenue, there were few dollars available to market the shopping malls. Secondly, without the marketing, there were not enough alumni visiting the online community yet alone the mall. I'd had enough experience at this point to begin to see the timing of this product was too early.

Online Community 2.0

There is an old saying, "The pioneers don't make it, the settlers do." I'm assuming this phrase was born out of the reality of the early American pioneers who had a better chance of getting an arrow in their back or dying from the extreme conditions they faced as they moved into the "wild west." However the settlers, those that came later, had a better chance of survival either due to reduced dangers from bandits and Indians or increased infrastructure of food, medicine, and law enforcement.

I spent a great deal of time sharing with you the "pioneer days" in online communities to give you a sense of its history, but more importantly to build the case that we are now living in a time when your online community has the potential of being enormously successful.

Now nearly a decade later, about half of all alumni associations are in the process of building or already offering online directories and communities to their alumni. The other half is waiting for a signal from upper management that their organization should invest in an alumni online community **and the half with online directories are not employing enough resources to make their online directories into true online communities.**

With the success of MySpace and Facebook, hundreds of new online communities are being introduced. Each is aiming for the same audience you are, your alumni. The success that MySpace and Facebook have experienced is being repeated in other countries with homegrown communities. CyWorld has captured a larger percentage of the Korean population than MySpace has captured in the United States. Orkut has captured the majority of the Brazilian population, yet it's barely made a dent in the U.S.

The early introduction of online communities in 1995, like The Well, AOL, and GeoCities, had anywhere from a thousand to a maximum of three million users. Today's 2.0 online communities like MySpace have over 130,000,000 users. Online communities are not fads; they are utilitarian, practical, technological tools that bring people together 24/7, anywhere in the world. The incredible and rapid growth of the 2.0 online communities is proof that user behavior has caught up with technology and will be pushing it to do more for them. Your alumni are among those millions.

To show you how hot online communities are, Nielsen Netratings, the organization that tracks web usage, reported in 2005 that only one out of the top ten web brands was a community-oriented site. They define a community-oriented site as one to which consumers contribute content. Only one year later Nielsen Netratings reported that five out of the ten fastest-growing websites were community sites.

This cannot be ignored. Your:

- Alumni are among the 130 million users of MySpace.
- Alumni are also part of the nearly 72 million users of YouTube.
- Students are part of the 13 million users of Facebook.

If you've not heard yet, 83 percent of your students are registered users of Facebook. Chances are, the same alum who is registered in MySpace, is also a registered user in Classmates.com and other online communities.

Some of your alumni are also more than likely members of many other established and emerging niche online communities. Here are few examples of the communities they may already be a part of:

- Prayer Communities

- Weight loss Communities

- News Communities

- Parenting Communities

- Career Communities

- Social Communities

- Dating Communities

- Professional Communities

And of course, we all hope they become a part of your alumni online community!

I understand you will still have to do business as usual by holding events, activities, and award functions. This doesn't change the fact that you and your staff must be taking a more active approach in developing your online community, as well as in the integration of all the department functions within it.

In my book, *Create a NET-Centered Alumni Office*, I show how the future of your alumni association will be built around your Internet strategy. Creating a written Internet strategy will be an important first step in leading your alumni association in a direction that will be more relevant to your alumni. Under your leadership, you have the opportunity to position your alumni association in a way your alumni will be able to relate to.

The future of your relationship with your alumni is online

Peter F. Drucker, author of 39 books on management and one of the originators of the concept of the "knowledge worker" that challenged Karl Marx's worldview of the political economic landscape, said in his book, The Age of Discontinuity:

> The important challenge in society, economics, and politics is to exploit the changes that have already occurred and to use them as opportunities. The important thing is to identify the "future that has already happened" and to develop a methodology for perceiving and analyzing these changes.

Peter Drucker would remind us to recognize when the future has arrived. Nearly 90 percent of college-educated alumni are online. Very close to 100 percent of graduates since 2001 are online. The companies they work for, the organizations they belong to, the nonprofits they support, and the firms they buy from are all changing the way they do business and building their relationships and expanding their customer service via various Internet tools and techniques.

Your alumni are showing you how you can build a bridge to your college campus that will keep them connected 24/7/365. Your job is to recognize how they want you to connect with them and build the tools and services that will keep them coming back. Your job is to build the community that will engage them, network them and keep them connected to your alumni association. Under your leadership, your alumni association will remain relevant to your students and your alumni. Failure to fully embrace an Internet strategy and build your alumni association around Internet technology will result in less frequent communication with alumni due to rising costs, decreases in participation in giving and the risk that the alumni association loses its value to alumni.

It makes a lot of sense for your alumni association to continue to invest in and develop your alumni online community. Your alumni are beginning to understand the value that online communities provide them, and as they do, they will begin to venture out of the "super communities" (MySpace, YouTube, etc.) to join numerous niche communities.

Connecting the dots

Steve Jobs founder of Apple, Inc., in one of the most incredible commencement speeches I have ever heard (and I've heard hundreds), told the 2005 graduating class of Stanford about connecting the dots in their lives. As he shared his journey in life and the momentous steps and decisions he made or were made for him, he reminded the students that you never know if the decisions you are making are the right ones. A seemingly foolish, unproductive action may years later prove to be a brilliant move or a stroke of luck. In his speech he reminded students that life happens as you make choices and suggested they follow their gut and intuition.

He told the graduates about his mother giving him up for adoption but insisting that the family that adopted him promise to send him to college. The couple who was lined up backed out at the last minute when they found out it was a boy. Hurriedly another couple was located, a working class family with limited resources. The family agreed they would send the child to college. Steve chose Reed College in Portland, Oregon. However, after less than a year, he decided he was wasting his parents' hard-earned money and decided to drop out, but drop in on courses that interested him. One course that he dropped into was a calligraphy class. Calligraphy was an admired art and communication tool at Reed. Later, as he and Wozniak were developing the software for the Apple, he decided the operating system HAD to offer fantastic graphics that would enable Calligraphic and other designs. His point to the graduates was, the core "culture" of Apple, the one thing they were able to hang their hat on, was a result of the course that he "dropped in" on!

He reminded the graduates that you can't connect the dots until much later in your life. It's only then apparent if the decisions you made were connected.

In this chapter I've shared with you a series of events and decisions I've made in my very short "Internet" career. Each of my decisions led me to the next step in my journey. At the time I had no idea where each would lead, but I had one underlying theme I was following. **I wanted to create online communities**. I knew it at the instant in 1995 that I was mountain biking down an old train bed, listening to the Rolling Stones, singing, "I can't get no satisfaction." My satisfaction lay ahead in creating online communities.

As I watched the slow adoption, endorsement, and investment in alumni online communities, I started to write white papers, newsletters and blogs, hold webinars, and to encourage organizations to more aggressively adopt Internet technology. After over 1,500 people attended various webinars we offered during a two-year period on subjects like "Facing UP to the Facebook/MySpace Generation" and "Internet Techniques for Annual Giving," I realized that our industry would benefit from practical, how-to instructions on creating an effective Internet strategy. That led to the creation of the Internet Strategies Group and my writing the book you are reading.

While none of us can predict the future, it is abundantly clear that the future of your relationship with your alumni is going to be via the Internet.

This chapter was designed to show you that online communities have been growing in importance over the last ten years and are becoming more important, more popular and more a part of your alumni's lives.

With the introduction of broadband, video, and other online news, content, and information, your alumni are going to be spending more time online. Research is already indicating this. In countries where broadband has a higher penetration than ours, Internet users are spending twice as much time online than Americans. Innovations like YouTube, and the emerging conversion of TV, movies, and other video being delivered over the Internet is only going to increase the time your alumni are online. That's great news for you because when they are hooked into the Internet, you are connected to them.

Research has proven your alumni are not reading newspapers and magazines. They don't have time to read long research articles. They like their news in small bits and for the 35-and-under crowd, they like it online. The magazine, newspaper, TV, movie, and music businesses have suddenly recognized this as they watched their ratings suffer and their advertising budgets affected. Most are cutting costs in their traditional print industry and ramping up their Internet divisions. You have the same options available to you.

If budgets are a concern, consider targeting older or significant contributors, producing fewer editions, and/or cutting back on the size of the magazine. At the same time, you should be integrating your alumni magazine stories online.

You have the benefit of connecting the dots today and recommend to your management a massive increase in funding and staffing in order to use Internet technology to connect your alumni 24/7/365 with your travel, membership, annual giving, career services, events, and advancement offices. You need additional funding to market your website to your students and alumni and to gain professional expertise to help you develop the right strategy the first time. You need additional funding to continue to increase the quality and usefulness of the technology and services you provide your alumni.

Now is NOT the time to idly move forward as most alumni and advancement have been doing that for the past decade! The future has already occurred and your alumni are living in it!

WHAT IS AN ONLINE COMMUNITY?

Most alumni websites do not qualify as online communities!

According to www.wikipedia.org:

> A **virtual community** or **online community** is a group of people that primarily or initially communicates or interacts via the Internet. The dawn of the "information age" found groups communicating electronically rather than face to face. A "Computer-mediated community" (CMC) uses social software to regulate the activities of participants.

The more successful online communities are built around defined concepts and provide users with practical information, interactions, and/or connections with others. There are online communities that focus on weight loss, collecting obscure items, sports, hobbies, etc.

An online community tends to grow organically around a single interest or niche. Within each niche, you'll find passionate members who are willing to put in a great deal of time and effort to share information and build the group.

The community's value comes from the members. Without a perceived value, you have nothing. If your community has value to your members, they will visit frequently and encourage their friends to participate. If your community doesn't offer much to your users, they will lose interest and rarely return.

The Marketing Faculty at the Kellogg School of Management wrote the book *Kellogg on Branding*. In the book they remind us that we need to concentrate on what our customers think of our products and services. The brand of your alumni online community is not what you say it is. It's what your alumni perceive it to be. The authors state:

> Brands are sets of associations linked to a name or mark associated with a product or service. The associations can be positive or negative, and anything can be branded, even water, cities, and people. In addition, brands have the ability to shape how people perceive products – they can elevate a product or diminish a product. As a result, brands are critically important; a brand with negative association will hurt a company, and a brand with positive association will help.

If your alumni are not returning to your online community you need to examine what value you are providing them. If they do not perceive value, they won't tell others and your community will not grow.

An online directory does not make an online community!

The typical alumni website includes information about the alumni association, events, and photos, along with a small link to the alumni online directory. Most directories today are password protected and require alumni to be authenticated to prove they are "who they say they are." This is a great idea because it enables alumni to share more information about themselves with a group of people they trust. Plus, it makes the online community more "exclusive."

But with exclusivity comes the risk that you make it too difficult for alumni to register in your online community. We've seen many alumni attempt to login to their community only to be told they have to authenticate themselves with their student ID number or with a crazy assortment of letters and numbers they had to use as students. No one remembers these, and few take the time to find out what they are. While their curiosity drew them to the community, the moat they had to cross to get in was just too wide. So they end up walking away.

An online directory, by itself, allows people to search on specific fields. For alumni associations, alumni would be able to find someone from a specific class year, major, and/or city. Online directories are essentially phone books on steroids. They don't do a great deal in creating community. After all, once you have completed a couple of searches, why would you go back?

The standard Internet tools and services offered by most alumni associations in their attempt to build an online community include an online directory, class notes, business card exchange, news, opinion polls, bulletin boards, photo albums, and in some cases, career centers.

For the most part, these do not make an online community.

When you refer back to the definition of online communities as offered by Wikipedia, few alumni online communities create environments where alumni are communicating and connecting in large numbers. Few alumni online communities see alumni collaborating and sharing information at a rate that increases participation to the level needed in order to keep alumni coming back to the website.

There are three fundamental reasons why most online communities fail to gain a large audience. First, an online community needs to provide value to the users. If they are not getting any value from the community they will rarely come back. Second, the sites are not promoted enough. And third, the website does not have enough interactive services.

So let's examine ways your online community can increase participation and registrations. There are six ways you can build a strong alumni online community:

1. Determine your purpose.

2. Build your online directory around career development.

3. Promote your community via admissions, orientation, graduation & employers.

4. Make your online community interactive.

5. Actively work to increase networking in your online community.

6. Analyze and track the effectiveness of your online community.

1) Determine your purpose

One of the first things you need to do if you are committed to developing an alumni online community is to determine why you are offering it to your alumni.

When I've asked alumni and development professionals why they created an alumni online community, some of the typical responses I've received include:

- Increase communication with alumni.

- Increase alumni participation within alumni events.

- Gather more data about alumni.

- Increase contributions.

Do you notice anything in common about these responses?

You are right! The comments all focus on what the online community will do for the alumni association – not what it will do for their alumni. If you want your alumni online community to be used by your alumni, you will have to build it around their needs.

Look at it from another angle. In their book *The Disney Way*, Bill Capodagli and Lynn Jackson share a quote from Walt Disney:

> You don't build the product for yourself. You need to know what the people want and build it for them.

Chances are if you are reading this book, you graduated from college. For just a moment, think about what YOU would like your college alumni online community to do for you. You probably don't need access to the campus library, or need to find a roommate too frequently, or discounts on insurance or rental cars, but what you might be interested in – is help in advancing your business career.

If you were indeed interested in that, more than likely you would ask for help in:

- Securing a better paying job or getting a new job.

- Meeting other alumni to do business with.

- Finding a mentor.

2) Build your online directory around career development

Remember there are now hundreds, if not thousands, of social networking online communities that your alumni can be a part of. Your alumni online community has to offer something unique that others cannot provide. It has to stand for something that other online communities cannot stand for and, as we discussed, it has to offer value to them. They have to benefit from participating in it.

For most of your alumni, I would venture to say that after family, their careers were the next most important part of their lives. Let's evaluate how you can create an online community that helps them transition to new jobs and do business with fellow alumni.

It's common knowledge that 80 percent of us get jobs through our network of friends and business associates. Your alumni association represents the largest network of people who passionately shared the same experience your alumni will ever be a part of. The alumni connection is a powerful job hunting tool, but when you end up in Peoria, Illinois, and you graduated from the University of Akron, the chances of you being able to use your college network to find your next job is, frankly, limited. With an online community it doesn't matter if your alumni is working in Peoria or in Bangkok. In either case, they would be able to get online, search for alumni who work within a specific industry or company or simply send out notices that they are looking for a job.

> There is nothing your alumni association can do that is more important to your alumni than to encourage alumni to hire each other and do business with each other.

Your alumni are currently working in tens of thousands of businesses all over the world. Each one of them would be more than happy to help fellow alumni with employment or to do business with their firm.

Case in point.

Steve Chin, Chad Hurley, and Jawed Karim founded YouTube in 2005 and sold it 18 months later in 2006 to Google for $1.65 billion dollars. Steve attended the University of Illinois, Urbana, but left college with only a couple semesters to finish in order to work at PayPal in the San Francisco area. Steve was drawn to PayPal because several University of Illinois, Urbana, alumni worked there, including the co-founder, Max Levchin. Steve turned out to be a brilliant programmer, but chances are he would not have been drawn to PayPal without the University of Illinois alumni connection. This single alumni connection changed his life, changed his fortune, and is changing the way all of us view videos on the web!

It is my personal opinion that there is nothing your alumni association can do that is more important to your alumni than to encourage alumni to hire each other and do business with each other.

You could be responsible for bringing together the next YouTube by:

- Adopting the philosophy that your alumni online community is a career and business development tool.

- Providing mentoring opportunities and promoting the alumni association as a career and business networking organization to your students.

- Promoting to your graduates they are joining a network of alumni who will mentor them, help them get a job and do business with them.

In the beginning pages of this book, we talked about the alumni industry first adopting online directories, and then later upgrading the directories to provide more social networking tools, and now we are suggesting that your online community become focused on helping alumni advance their business and professional careers.

Certainly there are career networking sites out there, but none have the unique connection among the members. Few will have people passionately willing to help others as much as your alumni will be willing to help fellow alumni. Focusing your mission around career and business development will not only provide a powerful tool to your alumni, it will give you all the data and information about your alumni that you ever dreamed of! As you do that, your marketing and promotion should focus on promoting that brand. Your marketing and promotion of this brand should start with prospective students and continue with students, parents, and alumni.

3) Promote your community via admissions, orientation, graduation and employers

The first area you should be promoting your online community brand is via your admissions office. Your admissions office should begin to promote to prospective students that your alumni association is an active network of alumni who work at thousands of great, well-paying companies around the world. They should be sending information to the prospective students' parents informing them about the average salary and the percent of students getting jobs, and highlighting some of the students who got great-paying jobs. They should also be bragging about the mentoring opportunities available to their son or daughter.

The second time you should be promoting your online community brand is the minute your incoming freshmen arrive on campus. Your alumni office should be welcoming them to the alumni association and continuing to inform them about the network of alumni who are already working that will be able to help them not only get jobs, but great-paying jobs. In keeping true to your brand, you should invest more time and attention in developing mentoring relationships between your students and your alumni. You should have a goal of pairing up every single student with one or more alumni. While it wasn't possible in the past to require that each student find a mentor, with Internet technology today, it's easy for alumni to participate as mentors to your students.

Your alumni association is YOUR career and business network.

A third way you can build your online community brand around career development is at graduation.

The photography company I founded put me at hundreds of graduation ceremonies. As a result, I heard many amazing speeches, but I also heard a great many that I could barely sit through! One speech that made the graduates roll their eyes was the representative of the alumni association.

The message was always the same – congratulations and don't forget to contribute to the annual fund. I could tell this was not something that students who were leaving college with loans to pay back wanted to hear. I had the unique opportunity to see and capture on my camera the expressions on the graduates' and parents' faces as these comments were made. It's probably no surprise to you that the lighthearted laughter and discussion among those students focused on, "Yah, I'll participate in giving after I pay back my loans."

At your next graduation ceremony, I'd like you to consider having the President of your alumni association say something like:

> "Graduates, welcome to the best career and business club you will ever have an opportunity to be a part of. The alumni association has 50,000 alumni working for thousands of companies around the world that are doing fantastic things in their marketplace. Our alumni have footprints in 30 other nations around the world.

> "You are now part of a group of people who have shared the same experiences as you, who have walked the same paths, taken the same courses, loved and disliked the same professors, who joined the same clubs and organizations. These individuals have made the transition you are about to take, and in effect, have paved the way for you

to help you reach your dreams and aspirations sooner, rather than later. Your alumni association is YOUR career and business network. We've invested in technology that will enable you to find a mentor, post your résumé, find an alum who can help you transition in a new town and who could introduce you to the right people in their company.

"Do you realize that 80 percent of the people looking for jobs find jobs through people they know? You may have heard it before, but it will mean a lot more to you today and in the near future when you start looking for your next job. You will not find a more willing group or a more powerful group of people who will go out of their way to help you in your professional career. I urge you to register in the alumni online community and to take an active part in it. The stronger we make our network, the more it will deliver to each of us. I wish you the best you can become."

Ok, you might not have gotten chills from this speech, but I think you got the point. In this situation, the representative for the alumni association reminds the students that the alumni association is a network of people who are there to help each other achieve more, reach their goals, and advance their career and business objectives.

It sets in motion a reminder to register in and use the online community to stay in touch and connect with alumni who are already in the workforce that can help them get a job!

A fourth way you can build the brand of your alumni online community is to create tools for alumni to build affinity groups around the companies they work for. You might have 1,000 alumni working for IBM, 200 working for the State of Ohio, 120 working for a local hospital, and so on. You should consider actively building affinity groups and encouraging alumni to become a part of these "clubs." Not only does it increase the visibility of your alumni association, but you create a bigger buzz in the company, which has the potential of getting more of your graduates hired there.

It doesn't take a $10,000 survey to determine what your alumni want the alumni online community to be. By focusing on career and personal development, specifically networking, mentoring and job placement, you will begin to build a powerful brand and beneficial service to your alumni.

4) Make your online community interactive

In addition to determining a purpose, your online community has to offer interactive experiences and technology. For example, class notes should be designed so alumni can be alerted when their friends post notes or when those from a specific college or graduation year(s) post notes. They should be designed so alumni can post comments and congratulations to alumni who have posted class notes. Alumni should be able to request that a friend post a class note, and alumni should also have an option of sending eCards that offer congratulations in response to the original class note.

The alum should have the ability to pick from a series of eCards relevant to the class note posted by the alum. If you posted a class note announcing the birth of your child, I would be able to present you with an eCard that includes the college mascot looking like a stork. Additionally, class notes should also show up on the private profile and public profile pages of the alumni who posted them. You get the idea! All of the services you offer today need to be revamped to have the interactivity described here built into them.

Later in the book we'll talk about PUSH/Pull techniques and viral marketing techniques your online community will need in order to grow. You can't invest in technology today and expect it to meet the needs of your alumni even a year later. You and your team will need to be looking at continually improving the user experience and the functionality of your products and services.

5) Actively work to increase networking in your online community

In addition to creating an interactive online community you need to continually work to increase the connections your members make.

The illustration below shows that a strategy built around providing news, information, and/or the ability for a person to find another is a recipe for a weak online community. In this type of community, individuals will visit the website on rare occasions.

However, in the case where you are providing techniques to network alumni for personal, career, or business purposes, your community will become more valuable to the alumni, which results in increased frequency of use of the website.

Strength of Community Building	
Searching for Someone	Weak
Posting of Data	Weak
News and Information	Weak
Network Based on Interests and Hobbies	Strong
Career Development	Strong
Business Development	Strong

But that's not all, you need to continue to add ways that your members can express themselves and feel connected. To do so, I would recommend that you begin to adopt any and all of the following aspects:

1. Providing users the ability to form their own groups.

2. Tools that enable alumni to find others with similar interests and hobbies.

3. Capabilities for alumni to reach out to others to get jobs and do business with each other.

4. Using Network Weavers (See Strategy 4) to connect unconnected alumni.

5. Ability to share their own content and information.

6. Give them the ability to make comments, vote on the value of content, and give their opinion.

6) Analyze and track the effectiveness of your online community

In my research over the past decade, I developed a methodology that allowed me to review a number of matrixes to identify whether an alumni association had an online directory or an online community. Some of the information I analyzed included:

- Percent of alumni registered.

- Number of alumni who created personal pals (buddy lists).

- Frequency of returning to the community.

- Number of services the average registered person used.

- Number of services provided to them.

- Number of class notes posted and read.

We developed a database to capture this information and we built in logic to quickly show if our client had an online community or simply an online directory. Armed with this information, we were able to help them better communicate to their board and to their president where they were based on the current investment, commitment, and staff, and where they needed to get in.

Why should my alumni association be in the online community business?

Over the years, I've heard some say they didn't believe their alumni association should be in the business of providing online communities. The position they held was that commercial companies can do it better, so why not concede the space to them?

When asked that question I usually offer the following seven reasons why every alumni association should be continually investing in their alumni Internet strategy. With a decade of experience and implementations, there is increasing evidence that alumni online communities:

1. Increase contributions.

2. Increase the amount of data collected from alumni.

3. Keep the alumni connected to the alumni association.

4. Provide faster, cheaper, and more frequent communication.

5. Increase the number of dues payers.

6. Increase participation at events.

7. Connect alumni in ways never possible before.

Research has shown that alumni who receive increased frequent communication from your college about things such as the administration, faculty, athletic teams, and what students are doing, the stronger the likelihood that they will not only give more – but that they will give more frequently.

We suggest that commercial social networking websites including Classmates. com, Linkedin.com, Facebook.com, MySpace.com, Youtube.com, and hundreds of others are your competion. Each are gathering information and data from your alumni that you will need to continue to personalize your stewardship message throughout their life.

Summary

Take a moment and reflect. Do you have an online community or do you simply have an online directory? Ask yourself the following questions:

- Why would alumni come back to the alumni online community?

- Are the tools and services you are offering being used? Do they match alumni needs?

- What benefits is your alumni online community offering your alumni?

- What services are you offering that create a dynamic interchange of ideas and information and/or encourage alumni to collaborate?

- What opportunities do you provide that allow alumni to network with each other?

Creating a vibrant, engaging alumni online community is not something you can expect to have by only offering an online directory and providing a few services. An indication that you have an online directory is low registration and participation rates. I can assure you that if your alumni are not returning, at least on a quarterly basis, then you don't have an online community.

I suggest that you set these or a modified version of these to benchmark your progress:

- Get alumni to return to your online community at least once a month.

- Encourage alumni to build a networking list of a minimum of 12 people.

- Get 50 percent of your alumni to volunteer and mentor.

In the coming chapter, I'll show you how to develop a strategy that will give you the funding to adopt 101 different strategies that will keep your alumni coming back to your online community on a frequent basis.

DEVELOP A STRATEGY!

Without a plan, your operations will be inefficient, staff will be stressed, funds will be wasted & alumni will be underserved

The purpose of this chapter is twofold.

First, I want to impress upon you that NOT creating a comprehensive Internet strategy is costing you a great deal of time, aggravation, and money. Secondly, I want to give you a twelve-step plan that will help you create a comprehensive Internet strategy for your alumni association.

Effects of no strategy

My research and interviews with alumni associations worldwide has shown that without a written Internet strategy, organizations are:

- Wasting a great deal of time.

- Investing in the wrong solutions.

- Burning out their staff.

- Failing to serve their alumni.

- Missing out on millions of dollars in contributions.

Without a plan, you and your staff will find yourselves in meetings talking about what you'd like to do, making decisions based on your feelings, not fact, with an outcome of investment in software, hardware, and third party solutions that are not needed. In the ten years I've worked with organizations worldwide, I've watched them spend tens of thousands of dollars needlessly.

I've seen organizations hire additional staff to handle technical skill sets that were not necessary, and I've seen hundreds of organizations follow other's leads in adopting the latest buzz, only to realize within a few years that the buzz was based on no facts and no value, and provided no real benefits to alumni. These costly missteps put undue workloads on staff, wasted limited resources, and, in a nutshell, confused alumni.

In the late 90's, as an example, a number of dot-com, venture-backed companies came out of nowhere with fantastic offers to alumni associations if they adopted their service. One example was zUniversity. The firm burned through $40 million dollars and left nearly 100 organizations a product that no longer worked or was supported. Instead of determining what their strategy was, the participating alumni associations followed zUniversity's strategy that was built on flaky dot-net thinking and not on the needs of alumni and alumni associations.

There is no one to blame for these situations. When change is forced on our organizations, we don't always have the luxury of knowledge, time, experience, and funding to figure out what to do right away. It takes time to forge a plan on how to incorporate new concepts into an organization.

When new concepts are introduced into your business, there are usually no:

- Business processes to handle the communication, input, and customer contact.

- Funding to support technology or staff.

Also, it is unlikely that anyone will be officially given the responsibility of implementing, maintaining, and improving the concept. In most organizations, someone will gradually step to the plate to handle the emerging responsibilities. If the organization is fortunate, that person is passionate about the new responsibilities.

However, there are a number of risks an organization faces as the responsibilities in this emerging area continue to grow. First, the person may not have the experience or the expertise to successfully handle the responsibilities. If they don't, the image you present to your alumni will suffer. Second, the increase in time commitments will require the person to set aside some of their previous responsibilities in order to focus on the emerging responsibilities to maintain and update the alumni website. The end result is that this staff person becomes stressed and management begins to wonder why they are no longer as effective as they were before. Sooner or later an event occurs that gets management's attention, and the organization has to focus on developing solutions.

I've spoken with alumni associations around the world and nearly every one of them is extremely proud of their alumni magazines. Over the years, nearly all have received the staffing and funding to improve them. Many I talk to mention they want to offer "world class" alumni magazines. However, those same institutions, **because of a lack of focus and strategy**, are offering mediocre, illogical and ineffective alumni web services.

When minimal attention is given to an emerging alumni online community, it will provide minimal results. Minimal investment in time and money will result in slow growth, little data collection, and underserved alumni.

This is caused by a lack of:

- Funding

- Staffing

- Marketing

- Technology

- Purpose

This is really not rocket science. The more you invest the time, resources, and funding into your Internet strategy the more you will get out of it. And of course you will NOT get the level of funding and resources you will need without creating a comprehensive written Internet strategy. Because this is a new emerging area, in most cases, management has not set aside funding. How could they? They have no idea what they should be investing in.

By creating a comprehensive written Internet strategy, you will be able to approach your board and upper management and clearly show them the level of funding, staffing, marketing and technology you will need to get 100 percent of your alumni registered.

Twelve Strategies

There are 12 primary strategies that I'd like you to include in your comprehensive written Internet strategy. The twelve strategies include:

1. Determine your mission and purpose.

2. Services strategy.

3. Registration strategy.

4. Partner strategy.

5. Volunteer strategy.

6. Goals and benchmarks strategy.

7. Student online community strategy.

8. Training strategy.

9. Marketing strategy.

10. Staffing strategy.

11. Funding strategy.

12. ePhilanthropy strategy.

Let's take a detailed look at each of the processes I'm asking you to include in your written Internet strategy:

1) Determine the Mission and the Purpose of your Online Community!

In the previous chapter we took a 30,000-foot look at determining what your purpose is. Now I'd like you to begin to drill into the details of how you can build a community that is unique to your organization.

The founders of MySpace decided that the Internet would offer a great way for bands to promote themselves. The founders of Facebook wanted to give students at Harvard a way to find out what was happening on campus. It was originally designed as an online directory, much like your online directory. Each started on a shoestring budget, but their focus was always on providing a community that people want to use. They knew if they gave something that people wanted, they'd attract more people and as more people came, they'd generate revenue from advertising.

In the previous chapter we asked you to focus on building your online community around career development. We think your online community will have an opportunity to thrive and grow when you focus in this area.

Now, however, I'd like you to consider finding other services you can provide that are totally unique to your college.

    A. Career Development.

    B. What makes you different?

    C. Lifelong learning.

    D. Making heroes of your alumni.

    E. Find Relevant content

Let's look at each of these in detail.

A. Career Development

We talked at great lengths about this in the chapter, "What is an online community?" It is our personal belief that this is one of the most compelling ways you can make your alumni online community a valuable resource for your alumni.

B. Focus on what makes you different!

As you continue to develop your Internet strategy, you need to remind yourself what makes your alumni online community different from others that your alumni can join. Your students and alumni will have a choice of many different online communities to participate in, so you have to offer something to them that is unique, that no one else can do as well as you.

There are a couple ways to do that. Think about the experiences that your alumni shared while they were on campus. For example, your alumni:

- Lived in the same residence halls.

- Walked the same paths.

- Had the same professors.

- Attended the same events.

- Listened to the same songs, bands.

- Experienced the same issues.

- Participated in the same clubs, sports, and groups.

- Took the same courses.

- Walked across the same stage on graduation day.

These shared experiences created a common bond among your alumni. In many different ways, their college experience has given them an opportunity to build affinity groups they will always feel connected to. This is something that puts your online community ahead of all others. Part of your purpose should be to develop and to foster these reconnections around their affinities and experiences. If this is part of your purpose, you should be adopting technology and services that will increase your alumni's sense of nostalgia.

Using these as examples, your strategy could include:

- Photos of events and activities during the time they were in college.

- Listing of music, movies, political, and social events that occurred.

- Information about current and retired professors.

- Access to some basic courses now recorded by professors.

- Ability to view yearbooks online and update information.

- Techniques to encourage discussion and collaboration.

Your alumni enjoyed many hours of fun and exciting experiencing that, in some cases, changed their lives. Your goal is to remind them of those experiences and to give them an opportunity to reminisce. NO ONE ELSE CAN DO THIS!

The Internet enables your college to build a relationship with your alumni that is so powerful, they will NEVER feel like they left campus. It would be a shame not to use this tool to build the bridge that virtually connects your alumni 24/7.

C. Lifelong Learning

You have tens of thousands of customers who spent tens of thousands of dollars, if not hundreds of thousands of dollars, on their education. You don't have to remind them that their education has elevated them from working in minimum wage jobs, to jobs and opportunities that are challenging and financially rewarding.

In the business community, it's commonly understood that a business will make more money from their existing customers than they will by going out after new business. It costs money to get new customers. Existing customers already know the quality, and they are more likely to buy from their current vendor. In the last decade, we've seen the rampant growth of distance learning colleges like Phoenix University, National University, and hundreds of others. **These organizations are growing at the expense of your college**. As our culture continues to become more complex and complicated, continual learning will become a requirement, not an option. In the past, cost was a definite deterrent to delivering these distance learning courses. However, courses that once cost $100,000 to produce a 60-minute lecture are now reduced to virtually nothing. You need to re-explore this strategy.

To continue to find ways to make your alumni online community unique and different from the hundreds of others your alumni can participate in, think about ways you can integrate educational opportunities for your alumni. You should identify how you can build learning communities around topics, interests, and/or hobbies that your faculty can be remotely engaged in. Meet with your faculty and staff to locate information that is already packaged so that you can offer introductory courses to your alumni. Don't expect an overnight success on this concept. You need to introduce it, market it to both students and alumni first. As they become more familiar with it, you will find their consumption of educational material will increase exponentially.

D. Make Heroes Out of your Alumni

Many alumni associations recognize alumni for contributions to the college, or they focus on the really high achievers in business, social, and/or political areas.

The web enables you to recognize a parent for raising four boys, a doctor who goes to Africa each year, alumni who volunteered at their church for 20 years, and the father who has coached Little League for 25 years. It's an important tool that enables you to effortlessly recognize ALL of your alumni for their wonderful achievements, contributions, and commitments to their families, work, community, and other nonprofit organizations.

One of the 101 strategies I'll suggest is that you have journalism students interview hundreds and thousands of alumni and write short essays about their lives and commitments. These can be posted to your website, along with photos shared by the alumni. This technique is a simple way to recognize your alumni and make them feel good not only about themselves, but their alumni association also.

E. Find Relevant content

Your college has an incredible wealth of photographs, news stories, articles, yearbooks, and information alumni have shared. You could repurpose that information by putting it online not only for alumni to consume but to interact with. Old photographs of events, campus life, protests, and significant moments could be posted photo albums where alumni could make comments and or email the links to their friends. You have recordings either in audio or video of famous speakers, dignitaries, or political/social figures that alumni would find fascinating. We'll share more about this in the 101 strategies, but for now, I think you get the general idea.

2) Services Strategy

In our early years at IAC, we suggested that clients adopt as many services as they could afford in order to give alumni the options and services that would most interest them.

An online community that offers basic services will initially generate traffic, but over time, it will need to:

- Deliver a variety of content.

- Build relationships and networks.

- Engage and involve alumni.

- Personalize the experience.

- Provide value to them.

Everyone has a different hot button. Your online community strategy has to be thinking about providing services and tools that will engage a very diverse group of alumni. As we discussed previously, the services you should consider offering need to align with your mission and purpose. Some of the additional services you might consider adding to your online community include:

- Surveys

- Private and Public Profile Pages

- News feeds

- Mentoring

- eNewsletters

- Personal Pals/Networking Groups

- eCards

- Screen savers

- Online Giving

- Blogs

- Podcasting

- Bulletin Boards

Following our own recommendations, think about the services that are fun, engaging, remind alumni of the times they had on campus, and will also help their business careers. When you start thinking out of the box, you'll begin introducing things like:

- Alumni recipes.

- Affinity pages built around alumni hobbies, clubs, and interests.

- Business networking opportunities.

- Online reunions and homecoming.

- Scanning your yearbooks.

- Deliver campus lectures online.

- Offer virtual reunions, homecoming.

Then you have to begin looking to the future to adopt new technologies that will assist alumni by:

- Accessing information via cell phones.

- Automatically updating their Outlook calendar with alumni events.

- Being alerted when a friend is coming to their town.

In consulting with clients, we encourage them to create a grid that outlines a three-to-five-year implementation of products and services. It's important to create a planned release of services as a way to keep alumni coming back to your website.

3) Registration Strategy

Without gasoline your car will go nowhere.

Registered users are to an online community what gas is to a car. Without a majority of your alumni registered in your online community it will run out of gas. Few will participate and even fewer will return to the community on a frequent basis. Technology is not the solution. Even the most advanced social networking software will fail to deliver the number of users your community needs to thrive.

Without participation, users will find little value and you will end up with a marginal amount of ROI and benefits you are hoping to achieve.

All of us in the online community industry are amazed at the huge number of alumni who are registered users of commercial websites. In the case of Facebook, for example, we know that an average of 83 percent of your students are registered on their website. When the students graduate, experience is proving that they are staying connected with their friends via Facebook. While some colleges are showing success at getting young alumni registered in their community, the vast majority are struggling.

Others are surprised to find that Classmates.com has more alumni registered on their site than their official alumni website offers.

In the case of Facebook, students found it to be a great way to connect and socialize with others. Because the value of the network was only as good as the number of people on it, the students invited their friends to participate. As more participated, more were invited. It didn't take long before the majority of students on campus were registered. Classmates.com is a different story. For the most part, their success in registering, in many cases, more alumni than the official alumni online community, is through relentless marketing. They were able to put their brand in front of the alumni continually until they registered.

You have to make your own way. Simply investing in the software that offers an online community will not ensure alumni will register and use it. You have to build a strategy to get them involved. To accomplish this, we recommend you create a registration strategy that includes the following five areas:

A. Launching

B. Generational Strategy

C. Marketing

D. Email Acquisition Campaign

E. Volunteers

A. Launching

After you've gone to all the work required to set up your online community, the very worst thing you could do is send one announcement to alumni to inform them about the online directory and community. Traditional marketing techniques suggest it takes up to six separate marketing efforts in order to get a customer to make a purchase commitment.

> **Simply investing in the software that offers an online community will not ensure alumni will register and use it.**

Traditional marketing also shows that a direct mail campaign may produce a one-to-three-percent response. Let's assume your alumni respond because of who you are. Our experience indicates that you'll be fortunate to get ten percent of your alumni to register on your first launch mailing. So, in order to really get your website to take off, you will need to invest in multiple mailings and multiple delivery channels and methods.

Before you even set up your online community, **I would advise you to have a budget that equals three to five times of what you have invested in your online community.**

B. Generational Strategy

Once your community is up and running, you will have a better chance of getting alumni to register if you speak to them in a language that complements who they are. For example, young alumni are not going to be as interested in estate planning information as your older alumni will be. A mom and/or a dad is not going to be interested in business networking as much as they will be with connecting with other parents who need a sounding board on how to handle the specific issues involved.

You need to recognize that not all of your alumni have the same needs and wants. You have to take the time to deliver a message to them that matches their needs at that point in their lives.

C. Email Acquisition Campaign

Another critical area to develop is an Email Acquisition Campaign. I'll detail this later as one of the 101 strategies, but in short, your EAC is an organized plan that identifies how you are going to get all of your alumni registered, who is responsible, and your overall goals.

> **You have to invest the greatest amount of resources in your registration strategy.**

We've had ten years to see the results of NOT having an organized plan to get 100 percent of your alumni registered. The vast majority of alumni associations have less than 30 percent of their alumni registered in their online community.

I see the EAC much like a capital campaign or annual giving campaign. Both have committees, goals, and people assigned with responsibilities. Your EAC needs to be structured the same way.

D. Volunteers

Later we'll share with you ten different things alumni volunteers can do to help you expand and maintain your online community. Here's a simple, effective and low-cost way to use them to increase registrations.

First, get a core group of approximately 100 alumni and ask them to find 20 classmates from their graduation year that were not registered in the site. Ask them to send a personal letter to each requesting them to help the college reach the goal of getting all alumni registered. The letter will remind them that helping reduce the cost to operate is another way to give back. The letter should also request the person keep the process going by sending a personal letter to another 20 people they know that are not registered in the community. A quick recap! Assuming that 50 percent register, the first 100 alumni would result in a net growth of 1,000 new registered users. If 50 percent of that group registered, the 500 alumni would then invite 20 classmates that could result in 5,000 new registered users. This is viral marketing at its best!

You have to invest the greatest amount of resources in your registration strategy. If you fail to have a written registration strategy and properly fund it, you will fail miserably at attracting enough alumni to provide them the experience that you could provide them.

4) Partner Strategy

Alumni professionals are stretched in every way possible. They have to write copy for websites, emails, and invitations. They need direct marketing skills to get alumni to participate in events and activities. They have to possess organizational skills to manage small and large events, and they are expected to develop their Internet strategy with no guidance or advice from management or experience.

With that in mind, I'd like to find ways for you get free help and/or advice from others both on and off campus. The bottom line is, you can't do this on your own and management shouldn't expect you to. Partnering with other groups and organizations will help you accomplish much more with less cost and effort.

Tom Sawyer is a great example of the benefits of working smarter and not harder. By pulling together a few meetings and enthusiastically showing why those at the meeting will benefit, you will be effectively creating a team that will do most of the "heavy lifting" for you.

For example, let's imagine you create a written strategy that identifies the following as potential partners to help you accomplish your overall written Internet strategy:

Partner	Delivers
A. Deans of Colleges	More registered users
B. Affinity Partners	Revenue and users
C. Faculty/Administrators	Student workers, staffing, funding

Now, let's look in detail on how each of these can help you.

A. Deans of Colleges

The deans of your colleges are terrific allies. First of all, your alumni will want to stay in touch with the departments and people they had the most day-to-day exposure with. While you act as the coordinator of the relationship, your deans and their staff could maintain alumni "approved" portals that include news, photos, information, and class notes about students within their individual college. Experience is showing that alumni are connecting more with the alumni association via these types of portals.

Just as I shared earlier that alumni are more likely to respond to a message from fellow alumni, rather than the alumni director, your alumni are also more likely to respond to participation requests from their deans.

The key to this relationship is that you are the sole source for address updates. While the deans are spending their hard-earned dollars mailing to their alumni, you need to agree to provide them access to emailing, as well as other tools that will allow them to continue to build their relationships with alumni.

B. Affinity Partners

Your affinity partners need you and you need them. Many are still doing frequent mailings to your alumni via the US Postal Service. Not only is this costly, but the overcrowded mailboxes and changing alumni behaviors could result in a declining response rate in the not-too-distant future.

In properly structured arrangements, your affinity partners could be including information about registering in your online community in the print mailings they do. In return for including your marketing materials that could include testimonials, endorsements, and why they should register, you could provide them access to periodic emailings to your alumni, or even more prominent banners. I advise clients to include opt-in opportunities in the registration process that encourage alumni to accept offers from your "approved" affinity partners at least twice a month. Your message could remind them that accepting these messages is the equivalent of providing a "micro" donation!

C. Faculty/Administrators

Your faculty could help you in a number of ways. First, they could provide your students the option to write articles about your alumni. Second, they could provide videotaped lectures that you could repurpose and make available to your alumni. Finally, they could make themselves available to be contacted by nostalgic alumni who need to feel attached to the college again.

Your administrators on campus need to understand your strategy and how every bit of it benefits the institution. Your admission office needs to know how your alumni can help them recommend, interview, and acquire new students. Your student services department needs to know how your alumni can mentor students, and your career services department needs to know how your alumni can provide job shadowing, internship, and employment opportunities. As you deliver more value to other departments, you can ask for a commitment in more staffing and funding.

Work smarter not harder. That should be your motto. Include this strategy for two reasons. It requires little setup and follow through, and it costs you basically nothing.

5) Volunteer strategy

Very few organizations are using volunteers to effectively increase participation and networking, update content or even maintain their online community. Not only are volunteers FREE, but they tend to be passionate and do a great job!

You will find volunteers to be helpful in increasing the number of alumni who are registered in your online community.

In the second strategy, "Registration Strategy," I recommended you use volunteers to increase the number of registrations. However, there is so much more they can do. In fact, I've outlined ten ways that volunteers will be instrumental in helping you grow and manage your online community. These include:

1. Welcome wagon greeters who show new registrants around.

2. Network weavers to pull interested alumni together.

3. Chat and bulletin board managers.

4. Blog managers who encourage alumni to link in their blogs.

5. Alumni interested in mentoring students.

6. Alumni to help admissions recruit new students.

7. Marketing oriented volunteers to help promote events and activities.

8. Alumni agreeing to post job opportunities within their firms.

9. Annual giving supporters.

10. Relocation advisors to help alumni settle into new cities.

I won't go into details on these in this section. Suffice to say, you will gain a tremendous boost by taking time to develop a volunteer strategy. You will learn in one of the 101 recommended strategies how you could gain 300 hours a week of volunteer time with a small number of alumni volunteers.

Using volunteers, like partnering with other departments, will benefit you in two ways. First of all, you gain the expertise and the work from hundreds of your alumni. Secondly, it doesn't cost you anything.

6) Goals and Benchmarks Strategy

You don't know if you've arrived if you don't know where you are going.

It is essential to set goals and benchmarks in order to know if your marketing plans are working. If the numbers are up, you are on track and may not need to make adjustments. If you are below your goals, by getting together and analyzing your numbers as a group, you can determine what you need to do over the next six months to bring your numbers back up.

I know it's hard to set goals and benchmarks when you've never set them before. However, I advise all of my clients to not get too hung up on setting the initial goals. Check in with peer institutions and do an assessment of what others are experiencing, identify your budget and the number of different departments who are helping to reach the goals, and then – just take a stab at it. You can always adjust them later. The point is to get something down and to build a business process that will enable you to keep moving forward.

Some of the basic goals and benchmarks you should consider tracking include:

- Percent of graduating seniors registered each year.

- Percent of (total) alumni registered.

- Frequency of alumni visits.

- Number of email addresses accumulated.

- Number of bad/undeliverable email addresses.

- Data updates.

- Number of alumni "connections."

- Number of class notes posted.

- Hits, views, and length of time on the website.

- Contributions.

- Most popular page.

To ensure you reach your goals, you will need to assign responsibility. I've worked with hundreds of organizations and thousands of people over my business career, and the one area everyone has trouble signing off on is responsibility. For many people, the goal of attending meetings is to walk away with no assignments!

Your plan has to assign responsibility to every single area of your plan. Everyone has to be committed and feel the pain if the benchmarks and goals are not met. Assign it, set a date for it to be completed by, and circle around to make sure everyone completes their assignments.

> **Parent Online Communities to give parents an opportunity to connect.**

The goal is not simply to track the above areas, but to analyze how you can continue to increase them. That requires someone to assume the responsibility, commit the time to accomplish it, and report back to the team.

Too few organizations take the time to meet even yearly to analyze the results of their progress and to make logical business decisions based on need.

7) Student Online Community Strategy

Nearly a decade ago, I suggested in my book, *Create a NET-Centered College Campus*, that colleges should offer online communities for all constituents of the college.

I shared with administrators that building gorgeous new buildings and facilities on campus may be a good strategy to stay competitive, but I stressed that colleges and universities should also invest in Internet technology to provide online communities for a generation that is going to be spending a significant amount of time online.

It wasn't hard to come to this conclusion. All you had to do was watch the success of commercial online communities in the mid 1990's and how people were connecting and participating in them. My suggestion then, as it is now, is that your college encourage and endorse the development of private, password communities built around the different phases students pass during their college experience.

I suggested a "**cradle to grave**" concept that included:

- **Prospective Student Online Communities** that would connect students who are evaluating a college, and give them the ability to see who else is considering going to the campus. This technique increases the number of visitors to the admission page, and keeps them there longer. Longer stay means you will be able to deliver more information and collect more data about the prospective students.

- **Orientation Online Communities** that widens the incoming students circle of friends to take away some of the anxiety of coming to college. Students are able to find others based on their hobbies, career goals, and skills. This technique benefits the college because it gets prospective students networking over the summer, reducing their "summer melt."

- **Student Online Communities** that give students the ability to find others on campus who have the same hobbies, interests, and goals. A student may find that a person who plays classical guitar, is interested in photography, and plans to go into law, lives right next door to him.

I also suggested that colleges and universities consider adopting Parent Online Communities to give parents an opportunity to connect with the college and each other. This generation of parents wants to be connected, and a community built around them will give your organization additional support dollars for your needs.

In hindsight, I only wish I had promoted this concept more vigorously as colleges today find themselves competing for their digital relationship with students because commercial websites like Facebook and MySpace have gotten a stranglehold on their students. In an attempt to raise more awareness to this matter, I issued a series of white papers and held webinars that attracted over 700 alumni professionals.

Our message was simple, Facebook:

1) Is stealing your brand.

2) Receiving valuable data that students update on their sites that would be beneficial to the advancement office in the years ahead.

3) Created student disciplinary issues for various departments around campus.

4) Was fundamentally altering the college experience for your students.

5) Leaving you with no control.

Colleges that want to control their brand, data, and relationship with their students and alumni are beginning to understand the necessity of providing password-protected online communities. The college-based online communities are not designed to compete with commercial social networking online communities but rather to provide unique services and networking that only the college could provide.

My firm, IAC, has been introducing these concepts to receptive admission, orientation, and student affairs offices around the world. Some might say that the educational market is slow to react, but once they do, they pounce with the tenacity of a hungry bear that just came out of hibernation! Within the next five years, every college will be following each other in a race to recapture their digital relationship with their students.

So how does this benefit your alumni association? By participating in college-endorsed online communities, your students will be developing a behavior that will make it easier for you to keep them engaged in your online community.

And in the bigger picture, your entire campus benefits in the following ways:

- Capture the data they were losing to commercial organizations.

- Protect their brand that commercial organizations were stealing and misusing.

- Educate students how to professionally participate in online communities.

- Develop a behavior in students that would carry over as alumni.

Don't sigh and tell me it's too late to engage your students in "college-endorsed" communities! Your students will be members of dozens of communities. You have a new crop every year that you can begin inculcating into using "college-endorsed" communities.

8) Training strategy

Your online community initiative is not only new to your alumni, but it's new to your staff. Your alumni will need to be taught, not only what the website will do for them, but also how to use it. They will need training on how to promote, manage, and engage users.

I can remember nearly 20 years ago when ATM machines were being introduced to banking customers, my future wife, Gae, spent time showing customers how to put a plastic card into the ATM machine sitting on a table in the lobby of the bank. Customers were confused and uncomfortable with the new technology. Even though ATMs were initially free, consumers today have found the convenience to be so immense that they are willing to pay for the service.

The point I'm trying to make is simply this – you might have the greatest new gizmo in the world, but if people don't know how to use it, they won't.

You, along with your online community providers, will need to:

A. Teach students before they leave campus.

B. Provide training via webinars, podcasts and videos.

As well as other tools to show your alumni how to use your online community to help them get jobs, do business with others, and find classmates.

A. Teach students before they leave campus

The earlier you teach students about what your online community can do for them, the better. You and your team need to spend time showing students how to find mentors, how to find people that can help them relocate to other cities, how to locate alumni that can help them get jobs, etc.

B. Provide training via webinars, podcasts and videos

While it might not be possible to interact with all of your students and alumni, in the spirit of working smarter not harder I recommend you develop some training and marketing materials to support your goals. It's easy to hold an online webinar to show alumni how to use the online community and what it will do for them.

Do it once, record it, and it will be available for hundreds of other alumni. You might consider interviewing some of your alumni who are frequent users of your website. It's easy to look at your stats and determine this. We've found some alumni who are on the site every week. They are using the site for networking. After you find this person, get a testimonial and do a podcast interview that others can download and hear at any time. Supplemental content like this will help you continue to grow your community.

A little training will go a long way in increasing the value of your online community to all of your alumni. Think about each person you train as part of your training and marketing strategy. The more they know how to use your site, the more people they will invite and invest their own time in showing them around and telling them what services to use.

9) Develop a marketing strategy

Once you have your site up and running, your number one goal is to increase awareness. The only way you can do this effectively is to create a written marketing plan. You have a great deal to lose if you skip this step. Experience has proven that alumni will not stumble on, and find your online community, in great numbers.

You'll hear me say many times, "If you build it – they will NOT come." Traditional marketing programs use different media, messages, and delivery mechanisms to promote a product or service. Your strategy has to include print, digital, peer to peer, testimonial, and all the tricks you can think of to promote your website. Plan this part properly and you will have a very successful online community.

There are eight key ways to market your website and your desire to get alumni to participate in events, activities, and fundraising campaigns:

    A. Traditional print media.

    B. Email marketing.

    C. Friend inviting friend (viral marketing).

    D. Through partners.

    E. Press releases and PR.

    F. Endorsement and testimonials.

    G. Phone marketing.

    H. Event marketing.

Let's take a quick look at the eight techniques:

A. Traditional print media

This area includes advertising in your alumni magazine, sending out letters, postcards, flyers, and more. We recommend that you spend at least four dollars per alumni in the early years of your online community to get your alumni registered in the community.

B. Email marketing

This is the easiest for most to adopt, but too many are not using email marketing effectively. For homecoming, reunions, and special events, I am suggesting to clients that they use a variety of email marketing tools like broadcast emails, animated emails, multimedia emails, and epostcards to increase participation in events.

C. Friend inviting friend (viral marketing)

More than just a link on your website letting alumni invite others to participate, you need to develop powerful friend-inviting-friend campaigns where your alumni will be actively inviting others to participate.

D. Through partners

Your deans, affinity partners, and others are important parts of your marketing program. Before you create a marketing program for a specific event, ask yourself how your affinity partner can help you, while at the same time benefiting them.

E. Press releases and PR

Simple press releases through traditional channels are effective marketing campaigns. Consider adopting your website so your alumni can identify which newspapers they read in their hometown. Using digital technology, you can deliver thousands of unique press releases to hometown newspapers.

F. Endorsement and testimonials

You have thousands of alumni who are already using your online community. Your marketing program should involve showing alumni practical reasons why the online community would benefit them. Hearing these benefits from peers makes the meaning much more significant.

G. Phone marketing

Automated Phone Calls are the tools political candidates use to capture our attention. While you and I ignore their message, a well-crafted message from famous alumni, athletic director, the president, or national celebrity, will be heard by your alumni. When their message is to register in the community, or come to homecoming, I can guarantee you will increase participation.

H. Event marketing

Some organizations have hundreds of events per year. You should consider taking a wireless laptop with you to each event and plan on signing up alumni in your online community. It's a good time to build interest in it and to show them how it will benefit them.

An effective marketing program requires a commitment of staff, resources, and funding and a great deal of creativity. Your marketing needs to reflect the mission and purpose of your community. It needs to focus on the benefits it provides the alumni, and when done properly, will put them front and center as satisfied users!

10) Staffing Strategy

You'll get tired of hearing me talk about how woefully understaffed online web strategies are.

I should clarify myself, however. If your alumni association does NOT have written goals or a comprehensive Internet strategy, your current staffing levels are probably fine. Not great, but adequate enough to get the job done.

When asked how much time is spent on maintaining their online community, many organizations admit to less than a couple of hours per week. As a result, their online community is underutilized, has few alumni participating, and is viewed as more of a chore from administrators because of a growing frustration of having to spend time and money doing something that is not offering a clear ROI.

There are two types of staffing strategies:

    A. "Fit it in."

    B. Strategically driven.

A. "Fit it in" staffing strategy

If your organization is like most, the following responsibilities are performed by one or two people when they can "fit them in."

- Authenticating users.

  - Handling users' issues.

  - Updating news and information.

  - Marketing the website to alumni.

  - Sending broadcast emails out.

  - Managing the technical aspects of your website.

We call this the "Fit it in staffing strategy." This strategy leaves little time for:

  - Involving other departments.

  - Strategizing on what you want to do next.

  - Meeting to determine if you are on track.

  - Engaging and involving students and young alumni.

B. Strategically driven staffing strategy

When you take the time to develop a comprehensive Internet strategy, you will have a clear picture of who has to accomplish what, and when they have to accomplish it.

When you are fully investing in a comprehensive Internet strategy, we envision you will need the following six positions:

a. Website Director

b. Volunteer Coordinator and Partner Coordinator

c. Content Developer

d. Marketing Coordinator

e. Career Services Director

a. Website Director

Your Website Director would be your alumni magazine's equivalent of the editor. This person is the visionary, whose ultimate responsibility is to see that the entire team stays focused on accomplishing the written Internet strategy. This is one savvy Internet user. This person is a member of many online communities, is well read on the topic, and can demonstrate leadership capability.

b. Volunteer Coordinator and Partner Coordinator

This person supervises the volunteers. We've identified ten different ways your alumni can volunteer to help you reach your strategic goals. Someone needs to manage, encourage, compliment, and acquire them. This is a very important position, as one person could be multiplied by 100 volunteers. Another major responsibility of this position would keep your partners engaged. We discussed the benefits of working with a number of partners in order for you to accomplish more with less. You need to have someone coordinate your partnerships with the deans, affinity partners, sponsors, and others.

c. Content Developer

Someone on your team needs to be focused on obtaining interesting content from as many different sources as possible. This person will be gathering content from alumni, faculty, administrators, and colleges, and positioning on the website content in text, audio, and video.

d. Marketing Coordinator

This is a critical position, because it not only develops the marketing copy, strategy, and execution of the written marketing plan, but is also responsible for coordinating the marketing program for partners and the colleges. This creative person has to understand the venues available to market the website, and should have a clear vision of the Internet tools and channels that can be used to deliver the message.

e. Career Services Director

Critical position! If you agree that the number one benefit you can provide your alumni is contacts and mentors to help them find jobs and advance their business careers, you need to invest in someone who can focus in this area. This person needs to understand they are responsible for connecting alumni and for building a culture that supports the overall agenda of alumni helping others.

Each of these positions should have well-documented job descriptions, deliverables, expectations, and goals.

Why do you need all of these positions? Think about the positions that have developed over the years in your alumni magazine. You now have an editor, writers, graphic designers, and photographers. While the very first edition of your alumni magazine probably was produced by one person as a labor of love, or simply assigned to "keep up with the Joneses," today's organizational chart has expanded to reflect the institution's support for providing the very best image to their alumni.

It's ironic that this same desire for quality is not extending to the alumni web presence.

11) Funding Strategy

Nearly every alumni association is under-funding their Internet strategy.

Ok, I'll have to qualify that statement again. If your organization does not have a comprehensive written Internet strategy, then you are probably funding your online community at the proper level.

After all – You get what you pay for!

If you have been developing your strategy in the order that I've presented it to you, you should have a pretty clear picture of how much money you will need to fund your Internet strategy.

The goal of your strategy will be to show management that the initial investment will immediately begin to pay off. Your web site will reduce the cost to communicate with alumni and increase communication to alumni, and as studies have shown, the more you communicate good news about the college, the more alumni will contribute, and more frequently.

I'd like you to do a simple exercise.

Pick up the phone and contact the head of your IT department and ask how much is spent each year on staffing, software, hardware, and consulting to provide your students the level of technology and service they have come to expect. Then, take that number and divide it by the number of students. For fun, let's assume that your organization spends $1,000,000 a year in technology and related costs. Let's also assume you have 10,000 students. When you divide the

$1,000,000 a year by the 10,000 students, you end up with a yearly technology expenditure of $100 spent per student.

Let's compare that number to what you spend on technology to support all of your alumni.

If you are like most organizations, you have a number of different people involved in maintaining your online community. The data person updates data, you handle event promotions and authentications, and another person handles the monthly eNewsletter. Let's assume that the time committed between all three people is the equivalent of one half-time person. Let's also assume with benefits and salary, the full-time pay for a position is $50,000. Because your team collectively is committing half of a full-time salary, the salary cost to manage your community is $25,000 a year. Now, let's assume that you are spending $20,000 a year for an online directory/community solution from a third-party firm. Based on the prior assumptions, your total financial commitment to your online community initiative is $45,000 per year.

Let's determine the investment/cost per alumni served. Assuming you have 30,000 alumni, divide the amount spent in software and staff to provide an online community by the total alumni base. When you do that for the example shown above, you end up with a yearly commitment of $1.50 per alumni!

Wow! You almost spend that much when you send them a letter! In the first example, we showed how students receive the equivalent of $100 a year in technology services. What kind of signal does that send to your prospective students, parents, and alumni when you are only spending $1.50 per year on them?

Let's look at it from another angle.

Let's compare your investment in your online directory and community to what you are investing in your alumni magazine. You have staffing, writers, photography, postage, paper, printing, and other related costs. Even if you were able to reduce your core cost per magazine, including postage, to a measly two dollars, a quarterly commitment to mail to alumni would be six dollars per year, and that doesn't include departmental costs.

The point I'm trying to drive at is your college is already making significant investments in other areas to serve your alumni. Management needs to step up to the plate and make corrective investments in your Internet strategy – or risk losing an incredible opportunity to more tightly weave alumni into the fabric of the campus.

I have to plug the fact that you will see a higher return of your investment from your online community than you do from your alumni magazine. Later in the book, I'll offer compelling reasons why you are wasting resources by continuing to print alumni magazines, and I'll offer indisputable evidence that you will get more back from your investment in your alumni online community.

But for now, for the sake of getting you to start thinking about your web investment as a rolling three-year commitment, here are just a few of the areas you need to be including in your funding needs:

	Funding	Yr. 1	Yr 2	Yr 3
• Technology				
• Software				
• Staffing				
• Marketing				
• Training				
• Consulting				
• Sending broadcast emails out				
• Misc.				
Total				

12) ePhilanthropy Strategy

If you have successfully implemented the previous 11 strategies, the final strategy will provide you the contributions you deserve!

Properly organized and followed, your ePhilanthrophy strategy will help your organization raise significant contributions and, at the same time, continue to cultivate a sense of giving and stewardship in each of your alums.

While there are many ePhilanthropy strategies you can develop, we'll share with you five basic strategies to get you started.

These include:

1. Annual Giving

2. Capital Campaign

3. Scholarship Online Community

4. Data Capture

5. Students and Young Alumni

Annual Giving

Over the past 50 years, the annual giving office has had the benefit of testing numerous techniques to increase the number of alumni contributing to the Alumni Association.

The industry initially focused on direct mail techniques to increase contributions. Today, alumni associations are adopting sophisticated telemarketing techniques to reach alumni and encourage them to participate in annual giving. The telemarketing calls to alumni are either outsourced to third-party companies or is completed by paid students and volunteer alumni.

While many organizations are increasing the total contributions each year, a growing majority are finding it difficult to increase the number of contributors. Well oiled annual giving machines are beginning to see a series of new issues that could significantly impact their ability to increase contributions in the future.

First, they are facing a growing number of alumni who use caller ID to screen calls. There was a time when every call was an exciting new communication from someone and it was answered! Today, however, most people look first at who's calling and make a snap decision if they want to take the call. This change in your alumni behavior has required you and your team to make more dials, which costs time and money.

Another issue you are facing is from your alumni, particularly younger alumni who are abandoning landlines and relying on their cell phones as their principal means of communication. This will continue to make it more difficult to reach this generation as they reach the "giving" age.

We are recommending that annual giving offices begin to adopt Internet technology to reach alumni who are becoming harder to reach by telephone and mail. Some of the techniques that alumni associations could be adopting include:

1. Developing interactive giving tools to reach alumni via the Internet

2. Encourage alumni to pay using their credit card online

3. Network their student callers with alumni to increase participation

4. Use online tools to recognize contributors

5. Adopt technology that increases challenge gifts between classes and peers

6. Develop an interactive annual giving portal page

Annual Giving offices who are adopting Internet technology to reach alumni will find themselves in a good position to begin to overcome these issues. Your alumni are already giving online at non profits. It's time to get them used to giving online in your annual giving program. More importantly, it's time to give THEM the chance to connect with your annual giving program – when they want. Adopting any of the techniques suggested will help your organization engage more alumni and increase contributions.

Capital Campaign

Capital campaigns can benefit from Internet technology by carrying the message to the alumni on a more frequent basis. We recommend that capital campaigns develop communication channels with their alumni based on what their alumni are interested in supporting and interested in knowing the results.

Your alumni should have the opportunity to opt in to a series of enewsletters that will keep them informed about the progress. Key individuals within the university should create blogs to update the progress to alumni. Each development officer could create a blog that would be dedicated to those alumni they are assigned to. A steady flow of personal, positive information and successes could be just what is needed to tip the scale.

Online Surveys are valuable ways to give alumni a chance to participate in the early phases of the Capital Campaign. Surveys will help you understand alumni moods, attitudes, and what areas they would be willing to support.

Online volunteer tools will help you find individuals willing to get the message out to fellow alumni in a more personal way. Using Internet technology you will be able to recognize the volunteers too.

Increasing participation in events, activities, and regional meetings will be important in the years leading up to your Capital Campaign. Use Internet technology to bring together alumni for virtual events that will engage and connect them to each other. Your online community can be used to identify alumni who are connected to each other. Armed with this information you will know which "giving" alumni to approach to ask their friends to participate in the Capital Campaign.

I've identified 40 other ways to use technology to increase participation in Capital Campaign by using technology. The items we've reviewed are a good place to start, however if you'd like to learn more, email me

Scholarship Online Community

Contributors today are interested in knowing how their contributions are being used. They want to see the results of their hard earned dollars, and they want to be able to determine where their money is used. When your alumni have thousands of different organizations who are willing to give them more flexibility in how their gift is used, and are willing to develop more customized giving programs built around the contributors desires, your development office should be moving toward Internet products and services to accommodate this trend.

One of the effective ways to increase the number of contributors, and the amount contributed in scholarship programs, is to provide contributors their own Scholarship Online Community. This program is highly effective because it enables individuals to stay in touch with the students who are receiving scholarships from the contributor. An effective Scholarship Online Community should include the following tools and services:

- Portal page with the contributors name, bio, photo, and history

- Profile pages of the scholars and class notes updating their success

A Scholarship Online Community is an effective way to build a lifelong affinity group. Students who are part of this affinity group will, over their lifetime, have an opportunity to update their successes and to mentor others who are receiving the same scholarship. As the students graduate, they will continue to have an opportunity to share what they are doing with their mentor/scholarship provider and others who received the scholarship.

It's a perfect way to build stewardship in students receiving scholarships and a great way to get them to contribute back to the same scholarship over time.

Here's how a Scholarship Online Community works.

First, you'll need to decide what level scholarship will receive a Scholarship Online Community. Let's assume you set the requirement at $25,000. Now your advancement team has an edge to "up-sell" prospects to contribute more.

Let's look at an example. If I contributed $25,000 to your scholarship program, you would create for me the Philabaum Scholarship Online Community. The Philabaum Scholarship Online Community would include biographical information about me, a photograph, and a comments section where I can share my philosophies about business, education, and giving back to the community. It would also include profile pages of the scholars; a photograph of each scholar and class notes where they can update information about the events activities and successes they are experiencing. Included in the scholarship online community is the ability for each scholar to network with each other along with me.

For a very small investment of time and Internet technology, your annual giving program could see dramatic increases in contributions to scholarship programs. It's a fantastic way for your contributors to see the results of their contribution. If you're not sure if this would be a valuable resource, ask your development officers who approach alumni contributions at this level. My guess is they would be thrilled to have this innovative tool as a way to encourage donors to not only contribute to the scholarship program, but to contribute more in order to qualify for a Scholarship Online Community.

Data Capture

Another area you will want to focus on in developing your annual giving ePhilanthrophy strategy is data capture.

The more information you know about alumni, the better opportunity you will have to personalize and ask questions. For example, if you knew that I was part of the Daily Kent Stater, was involved in the campus radio station, engaged in protesting on campus, and lived in the Tri-Towers dorm, you would have a number of powerful ways to personalize what you ask me.

Knowing that I was involved in the campus radio station, your development team would be able to contact me with specific appeals to support the needs of the campus radio station.

Research is showing that alumni are willing to give scholarship programs, but they're not willing to give to large buckets of undefined needs. By developing an active alumni online community that captures the information as described above, your development staff will be able to data mine the information and either send e-mails letters or initiate compelling personal conversations.

Remember you will have a lifetime to capture data from alumni. As they continue to come back to your website, you should be asking for additional data that will give you an opportunity to personalize your questions in the years to come.

Students and Young Alumni

In a previous business, my firm photographed nearly 200,000 students each year as they received their diplomas on graduation day. As a result, I sat through many graduation ceremonies, heard many graduation speeches, and listened to nearly every graduate groan when the President of the Alumni Association reminded them to be watching for an envelope from their alma mater, giving them an opportunity to participate in the annual giving program.

While it seemed to be an appropriate thing to say - the timing could not be worse. As you know, students are leaving college with large loans they have to pay back over the next couple of decades. Few students think they have an obligation to give back when they are facing monthly payments to pay off the loans that, in their mind, paid the expenses to run the college while they were on campus.

While students have limited resources within the first decade after college, studies have shown that students have more free time available to help the institution. We are suggesting that you develop Internet techniques to engage and involve students as volunteers to increase contributions.

One of the ways this could be done is by encouraging student volunteers to become part of the annual giving calling campaign. Instead of requiring young alumni to come to campus to make the calls, technology is available today where the young alumni can identify who to call via online call management tools, and update the results after hanging up their cell phone.

There are many additional strategies you can implement in developing your ePhilanthrophy Internet strategy. The ideas and suggestions we've discussed here are some we think you could get started on immediately.

It's a good place to start to engage, involve, and create a culture of stewardship using Internet technology.

Summary

Your alumni online community has the potential to completely transform your alumni association to one that offers a multidimensional connection between your college, alumni, and their classmates.

I guarantee you that with a written Internet strategy that relates information about the return on investment it provides, you will receive the resources you need to accomplish your plan.

There are many examples of alumni associations who are receiving hundreds of thousands of dollars a year in unsolicited online contributions. Others are communicating more frequently with alumni at less cost. And then there are even others who are increasing participation at events with more email marketing and by showing who is attending. Few are accomplishing all of these because of limited staffing and funding.

Creating a written Internet strategy will help upper management understand the revolutionary potential of your alumni online community. Once you have their commitment, the increases in staffing and funding will enable you to fully execute your strategy.

When necessary, you may need to bring in outside expertise to help you build a strategy that supports your college and departments' missions and goals. Keep in mind that the Internet is a relatively new thing to those on your staff, and few have had the background that will provide guidance on how to draft your Internet strategy.

If your organization finds value in bringing consultants to help craft directions and goals for annual giving and capital campaigns, you will also benefit from gaining the advice and consult of experienced professionals to help draft your Internet strategy. Consultant fees can be justified by helping you get where you want to be faster, because they can help you avoid making costly mistakes, and because they help you and your team focus on your core mission without getting too sidetracked while developing the written Internet strategy.

In the next chapter, we'll talk about how to identify and communicate what your return on investment from your alumni online community will be to support your request for more staffing and funding.

You can quantify savings, visits, contributions,
data updates with alumni online communities.
What can you quantify with your alumni magazine?

ONLINE COMMUNITIES PROVIDE SIGNIFICANT ROI

How much time and effort do you spend in determining your return on investment from any of the following:

- Events like homecoming, reunion and award banquets.

- The Alumni Magazine.

- Newsletters and other mailings sent to alumni.

From my conversations with industry leaders, only a few are performing break-even analyses on these. Even less are determining if alumni are reading the alumni magazine or newsletters. In most cases organizations don't have the time, in others they don't have the analytical expertise and in yet others, they don't want to spend the money!

With magazines and print newsletters you can't tell how many alumni are reading the magazine or which stories were the most popular, and/or gather feedback from alumni regarding the stories. Nor would we be able to tell how long alumni spent reading the magazine.

Events, the alumni magazine, and newsletters are traditional tools that have evolved over the last five decades to help alumni relations advance their missions and goals. Think about the events and activities that you have and identify the cost to hold those events versus the revenue they produce. In this exercise, identify the costs to provide the following events and services. List other activities that you can think of also, including travel programs, speaker series, or student alumni programs.

	Cost	Revenue Generated		Profit/Loss
Home coming	_____	_____	=	_____
Reunion	_____	_____	=	_____
Alumni Magazine	_____	_____	=	_____
_____	_____	_____	=	_____
_____	_____	_____	=	_____
_____	_____	_____	=	_____

I'm interested in you doing this simple exercise for two reasons.

First, to get you thinking about whether your traditional alumni programs are providing you a return on investment. As you review the data you filled in the fields above, I'd like you to begin to question if they are worth the investment. Obviously, I am not going to suggest that you stop holding homecoming or reunions. However, I would like you to think about secondary events and activities that you do each year that are costing more to produce than revenue collected for the event.

Secondly, I want you to begin looking at **what you are investing in these and evaluate if these are worth the time and effort you are putting into them.** If they are not, I would suggest you commit those funds to your Internet strategy. Nearly every organization should be able to find a dozen activities/events they can cut that would free up $10,000 to $50,000 to invest in their online community strategy.

You would not be reading this book if you didn't think that the Internet will become the heart of your relationship with your alumni now and in the future. In a time when there are limited dollars available to you and your staff I want you to be entrepreneurial in thought and look for ways you can develop an Internet strategy with money that is ALREADY in your budget!

What's the ROI of your online community?

While there is some anecdotal evidence that investments in events, alumni magazine and newsletters increase contributions, few provide as immediate and qualitative evidence as that supplied by an alumni online community.

With online communities you can determine how many alumni visited your website, how long they stayed, what they read, which page was most popular, what hour of the day had the most traffic. Imagine if you had 8,000 alumni knocking at the front door of your alumni house each month. Within the first three months, you'd have to replace the door and the carpets, and of course hire more staff to greet the alumni.

There are five primary ways you can determine if your online community is providing you a return on your investment:

    A. Savings by communicating via email

    B. Contributions per email address.

    C. Increased number of data updates.

    D. Labor savings.

    E. Soft savings.

A. Savings by communicating via email

This one is easy. All you have to decide on is what an email address is worth to you. The formula to do this is fairly simple.

Identify how many times you will be communicating with alumni by email over the course of one year.

Determine how much it would have cost you to communicate by the mail.

For the purpose of this exercise, lets assume it cost you $1 in labor, postage, printing, graphic design, envelopes, paper, etc., to communicate with alumni via letters and newsletters. If you were sending a letter or newsletter twice a month to your alumni you would save $24 per email address per year.

B. Contributions per email address

Nearly all alumni online communities we've evaluated generate unsolicited online contributions from alumni. If, for example, you received $20,000 in online contributions last year, and you had 5,000 alumni registered in your online community, the contribution value of each email is $4.

Add the savings value and the contribution value and the email address is now worth $28 each year.

C. Data Updates

Now you have to identify the value of each data update you get from alumni. All alumni and development offices invest in a variety of tools and services to get updated email and physical address changes.

It's a bit more problematic to determine the savings on having alumni update data online, but try it from this angle. Let's assume that it costs two dollars in staff time to open a letter and read the information, analyze what to do with it, and then update the address change in your database. You can develop your own formula based on how many per hour your staff currently handles. With a little research, you find that your colleagues are averaging five hundred address/email changes monthly. Your online community in this case would deliver $12,000 in savings per year, as well as making it easier for your alumni to update their address changes. In our example lets assume we have 10,000 email addresses. The savings from data updates will add another $1.20 to each email taking our new total to $29.20 cents.

> **The benefits from the self service cost now take the value of an email address to $29.70.**

D. Labor savings

Another, less obvious benefit, is savings that result from alumni "self servicing" themselves. With Internet technology, besides updating their address and career information, your alumni can register for events, pay online, and handle other transactions. Each of these steps would have normally involved your staff. What is the value to you to be able to save time, and to help your staff concentrate on more productive responsibilities? If you put a value of each self-service event at $5 and you had 1,000 alumni "transactions" you would save $5,000 each year. The benefits from the self service cost now take the value of an email address to $29.70.

E. Soft savings

There are other ways to evaluate the ROI of your online community that may not be as easy to put a dollar figure to. For example, if sending three to five requests to attend events and activities or to contribute increases participation, then each email has an increased value to you.

There are other areas that you benefit from, but you can't put a finger on the actual savings. You would have to determine what the value of the following works out to be:

- Staying in touch with alumni more frequently.

- Connecting alumni with others.

- Helping alumni find jobs via your online career center.

- Providing students with mentoring opportunities.

Each of these areas has a positive effect on your alumni, which can result in an increased sense of stewardship, involvement, and connectedness with the university and their classmates. To paraphrase a recent credit card commercial, the value could be "priceless!"

Calculate your ROI

To help identify your ROI from your online community, consider displaying the financial benefits in the following manner:

Savings & Revenue			
	Yr. 1	Yr. 2	Yr. 3
Saving in postage, paper, and printing	$100,000	$120,000	$150,000
Contributions received online	$12,000	$18,000	$30,000
Increased number of data updates	$12,000	$18,000	$25,000
Self service	$5,000	$5,000	$5,000
Soft Savings	$?	$?	$?
Total Savings	$129,000	$161,000	$210,000

This example would justify an investment of $166,000 (result of adding all totals and dividing by 3) a year on the alumni Internet strategy. Try this and see if you are already getting more benefits than you are investing in your online community.

If you are not investing at least as much as you are receiving in benefits from your alumni online community than you risk your alumni online community initiative failing!

A major goal of this book is to encourage all those who are involved in developing alumni online communities to petition to management for greater funding, staffing, and commitment to develop a comprehensive strategy in order to fully take advantage of the benefits the web will provide the organization. If you are not investing at least as much as you are receiving in benefits from your alumni online community than you risk your alumni online community initiative failing! Not only to achieve your goals, but also by simply falling off your alumni's radar and becoming more of a ghost town than an active, engaging website community.

This may seem like a lot of work, but if your college wants to have an Internet strategy, if your administration wants YOU to better serve alumni, if your administration wants YOU to increase communication, save money, and increase contributions, you've got to do it. Asking for money when you have a solid plan is easy. You are more passionate about the request because your plan will easily pay for itself.

Summary

In business, we have a phrase; "Spend time developing your business, not working in it." You are not leading your organization if you are toiling away on the daily tasks. Your leadership will truly shine when you help your alumni association develop a comprehensive written Internet strategy that includes providing a positive return on your investment of Internet technology.

In this chapter we identified five ways to show that you are receiving an ROI from your online community. These include:

- Savings by communicating via email

- Contributions per email address.

- Increased number of data updates.

- Labor savings

- Soft savings.

The example we walked you through in this chapter showed where an alumni association was realizing a savings and other benefits from every email address. The value we determined of each email address was $29.70 per year.

We said in our example that we had 10,000 email addresses. Looking at it another way, our online community provided us $29,700 savings ($29.70 x 10,000) and other benefits in just one year. Over a decade that would represent $297,000. ($29,700 x 10 years)

When you start thinking about the value of an email address this way, it becomes easier for everyone to begin investing to acquire all of your alumni email addresses. If the 10,000 email addresses we used in our example represented only 20 percent of our alumni base, that means we have 40,000 alumni that we are not reaching by email. That means we are losing $29.70 X 40,000 or $118,800 in benefits each year.

Doesn't that make you want to go out and get more alumni registered!

ALUMNI WEB STRATEGIES

101 Strategies to Build Online Community

This book owes the early pioneers of alumni online communities a great deal of gratitude.

Over the past decade, visionary alumni professionals have taken a leap of faith and implemented a number of Internet-based ideas and concepts in order to better serve their association and their alumni.

Based on the work of these early pioneers, we are better able to determine what we should include in our online communities and what we need to avoid. Their work, investment, and persistence have provided us a roadmap on which we can build our Internet strategies today.

Like you, they have struggled with what they wanted to do versus what they had the resources to be able to do. Like you, they were already working 40-plus-hour weeks, had 15 other responsibilities listed on their job descriptions, and were required to keep decades of old programs running successfully. Somehow, along the way, they found the ideas and concepts that worked.

Many of these views are included in the 101 ideas and concepts I am sharing with you.

While you are absorbing the 101 strategies, visit **www.internetstrategiesgroup .com**, where you can create web procedures for your organization that include your favorite strategies.

And now, let's take a look at the 101 ideas to build your online community!

1 FUN FACTOR

Andy Sernovitz in his book, *Word of Mouth Marketing*, reminds us that your product or service has to excite your customers. If you really want to excite and take advantage of viral marketing (word-of-mouth marketing), you need to exceed their expectations and provide an experience they won't forget.

In his book Andy says:

> In many cases, word-of-mouth marketing isn't actually "marketing" at all. It's about great customer service that makes people want to tell their friends about you. It's about fantastic products that people can't resist showing to everyone.

Making your website FUN is another way you encourage alumni to engage and involve their friends.

Nearly every alumni association I've encountered looks at itself as a fun organization that works tirelessly to build relationships with and between alumni via social events.

As you continue to build your web strategy, your Internet site should keep abreast of these core values. Just how fun is your website? Keep reading and we'll ask you to take our "FUN" test.

Imagine how you could make it more interesting by letting alumni search for:

- ONLY those online at that moment or within the last day.

- Alumni who have photographs posted of family or of themselves on their profile page.

- Alumni who have posted class notes.

- Alumni with the same affinity groups or hobbies.

Or you incorporate interactive tools that include:

- Allowing alumni to post comments to fellow classmates class notes or photos.

- Online blogs created and maintained by alumni.

- Automatically recommend others to meet those that match their interests.

- eCards they can send to each other.

Suddenly, we've added another level of activity that is designed to engage and involve alumni.

Contests are a great way to increase participation and awareness. You might consider holding a baby picture contest where both the alumni parents and grandparents can post their children or grandchildren's baby pictures. Then, hold a contest for who will represent the alumni association that year as the adopted (mascot) baby of the year! Photographs could be voted on by other alumni with the top vote-getter being the winner. Consider doing this with alumni posting photographs of events or parties from the days they were in college.

This contest might be focused to build more awareness in alumni who graduated within specific periods of time. For example, alumni who graduated from 1980 –1985 where photographs that depicted cultural attitudes, clothing, and events would be most appreciated. Imagine the fun alumni from 1970 would have when posting photographs of their friends and themselves with vastly different hair styles (assuming some still have hair), clothing, and accessories!

Your website could be designed to enable alumni to not only post photographs, but to also include captions and statements about the photographs and what they represent. To make this contest more interactive, consider adding a bulletin board feature where alumni could post their comments or reflections related to EACH photograph. This could be a fun online experience which will go a long way in helping you connect with each GENERATION of graduates with experiences that are unique to them.

As you continue to create and build your online community, think about your audience and build in as many fun elements as you can. Include ideas and concepts that will make them laugh, share with others, and encourage them to want to return to your site. You want alumni feeling good about your organization.

Think FUN first and your alumni will follow! Making it fun will enable you to increase viral marketing, which is low cost advertising!

Does this make CENTS?

Find out how much you are currently investing in IT, staff, software, and hardware to provide state-of-the-art Internet technology for your students. Divide that number by the number of students you have. (Example $1,000,000/2,000 or $500 per student). Now do the same for the technology you provide your alumni. Let's assume you spend $30,000 a year on technology for alumni. ($30,000/100,000 or 30 cents per alumni!) Get the point?

2 FIND MORE RESOURCES

Alumni professionals are finding themselves in a catch 22.

There is an urgent need for more staffing and funding, yet management is not going to provide additional funding unless they see how it will help support the university and departmental goals. In addition to providing management with a written Internet strategy, you need to draw some comparisons to the funding of established projects.

When talking to management, you must remind them that departments such as annual giving and the alumni magazine were at one time poorly staffed and funded, and that over the years, these departments grew to reflect their increasing importance to the overall mission and strategies of the college.

You know better than I that there was a time when your annual giving program consisted of nothing more than letters being hand typed on typewriters. Then, over the years, colleagues shared best practices, vendors developed techniques to get more contributions for less effort, and consultants came into the market to help organizations jumpstart their program. Today, annual giving has predictive modeling, goals, and benchmarks that clearly show management the return on their investment.

Your alumni magazine, more than likely, had a similarly inauspicious beginning. The first magazine was probably a sophomoric production based on the amount of funding and collective experience of your staff at the time; it was the best you could do. Today, your alumni magazine is a professional-looking magazine produced with the finest paper, excellent writing and photography, and delivered right to your alumni's doorsteps.

To most colleges, the alumni online community initiative is less than five years old. It hasn't become a line-item budget, it doesn't have dedicated staff, and your staff has little experience in creating and managing it.

It is essential to find a way to get management to understand the extreme importance today of fully funding a comprehensive Internet strategy. No new building, facility or donation is as important as your Internet strategy. It will be your job to become the squeaky wheel and to do whatever it takes within your organization to help everyone understand why the college should be diverting more resources into your Internet strategy.

This is such a critical component that I included it within my top ten!

Does this make CENTS?

When you launched your online community you or your colleagues were probably giddy with the realization that you could send an email to thousands of alumni, or target smaller groups with no computer experience. Not only were you thrilled with the ease but with the fact that it cost you next to nothing. You can measure your return on investment from savings in postage, printing and increased contributions. You can measure your return on investment from increased data updates. You can't look at your magazine and see immediate ROI. Doesn't it make "cents" to invest more resources in your Internet strategy?

Develop a plan to increase resources that management can't refuse.
The online course "Create a Comprehensive Internet Strategy"
will give you all the ammunition you need.
Visit www.internetstrategiesgroup.com and click on Courses.

3 EDUCATE YOUR USERS

You remember the phrase, "You can't see the forest for the trees"?

Most of us who are creating, maintaining and populating online communities make the mistake of thinking, if we know something, our users will know it too. The problem is, they don't!

To alumni who are 30 and older, online communities are new Internet tools they have had little to no experience in using. They might use the online directory a couple of times to find an old roommate, girlfriend, boyfriend, or classmate, but after that, they won't know what to do next. If you want to keep this group engaged, involved, and coming back to your website, you will need to show them what they can do in your alumni online community.

Students who are growing up on social networking websites like MySpace and Facebook will need extra training, propaganda and information to remind them of the benefits of your alumni online community. A young alum looking for a job will quickly learn to utilize your alumni online community!

The point that I'm trying to drive at is if your graduating students and alumni do not have a clear understanding of what they can do in your alumni online community, they won't use it. When something is new, you have to spend time educating them.

There are a number of tools you can use to educate your alumni on what they can do while they are using your online community. Some of these include:

- Videos

- Power Points

- Webinars

- Audio

Your training doesn't have to look like it was done in Hollywood, but it does have to be able to tell them what they can do on the website. For instance, you should employ a variety of techniques to tell them they can:

- Get jobs.

- Do business with each other.

- Find others with similar hobbies and interests.

- Relocate to new cities.

- Post class notes.

- Register for events.

- Find classmates.

- Post photographs, etc.

To do that, we suggest you take very active steps in teaching your alumni:

1. The purpose of your alumni online community.

2. The services you offer.

3. The benefits these services provide.

4. How to use the services.

Here is a five-step strategy you can adopt to teach your **students** about the purpose, the benefits, and how to use your online directory. These steps will initiate a behavior pattern that will make it easy to get them involved after they graduate:

1. Develop a program that introduces the alumni online community as a career, business networking community that will help students get a job, do business with others and provide mentoring opportunities THE MINUTE they arrive on campus.

2. Modify your online community so EVERY student has their own profile page that they can update with classes taken, organizations they were involved in, professors they liked, etc. Your goal is to differentiate yourself from Facebook/MySpace and to reinforce that their profile page will be their professional networking tool.

3. Hold events and activities on campus to remind students to update their profile in your online community at least once a year.

4. Build a stronger mentoring program so students have access to alumni, and begin to experience the value of the alumni network, early in their educational experience. We suggest you require students to begin contacting alumni asking them about specific careers and opportunities during their freshman year. The more exposure they have, and the more they use your online community while still enrolled, the greater the chance they will continue to use it when they graduate.

5. Create a special area on your website for graduating seniors that focuses on these three areas:

   a. Relocation Assistance

   b. Employment Services

   c. Finding a Roommate

Your older alumni will have a more difficult time acclimating because it will be harder for you to get the message to them. They lead busy lives and are less oriented to online communities than your students, graduating students and young alumni. You really have a challenge to get them involved.

Here is a four-point strategy we suggest you adopt to teach **alumni** about the purpose, the benefits, and how to use your online directory.

1. Establish a specific budget for marketing to alumni the value of your online community as a "professional" career, business development, and mentoring network. You have to spend money to build the brand. This will require multiple mailings, articles in your alumni magazine, and emails to your alumni.

2. Hold online Webinars that will educate alumni on how to use your

online directory to network and do business with others, to search for jobs, and to locate new contacts.

3. Show on your website testimonials of others who have done business or gotten jobs as a result of their participation.

4. Adopt services that provide real benefits to alumni.

Educating your users as to what you offer and how it will benefit them is very important.

60 percent of Americans consider themselves
shy! Your job is making them feel comfortable
and expanding their circle of friends!

4 NETWORK WEAVING

Do you realize that 60 percent of the general public consider themselves shy?

According to The Shyness Clinic at Stanford University, the above statement is absolutely true! All of us have experienced shyness from time to time. The reluctance of putting ourselves in social meetings, which often involves introducing ourselves and then following up on meeting someone, is very common.

I can remember being fresh out of college and deciding to visit a local marketing networking group. I arrived at the restaurant where the event was being held, walked into the meeting room, and witnessed everyone partnered up or engaged in conversation with another. It took all of three minutes for me to feel uncomfortable enough to turn around and walk right back out the door. I was frightened being in a room of complete strangers and I hadn't developed any skills on how to professionally network.

Would my life be different today if I had not walked out so quickly? Possibly. Who knows what contacts may have been made that would have taken my career in a completely different direction? As a result, I might not have written this book! Or I might have developed a friendship that would still endure today.

Let's look at that situation again. What if I had arrived at the marketing meeting and someone had met me at the door to take me around to introduce me to others? That I could have handled! All I needed at that point in my career was for someone to engage me in a short conversation to learn a little about me and then introduce me to people they felt I would find interesting. It's all about finding the right comfort zone.

Shyness, while obviously an issue in the real world, does carry over into the virtual world.

The research that Robert Putnam did for his book *Bowling Alone* showed that nearly all traditional civic, social, and fraternal organizations (which he typified with bowling leagues) had undergone a massive decline in membership while at the same time the number of people bowling had increased drastically.

In his book he talks about two kinds of social capital: bonding and bridging capital. Bonding happens when you are connecting with people similar to you, same college, same job, attend the same restaurants, age, etc. He suggests that the second form of social capital, bridging, is necessary to create diverse multi-ethnic societies. Bridging occurs when you are introduced to or submit yourself to people outside your norm via events, activities, and organizations. In his book Putnam says:

> Americans of all ages, all stations in life, and all types of disposition
> are forever forming associations. There are not only commercial
> and industrial associations in which all take part, but others of a
> thousand different types – religious, moral, serious, futile, very
> general and very limited, immensely large and very minute...

In the context of this discussion, however, I want to focus on the importance of helping your alumni connect with each other. Because a majority of your alumni are shy, we believe you need to actively work to help them "bond & bridge" with others. As you create bonds and build bridges between members, you increase the likelihood of them creating long-lasting relationships.

One way to do this is to adopt our Network Weaver concept. This concept will:

1. Widen your alumni's connections and friendships and make them more active within the online community.

2. Help alumni who have just registered, or have already registered, on the site to connect them to others with similar interests and hobbies.

What exactly is Network Weaving? Network Weaving is a technique where trained volunteers look for alumni with similar interests, hobbies, and careers with the intent of introducing them to others like them. A slight modification of your online registration tool will enable alumni to indicate who they want to meet.

For example, your online community could give your alumni the means to identify what they want to do within the online community. A drop down menu might say:

I'm here to meet others with similar:

- Interests

- Hobbies

- Professions

- Titles

You could also give them the opportunity to identify specific groups of people they would like to meet. For instance, alumni could identify that they are interested in meeting others from the same graduation year, who participated in the same groups and organizations, clubs, or sports teams.

Armed with this information, your volunteer Network Weavers could begin to use simple search tools to find others and introduce them. **Think about this for a second.** Your volunteers can be at any computer, anywhere in the world, and they can search the online directory, connecting alumni. We like to call the volunteer weavers "the gracious hosts" who bring people together.

More connected alumni will lead to alumni who are doing business together, helping each other get jobs, recommending more prospective students to your college, and in the end, increased support and revenue for your annual giving and capital campaigns.

As the value of your online community increases, the alumni and advancement office will benefit in the following ways:

- Increased registration, participation, communication and data updates.

- Identifying the connected alumni who can assist in getting your message out to support funding needs, campus issues, and campus objectives.

- You will generate more contributions.

    While it will be important that your team, and our team, continue to market the site to attract new users, we are also

suggesting that we spend additional time improving the
experience for those who are registered within the community.

Growing from within will ultimately create a snowball effect. By giving current
registered users a better experience and more value, they will attract others to
register and use the site more frequently.

Adopting a Network Weaver concept will require the following five steps:

1. The modification of your online directory so alumni can identify
    what they want from the online community so Network Weavers
    can accomplish their goals.

2. Developing a core group of 10 to 20 volunteers who will network
    alumni.

3. The creation of your network map. In order to understand your
    network, you have to take an overall snapshot of your network so
    you can see:

    •   Who IS connected

    •   Who IS NOT connected

    •   Who SHOULD BE connected

4. Training of Network Weavers so they understand their role,
    responsibility and objectives, as well as what tools they have at their
    disposal to make it happen.

5. A quarterly analysis of who is connected and who has scheduled
    webinars to help volunteers see how they are doing, as well as who
    they need to network with and connect to in the coming months

I'd like to drill into the third point a bit more.

Creating a network map is accomplished by a specialist in the social networking
analysis field. A social networking analyst will take the data in your online
community and analyze it, as we indicated above, to find out who is connected,
who is not connected, and who should be connected. Think of this as a regular
checkup with your doctor. In this case, the results will tell you how healthy
your virtual community is. If your community has less connected people, it is
unhealthy, and chances are your members are not gaining much benefit from it.

An online community that shows alumni are connected is exactly what you want to achieve.

Armed with the report from the social networking analyst, your Network Weavers can zero in on people and begin to connect them.

Here are some examples of what your Network Weavers will be able to accomplish:

1. You visit the public profile page of alumni who work for a company you've wanted to do business with. You don't want to go directly to them with an email, so you elect to click on the menu selection that results in the Network Weaver introducing you and asking the alumni if they would be willing to take a call from you.

2. The Network Weaver does a search on all individuals who mentioned the word **photography**, and invites them to join an affinity group that is run by two photography faculty at the university. The group uses photo albums to show work and to offer guidance. Alumni are encouraged to use their personal photo albums to update with their photos and share with others. Your travel program now targets this affinity group and builds a trip to Europe based on participants' love of photography. (This can be repeated for bicycling, rafting, running, etc.).

3. The Net Weaver identifies three hundred people who do not have any Personal Pals. He/she makes contact and over a series of emails, phone calls, and letters encourages them to create their Personal Pals. Experience proves that people need coaxing in creating these as most are shy, not technically savvy, or just don't know who to invite. The Net Weaver will share ideas of who they could be inviting to their Personal Pals.

4. Event weaving will become an important area of strengthening your network. The new Event Registration tool could be modified to give alumni the ability to see others they should meet at the event. For example, as alumni are completing the online registration, they may be asked, "What kind of people would you like to meet at the event?" with their choices being, Classmates, Major/Minor, Similar Interest, etc. A report would print from their printer that would identify the names of "matching" alumni. The idea is for

them to take their report and wander around, networking with the "matched" individuals.

5. Another example at an event would be the introduction of VERY connected people to expand their networked circle. The Net Weaver would identify VERY connected individuals who might be attending an event. Those responsible for the event would plan on introducing these very connected people and would encourage them to connect within their Personal Pals. People who are very connected like to expand their groups, and will feel like the event was more meaningful for them if they were able to build their "connections."

I am firmly convinced that your alumni association will have a successful online community when you spend time bringing your alumni together and giving them an opportunity to build their own career networks. While Robert Putnam, in his book *Bowling Alone*, warns us that alumni are abandoning their participation in traditional groups and organizations, through the Internet they are rapidly increasing their social networking through niche communities. You want to be where your alumni are.

By adopting a policy to actively connect your alumni, you will put in place a program that will build bridges between your alumni, creating a connection that will lead to increased bonding and a growing sense of nostalgia. I don't need to remind you that alumni that feel good about their alumni association are more likely going to participate in annual giving and capital campaigns.

Later in this book, we'll talk about how you can use technology like Facebook and MySpace do to enable your alumni to build "instantaneous" affinity groups around everything from alumni who lived in the same dorm or had the same professor to those who frequented the same bars.

This is another strategy that I included in my TOP TEN!

 Receive a free white paper, "Smart Communities via Network Weaving." Visit www.internetstrategiesgroup .com and type in "Weaving" in the Net-Tips search box.

5   RSS Feeds

RSS = Really Simple Syndication!

Or, you may hear someone say, Rich Site Summary or even RDF Site Summary.

Regardless, RSS has been around for years, but few organizations are using it effectively.

Exactly what does it do? In as simple terms as I can state, RSS gives you the ability to go to a website that supports RSS and automatically "pull" that information from their site to your site, whenever new content is displayed.

Sounds simple right? Hence its name!

The real beauty of RSS is that, if used properly, you could have constantly changing content on your website without ever typing a word. One of the biggest challenges any alumni office has is continually updating content on their alumni site. Few alumni professionals were hired in their current job to create and maintain their website, but whether they liked it or not, it became a task assigned to them.

The site may go for weeks or months without any current news stories or information because the person assigned with the responsibility is handling the 43 other duties on their job description. Anyone that finds themselves in this situation needs to get their IT team together to give them the ability to utilize RSS feeds. Adopting RSS feeds will:

- Save you time and money.

- Provide continually changing content.

There are two ways you will use RSS feeds:

- To update your website from other websites.

- To give alumni the ability to receive updates.

Update your website from other websites

In order to use RSS feeds, you will first need to modify your website so you can drop the RSS feeds into specific fields. I recommend that your front page become more of a portal that grabs information from different departments on campus. When news changes on their sites, the news will change on your site.

For example, let's say you create three columns on your alumni front page. One column is set up for you to grab information from the director of public relations/communication page, another grabs a story from the athletic department page, and the final one grabs the story from the capital campaign. All three will update on your site automatically!

Give alumni the ability to receive updated content

RSS was looked at as a potential solution to spam. Currently, 20 percent of all email fails to reach the intended recipient. Send 1,000 emails and only 800 alumni get them. Ouch! What if the 200 "lost" emails included a couple of prominent donors, or board members, or key committee people?

You can also set up your website so your alumni can "subscribe" to the news posted on your site. In this way, you bypass email completely, because when news is posted on your website, your alumni will automatically receive it via their RSS subscription.

Compared to websites, RSS feeds have a few advantages for the user experience:

- Users can be notified of new content without having to actively check your website.

- The information presented to users in an aggregator is typically much simpler than most websites. This spares users the mental effort of navigating complex web pages in order to find the information.

Your alumni can receive RSS on personal pages they maintain at Google, Yahoo, and MSN.

Adopting RSS feeds to constantly change content makes a great deal of sense for your alumni website. However it is going to take another five years or so for RSS feeds to be actively used by your alumni. Experts see a useful future for consumer use of RSS but acknowledge there is a great deal of training that will be required. We are suggesting that you consider holding simple Webinars that teach alumni how to use RSS. After all, you are in the education business, right?

Adopting RSS technology today will help you get the message out to your alumni ands increase participation in events, giving, and data collection.

Looking for proven ideas?
Visit www.wiredcommunities.com for
industry Best Practices!

6 BLOGS

We've heard a lot about blogs, and frankly, only a few alumni associations are using them.

In an October 2006 report, "State of the Blogosphere," the CEO of Technorati, Dave Sifry, counted just under 20 million blogs, but said that number was doubling every five and a half months, leading to the prediction there would be over 80 million blogs by the end of 2006!

Blogs are giving a new generation of "part time" journalists a chance to use their skills.

Traditional print news businesses have been whacking away at their costs and are cutting positions that once covered state politics, local politics, and community news. In their place, a new breed of reporters is rising and publishing their news on their own personal blogs. In most cases, bloggers are doing a better job at reporting news because they tend to be focused on a smaller niche. Unlike a journalist, they don't have to go out in the marketplace and be a jack-of-all-trades knowledge expert.

In the business world, corporations are beginning to understand the enormous benefits of blogs. Blogs are helping companies:

- Market their products and services.

- Connect directly with their customers.

- Control crises and issues

- Build their brand.

Even your alumni are creating blogs around their own interests, hobbies, and expertise. So if everyone is getting into it, and everyone loves it, why isn't your alumni association blogging?

While there are many different ways you can utilize blogs, here are five easy strategies:

1. Create a daily blog to share with alumni with whom you talk. You interact with the President, development office, athletic staff, students, and alumni. Your blog should be conversational and informational about the people who make up the alumni association. If you do it right, alumni will be contacting you just to be mentioned in your blog.

2. Find a professor willing to create a blog to talk about issues in his field, his profession, or simply to use it as a distance learning platform. Alumni interested in Geology will "tune" in to sharpen up their skills and knowledge

3. Give a camera to a couple of students whom you want closely aligned with the alumni association when they graduate and ask them to keep an online "diary" of their college experience.

4. Send an announcement to all of your alumni that will encourage them to share the addresses of their personal blogs. Simply link these addresses in an alumni blog that is dedicated to aggregating all alumni blogs. By using RSS feeds, you could feature ten alumni feeds on your blog automatically every day. Blogs' popularity increases when they're connected to other websites. Merely doing this will help your alumni get exposure. More importantly, once you have it set up, you won't need to add content, your alumni content will be updated automatically.

5. Create a blog for each travel group. Let's assume you have a group heading to Greece. You can create a blog where all members can contribute their daily observations and attach photos. At the end, you'll have a collaborative photo and travel album that will entertain

those who went on the trip, as well as family and friends who are interested in tracking their experiences in "real time".

I'd like to see you adopt all of these ideas; however, I realize you have to walk before you run. My suggestion is to adopt number four, a blog that aggregates all alumni's blogs as your first step. Your only investment is the time it takes to set it up.

The benefits are obvious. You get fresh, new content everyday and you help promote your alumni's blogs.

STRATEGY 7 SCAN YEARBOOK PHOTOS

I like this idea a lot! Take all of your yearbooks, scan the photos, and put them online.

In the scheme of things, it really doesn't require that much effort compared to some of the other initiatives we'll discuss. Google, for example, is currently scanning millions of books to create an online repository of knowledge that will do more to disseminate knowledge creatively than Carnegie did by contributing to the construction of libraries around the country. Scanning those books will take decades and cost a great deal of money, but in the end, all of us will be able to access even the rarest book with the click of a mouse.

Although you don't have the resources of Google, I think your President can find the funds to accomplish this important community-building technique. Your yearbooks are rich depositories of information and memories the longer your alumni are out of college, and yearbooks remain powerful nostalgia-building tools. Repackaging their content online will engage alumni, spark a sense of nostalgia, and help you generate increased contributions in the future!

Ok, did I say the right things to help you get funding for this little project? Good!

You have a couple of different ways you can approach this task. You can:

- Outsource the project to a third party provider.

- Hire a student.

I'd recommend you find the funds to outsource the work to a third-party provider. First of all, you will get state-of-the-art scanning as well as professional techniques that will let your alumni interact with the data. There is technology available today that will automatically scan and turn the page.

Secondly, by outsourcing, the project will get done within a deadline. If you attempt to do a project of this scope in-house, you will add yet another responsibility to your already overloaded job description. Managing this in-house will require you to figure out the process, hire the student(s), supervise the student(s), and be accountable for the results. This is not your expertise and could possibly generate additional issues you'd have to find the time to deal with.

However, adopt either option and you will, at the very least, create a fun way for your alumni to interact with your website and content. If you do nothing else, consider this low-cost method to add content to your site and engage alumni.

There are a number of things to keep in mind so you do this right the first time:

- Don't just scan the photos; include captions, names, etc.

- Add technology so the viewer can post their comments.

- Make sure the photo and captions are searchable.

- Give alumni the opportunity to print the photos to their printer.

- Create technology where alumni can "collect" selected photos and include them in their own profile page.

- Consider giving alumni the ability to post their "now" picture next to photos in the yearbook.

The Colorado School of Mines picked up this idea nearly a decade ago at the suggestion of Brian Dowling (one of the founders of www.supportingadvancement.com). To this day, their online yearbook section remains among the most popular pages on their website.

> **Happy older alumni, who are feeling more nostalgic, will be increasingly receptive to supporting scholarships and capital campaigns**

There are some side benefits of this project too. If you get a call from alumni who were on the 1956 football team, you could engage them by saying, "Are you on the computer right now? I'm going to send you a link to see your football team photograph." You won't believe how much fun you and your alumni will have with this. You'll want to encourage them to leave a comment and, of course, upload their own photographs.

Remember! Happy older alumni, who are feeling more nostalgic, will be increasingly receptive to supporting scholarships and capital campaigns. To me, funding this initiative is JUST as important as funding the alumni magazine. Unlike your alumni magazine, you will gather data and be able to analyze how frequently it is used. Unlike your alumni magazine, your alumni will be engaged and involve when they use it. Unlike your alumni magazine, you will be able to view statistics to see how often it is used.

Interested in details?
Visit www.internetstrategiesgroup.com and click on
"Yearbooks" in the NET-TIPS search box"

8 # EMAIL ACQUISITION CAMPAIGN

When you think about it, spammers have the email addresses of nearly 100 percent of your alumni who are on the Internet. Everyone seems to end up on spam lists. Even when you get a new position or change Internet providers, spammers seem to quickly catch up with you!

However, most state colleges and universities are struggling to reach a quarter of their alumni email addresses. Private colleges have been much more successful in acquiring the email addresses of their alumni, but few have acquired more than 50 percent of their alumni email addresses.

To me, this represents a HUGE missed opportunity.

If your alumni association had 100 percent of the email addresses of alumni who are on the Internet, you would be able to communicate more frequently – with less cost and hassle. With studies showing that alumni who receive a steady diet of "positive" campus news not only contribute more, but more frequently, it makes sense to develop a strategy to get as many email addresses of your alumni as you can get. If you don't you are leaving a lot of money on the table!

I know what you are going to say. "I'm in the alumni business. I don't have time to collect email addresses!" You are right, the only problem is; somebody has to step to the plate to gather email addresses. I'm not saying you have to be in charge of this, but if you include this in your comprehensive written Internet strategy, you can gain the necessary support for other departments to handle this responsibility.

There are a number of reasons why you don't have email addresses for alumni. Among them:

- If your college is like most, soon after graduates walk across the stage to get their diploma, the IT department cuts off their campus email address.

- There is no concentrated plan on getting graduates registered in the online community.

- No goals or responsibilities are set, nor is there a written strategy to acquire alumni email addresses.

Just like everything else, it's going to take time, money, and work to acquire all of your alumni email addresses. As in the rest of life, nothing happens without a plan.

That's why you should seriously consider adopting an Email Acquisition Campaign. An Email Acquisition Campaign (EAC) is an organized plan that has goals, assigns responsibilities, and schedules meetings to analyze the results. I like to compare it to capital campaigns. Capital campaigns are pulled together periodically to reach out to alumni to support the long-term mission of the college. In this case, you are organizing a team around a common goal of getting 100 percent of the email addresses of alumni on the web.

Like capital campaigns, your EAC will require you to engage and involve your alumni to help you reach your goals. Your EAC should have a life cycle of three to five years. Alumni can help in many ways:

- They can search the directory for classmates not registered and send a letter inviting them to register.

- They can contact alumni whose email addresses are coming back undeliverable

Why should you do this?

Because you will be able to communicate more frequently at less cost! By now you know there is a direct correlation between frequent communication and increased contributions.

This is a critical element of your web strategy. Fail to do this, fail to do it properly, and your website will not provide the benefits it could to your alumni. And if it fails to do that, it will fail to deliver the potential data updates, increased contributions, and the alumni engagement that could happen. Are you feeling the pressure?

You organization should consider an EAC immediately. I consider it SO important that I included it in my Top Ten Strategies.

Does this make CENTS?

Your organization, like others, has developed incredible expertise in raising money. Whether it's 4 billion dollars or 10 million dollars, your management team puts out an enormous number of resources to achieve their goal. In a day and age when spammers have 100 percent of your alumni email addresses, your alumni association should have at least 80 percent of your alumni registered in your community. We know increased communication results in additional contributions; doesn't it make "cents" to create a campaign to get all of your alumni registered in your online community?

Net Tips Interested in learning how to increase the number of email addresses? Take the course, "Triple Registrations in 9 months!" Visit **www.internetstrategiesgroup.com** and click on Courses.

9 PODCASTS

One of the goals of your website is to provide continually changing content. While slow to catch on in the alumni industry, podcasts have the potential to provide rich audio content for your alumni's consumption.

As you probably know, podcasts can either be listened to on your computer or downloaded to your iPod device. This flexibility allows the listener to take advantage of podcasting while they are exercising, traveling, or even waiting at the doctor's office.

One of the reasons alumni associations have NOT adopted podcasts is because it requires a bit of technical tinkering in order to do them. There are now programs available on the market configured to bypass the technical difficulties. The new generation of podcast tools requires you to pick up a phone, spend a few minutes interviewing someone, and then hanging up. This podcast is instantly available for others to listen to!

There are many different types of Podcasts your alumni association can offer. Some of these include:

- Interviews of ordinary and/or famous alumni.

- Current speeches held on campus can be recorded and repurposed as podcasts.

- Many colleges have recordings going back decades of very famous people that might be interesting to repurpose as a podcast.

- Interviews of sports figures on campus.

You don't have to be the person who creates your podcasts!

Your job as an administrator is to just make sure it gets done! I would suggest you look around campus and within your alumni association for people who would be thrilled to have the opportunity to interview others and, in the process, become recognized for their participation. Your volunteer "reporters" can do the interviews from any phone, anywhere in the world – and interview alumni anywhere in the world!

It shouldn't take too many phone calls to find a student in the Speech/Communication/ Journalism or TV/ Radio Broadcasting departments who would LOVE to interview alumni, or sports figures on campus.

> **You don't have to be the person who creates your podcasts!**

Students are pretty tech savvy and will be able to handle both the interview and posting it online.

Using volunteers to handle your podcasting benefits everyone:

- Students gain practical "real world" experience.

- Alumni volunteers get a chance to use skills they are not using in their current job.

- Alumni are honored to be interviewed and will share the experience with family and friends.

- You gain a tremendous amount of content with minimal effort.

Why are we doing this again? Remember the discussion about PUSH/Pull techniques and changing content? This simple strategy will pull alumni back to your website to hear the interviews. A community with changing content looks more lively and exciting. No one wants to hang around a "dull" website!

For all the benefits provided, for virtually NO cost, why wouldn't you adopt podcasting as a way to engage and involve alumni?

10 CAREER CENTER

Your career center should be the heart of your alumni online community.

After all, it's what your community should be all about. You need to build your alumni online community around something that is unique, something no one else can offer your alumni.

No other online community or organization in the world can claim to be what your alumni association represents to your alumni. No organization in the world has the opportunity to assemble people who have shared the same experiences, classes, professors, and organizations like yours. None have the opportunity to develop a fervent, passionate desire to help each other achieve as a result of these shared experiences. None have the ability to remind their members that the better everyone does, the better your college is viewed by the business community. As everyone becomes more successful, the value of their diploma increases.

How does your alumni association approach alumni career development?

Some turn the responsibility for career development to the campus career development office. This model has worked well for students who are graduating, but it tends to be underutilized by alumni. Others are including Internet technology in their online communities that allow alumni to:

- Post their résumés.

- Be alerted when a job matching their interests is posted.

The biggest drawback to this kind of career center is it requires a lot of effort from the alumni association to reach out to employers and remind them to post the job opportunities or for someone in the alumni office to proactively find job opportunities and post them.

What I'd like you to consider is offering alumni the opportunity to post "unofficial" job opportunities.

> **As everyone becomes more successful, the value of their diploma increases**

Your alumni work for thousands of different companies. In many organizations, staff is often aware of a job opening long before it is posted. The grapevine is a proven way to find a job. If you can harvest the power of the grapevine to identify jobs before they are officially posted, you give your alumni an inside track to get the job. Your career center should have technology that enables them to post whenever a position is about to be created or vacated. This simple change in the way you run your career center provides the following benefits:

- More job listings.

- More use.

If you have an interest in generating revenue from this function, you have two options:

- Charge companies to post job opportunities.

- Charge alumni who post résumés.

I've had clients that do one or the other. If you are looking to get maximum participation from your alumni and employers, you might consider keeping both free.

Also, keep in mind that when there has been no tradition by the alumni association or college to help alumni get jobs, it will require dedicated marketing to educate them.

When you build the brand of your alumni online community around career networking and development, your community will have a special purpose. This is another strategy that I think is so important, it can make or break you. This strategy made it to my Top Ten Strategies.

Another technique to provide career and networking opportunities to alumni is to partner with third party websites like Linkedin. Andy Shaindlin, Executive Director of the Caltech Alumni Association at the California Institute of Technology worked with Linkedin to create a private Linkedin networking group just for Caltech Alumni. The successful program uses proven technology and requires little effort by the alumni association. Creative ideas like this will engage alumni and increase participation.

A picture tells a thousand words, and with Internet technology, it engages and involves alumni!

11 PHOTOS AT EVENTS

Today's electronic cameras provide a perfect opportunity for alumni associations to engage alumni. Contrary to traditional cameras, once you invest in the camera, there is no film, film processing, or any development or printing costs. With digital cameras you can snap as many photographs as you wish without a concern for cost.

I like to remind alumni and development officers that a comprehensive Internet strategy should include viral marketing as well as PUSH/Pull techniques to bring alumni back to the website. Taking digital photographs of alumni at club events, reunions, homecoming, and other special events does both.

And it's easy to do!

When you upload the photographs from events and send an email, you'll be amazed at how many alumni will come back to view them. This is when viral marketing kicks in as alumni send emails to others to look at the photographs.

There are five types of photographs you could take at your events:

1. Candid smiling shots of alumni.

2. Posed photos with dignitaries, famous alumni, athletes, or campus administrators.

3. Couples shots (proms, etc.).

4. Table shots.

5. Speakers and program shots.

Let's talk about number two, the posed photos with dignitaries, famous alumni, athletes, or campus administrators. If the President of the university is attending an event, I would ask him/her to greet each alumni as they arrive at the door. Then I would have a photographer take a photograph of them shaking hands. Plan on having an assistant help with this to record the names of the alumni in the order in which they were taken. You might consider giving a card to alumni as they are nearing the President, and ask them to fill in their contact information so you can send an email to tell them where they can see their photo online.

Here is an easy way to incorporate number three, couples shots. An alternate idea is to have alumni pose in front of a backdrop with the university logo and/ or mascot on it. Your graphics staff can put together a special banner to use as the backdrop. (Kinko's and other companies can create eight-foot by three-foot banners for about 100 dollars). Your photographer can take photographs of alumni throughout the event. You'll be amazed at how much alumni will appreciate these photographs.

The last thing you want is for alumni to come to your website and not be able to see their photographs. Your team should make it a priority to post photographs taken at events, if not immediately after the event, within a day at most.

Once all photographs are posted, it's always a good idea to send a reminder email to alumni to visit the site to see their pictures. Most alumni professionals we've queried encourage their alumni to print their photograph – and some even offer to print it for them.

Take this idea and turn it into a fundraiser!

There are a number of photofinishing companies that allow you to upload unlimited photographs of your event for a one-time fee (approximately 40 dollars). They provide eCommerce software that enables you to charge alumni for each photograph. Alumni can order as many photos as they want; the third-party firm processes their payment and then prints and mails the photographs to your alumni. You get a cut of the money collected.

With these systems in place, you can decide how much you want to charge alumni for the photograph. Is an 8x10 photograph of the alum with the football coach worth 20 dollars? Probably. So after an alum orders a photograph and pays the 20 dollars plus postage, the photofinisher prints the photograph, mails it, and takes a two-to-three-dollar processing charge. You keep the rest. Wow! Simple and hassle free!.

Imagine photographing 150 alumni, of which 100 order a print at 20 dollars each. Total sales would be $2,000 minus the $400 processing charge and the 40-dollar upload fee. Not only did you make $1,560 but you gave something to alumni that they will cherish.

12 LIFELONG LEARNING

In the mid to late 1990's, I watched as colleges and universities raced toward the big unknown – distance learning. Millions of dollars were invested in fiber optics, software, and other technology to help organizations develop a platform to develop their distance learning programs.

The next steps were difficult. What courses should be offered? Who will teach them? How do you teach online? Professors who first stepped into this new world found themselves spending a great deal of time developing their distance learning courses. It was common knowledge in 1998 that it would cost nearly $100,000 to create a one-hour class for online distribution. Sensing an enormous amount of work with little payback, faculty at colleges around the country brought some sense of sanity to the table and refused to be required to produce distance learning courses. However, times are changing. The cost of producing online learning is going down dramatically. A simple video recording of a professor's lecture provides the seeds for distance learning.

For the most part, colleges and universities, although they had more content and better professors, have lost the distance learning race to entrepreneurial organizations like National University and Phoenix University. These and other colleges have learned how to deliver low-cost, dependable education for your alumni who are interested in advanced degrees.

There is another area where your college can reconnect with alumni and build a bridge to the campus to provide them courses. I'm not referring to distance education but recreational lifelong learning. Internet technology is now available for you to give access to your alumni the same courses that students are taking. College professors now understand the value of capturing their courses in video. Not only does this give students the ability to re-review the lectures, but it also gives the students the ability to catch up on classes they missed. I'd like you to think about delivering this same course to your alumni for free!

Yes – FREE!

When we go back to identifying what value your alumni association can provide, consider being the conduit to deliver additional education. The first step is easy – find professors who have videotaped their courses and are willing to offer these courses to alumni. The next step is to list all the courses alumni can take and then market the opportunity to your alumni.

Alumni who enjoyed Psychology, Math or Geology would be able to pick up on the classes and take them at their leisure. Remember, the goal is to provide alumni the opportunity to take these classes for fun.

13 SOCIAL NETWORKING

We've already discussed adopting business networking and focusing your alumni association around helping alumni get jobs and do business with each other, now let's look at how we can expand their relationships using social networking.

To a limited degree, if you have an online directory you have the basis for social networking. If alumni can find each other and connect with each other, you are offering social networking 101. However, social networking software today extends far beyond this basis. Assuming that you have a simple search function that allows alumni to search on words like "golf," "photography," and others, you have the basics of a social networking community.

We'll talk about some of those options, but first I want to strongly make a point. Before you incorporate social networking software into your online community, you need to make a commitment to promote and market your site. A network is only as strong as the number of people who participate in it. Social networking sites like MySpace, Friendster, LinkedIn and others, have a huge population base to build from. You do not!

I'm seeing a trend where organizations are spending a great deal of time and money to adopt social networking software (essentially a second online directory) in lieu of actively promoting and marketing their current online directory.

Should you spend too much time purchasing and installing social networking software and only have 20 percent of your alumni registered, you are wasting your time and money. Beyond that, you will not achieve the results you want.

The term "social network" was first coined by J.A Barnes in *Class and Committees* in a Norwegian Island Parish, "Human Relations." Typically, social networks tend to be built around an average of 124 to 150 people. When you think about networks, keep in mind that you can have multiple networks with different focuses:

- Business Networks

- Social Networks

- Entrepreneurial Networks

- Old Boy Networks

Your network would include everyone you know within any and all of your organizations, extended career contacts, friends, neighbors, people you know from church, and all other organizations. As you build your network, you'll find that some of your members will overlap into other networks. If you knew "who knew who," you'd be able to reach people in other networks that you'd like to meet via an introduction from someone

> **A network is only as strong as the number of people who participate in it**

in your network. This is the basis for the phrase, six degrees of separation, which was popularized by the trivia game, *Six Degrees of Kevin Bacon*. This game is based on a variation of the concept of the small world phenomenon, which states that any actor can be linked through their film roles to Kevin Bacon.

Let's look at examples of how your alumni might use social networking tools to connect with each other.

Get jobs and find mentors

Alumnus Kyle has just gotten laid off from his job as Vice President of an international company that specializes in rubber molding and extracting. A fellow alumnus, Bill, reminds Kyle to visit the alumni site to see if he can find another person in the industry who might be able to help him get a job. Meanwhile, alumnus Bill uses the online community and locates three alumni in his industry – plastic injection molding. Bill tells them about Kyle's skills in an email exchange, and then one of those alumni set Kyle up to interview with the Human Resource Director at her company, where they offer him a job – which he decides to accept.

Increase their income

Kier has been trying for years to do business with MicroNET Corporation, but he can't get past the traditional gatekeepers. An outreach mailing from his alumni association introduces the online community which Kier uses to look up MicroNET. Upon finding three other alumni who are employed there, Kier reviews their profile pages, takes a gamble, and sends a blind email to Julie, who works at MicroNET's Chicago headquarters. Julie's quick response to fellow-graduate Kier reveals that she's best friends with the local purchasing agent, and will be glad to mention at lunch that Kier will soon be calling!

Build strong affinity relationships

Alumna Tammy has just moved to Chicago. She misses the friends she used to crochet with in Akron, Ohio. Chicago is great, but sometimes it seems like a big, cold place where it's hard to find people who want to move beyond the acquaintance stage and become friends. Realizing that she forgot to update her address information at the alumni website, Tammy visits the alumni online community. Using the simple interface, she poses this question online, "Anyone in the Chicago area interested in crocheting?" Lo and behold, she is instantly presented with ten alumni names. After reviewing their profile pages, and finding that one of them lives just a block away, she sends five of them email invitations to join her in her new apartment for a housewarming crochet party!

Help young alumni get settled in new locations

You know it's good business when your graduates and young alumni get involved with their alumni association. And up until now, it hasn't been easy to do. But now, through an advanced online community, young alumni can easily find others who are moving to the same city. They can use it to find a roommate, land a job, or locate a place of worship. They can even use it to review comments from other alumni on where to go for drinks on Friday night! Imagine the sense of belonging and camaraderie you'd be helping to create by making it possible for groups of your young alumni to get together at local bars and entertainment spots!

While social networking IS something you need to build into your long term strategy, it's not the most important thing. What is actually more important is that you use the current technology you have along with social networking analysis techniques to find alumni who are connected, and not connected, and then have your Network Weavers strengthen your network.

14 BUILD BRIDGES TO OTHER DEPARTMENTS

Remember the old saying, "Two heads are better than one!"? When it comes to your campus, eight heads are better than one!

This sage advice from eons ago still makes sense when you apply it to your online community. Colleges, like businesses, develop departmental silos that prevent each other from creatively collaborating on projects and initiatives.

This lack of cooperation is:

- Quadrupling the cost to maintain databases and web strategies.

- Prevents each organization from focusing on their core competence.

- Sends mixed signals to alumni.

With everyone running full steam ahead, there is little time to meet and develop strategic alliances with peers around the campus. As a result, it's not unusual to find multiple departments:

- Collecting email addresses of their alumni.

- Maintaining a database separate from the alumni association.

- Sending emails to alumni.

In this scenario, you will find the athletic department collecting the email addresses of all alumni supporters and soliciting them whenever they find it necessary, and at the same time, the law and engineering schools are developing a customized database that tracks address changes and career information. Each of them is interested in controlling their own destiny and being able to do what they want to do when they want to do it. This creates a scenario where everyone is doing the same work and getting less than spectacular results.

> **Ten departments finding 100 volunteers equals 1,000 volunteers, who each commit to call 100 people, which equal 100,000 alumni**

The end result is a campus divided. Address changes in one database are not updating on others, and alumni are expecting that if they provide their email address change to the law school that the alumni office will receive it. This scenario has occurred because there was no initial discussion or coordination with the departments, and it will continue until you can meet with them to share the benefits of a centralized online database and a coordinated email use policy.

However, the entire campus has a lot to gain from your department working cooperatively with others to develop a comprehensive Internet strategy that will benefit everyone.

For example, the:

- Admissions office could benefit from alumni recruiting new students.

- Athletic department could promote events to the entire alumni base.

- Student groups and organizations could update alumni on what their group is doing and request mentoring and financial help for small purchases.

- Career office could use the alumni reach to deliver services to all alumni.

- Academic departments could get access to the latest address updates without staff committed to maintaining them.

With a minimal amount of effort and meetings, you can turn this situation around and get all departments on the same page. Your strategy should include meetings with:

- The Athletic Department

- Each Academic College

- Admissions

- The Career Center and other divisions relevant to your campus

Before you do anything, create an overall vision and plan that will help everyone understand why you should be working together to develop an integrated Internet strategy. Things you should consider discussing are the benefits of:

- Using the same technology, but providing everyone online access.

- Working from the same database.

- Coordinating the communication with alumni.

- Working together to get more email addresses from alumni.

- Working together to help each other reach their goals.

When you have your plan together, you are ready to visit the different departments on campus. Consider developing a PowerPoint presentation to help guide the discussion. Your presentation should provide strong evidence on the benefits of using the same technology, database, and schedule of communication with alumni.

Create a "Kick off Survey" and share the results

One of the first ways I would suggest you consider to help "break the ice" between your departments is to offer to do a survey of alumni – and include questions and information that the deans would be interested in gathering.

The goal is to get their input and buy in, so you can ask each of them to find 100 alumni who would volunteer to contact ten alumni each month for over a year.

Ten departments finding 100 volunteers equals 1,000 volunteers, who each commit to call 100 people, which equal 100,000 alumni. Wow! That was easy enough! We like to see you work "Smarter, not harder." Spending time either visiting your deans OR bringing them together for one presentation will produce far greater results than if you did this on your own. You also benefit because:

- You are building bridges between your department and theirs.

- You are centralizing the database.

- You are increasing the number of alumni registered in your online directory.

- Ultimately, you will develop an email use policy that will involve them too!

After you have gotten their participation, you are now ready to create your survey. This shouldn't be too difficult with the input you've received from your deans, and by utilizing and adapting the last survey you used for your print directory. You and your staff can spend an hour or so checking to see if there are any new relevant data fields you want to capture.

Your alumni deserve 15 minutes of fame
for their achievements, contributions, and
commitment to their passions and careers

15 ALUMNI LIFE STORIES

Everyone deserves 15 minutes of fame! I love this idea because it requires your alumni to provide content that your students can edit and post online. With this concept, everyone wins. Students get real-world experience, and alumni get their egos stroked along with the 15 minutes of fame you provide them.

You have thousands of successful alumni who have left campus with no idea where their future was going to take them, only to find themselves leading corporations, organizations, and congregations, and doing great things for their family, friends, and community. They deserve your attention!

The web provides a forum for you to inexpensively make heroes out of your alumni.

How? I'll show you in three easy steps:

Step One

First, contact faculty that teach writing, journalism, public relations, and/or English skills, and have them ask for student volunteers who would be willing to take information provided by alumni and rework it so it can be posted online. Remind the faculty that the students will receive "real world" experience and examples they can include in their resume and portfolios.

Step Two

Next, put an online form on your website that ask alumni to share the following:

- What have you done since graduation?

- What do you consider your most significant business achievement?

- What achievement brings you the most satisfaction?

- What insight training did the college provide you that helped you prepare for your career?

- What advice do you have for students?

There is nothing sacred about the questions above. If your team finds others that work better, by all means add them.

Step Three

Finally, promote the opportunity to your alumni. Send out broadcast emails and ask alumni to participate. Alumni who are featured will have something they can add to their "résumé" packet and share with family and friends. Bottom line, they will be honored and feel great when they see their "life story" about themselves on your website.

The real trick to make this work for you is to automate the process in which students can grab the information that alumni post, turn it into stories, and then post the stories online. Additionally, alumni should automatically be notified when the articles are posted. If you trust your alumni are competent to write their own "life stories" you can bypass step one.

Keep in mind, you don't want to have to coordinate this process. It needs to happen 24/7 without your intervention. While it may take a bit of work to get set up initially, besides providing benefits to students, your alumni and advancement office will benefit from the positive feelings and effect this has on alumni who are interviewed. This is another example of how you can use PUSH/Pull technology to keep your alumni coming back to your website.

If you want to take full effect of these benefits, you should set a goal of 20 alumni "life" stories to be posted monthly. I can assure you this area of your website will have loads of people visiting it, including the parents and relatives of your alumni!

16 AUTOMATED PHONE CALLS

A lumni and advancement professionals have more stress today than the people that held their positions 30 years ago.

Everything is different today. Not only do alumni associations have more alumni to serve, but they have more responsibilities and demands. Everyone is constantly challenged to hold more events, get more data updates, raise more money, cut costs and do everything more professionally!

Communication is one of the challenges that will continually get even harder. Postage is rising, the number of alumni is increasing each year, alumni are hiding behind their caller ID's, and young alumni have abandoned land lines for cell phones. So how are you going to INCREASE contact with alumni to reach your goals with all of these issues?

One way to do this is with a new technology called Automated Phone Calls.

Phone blast technology allows you to make 100 or 100,000 phone calls in a matter of minutes. Similar to what candidates have used in the past, alumni associations are picking up on the idea, sanitizing it, and making it suitable for promoting events and activities.

Marketing for alumni events and activities has been determined by the budget. Should we send a nice invitation, a letter, a flyer, or a postcard? Rarely do events other than homecoming and reunions get a second mailing. However, the cost of Automated Phone Calls is so low, it's hard not to add them into your marketing program. Street pricing to make 10,000 phone calls is as little as 10 cents per call.

Compare that with the minimum cost of 25 to 30 cents per postcard!

Here's how it works.

First, you'll want to identify what events and activities you want to use this unique promotion technique on. In this example, you are using the Phone Blast as a secondary marketing piece to follow up on a print piece. Let's assume you are going to target only alumni from your state.

Then you have to decide who to use to make the call. Some options include:

- President

- Alumni Director

- Athletic Figure

- Famous Alumni

- Students

Once you've decided who is going to carry the message, you'll need to write the copy. Keep the message to 30 seconds or less. Companies enable your "talent" to call in to a specific number and record the message, or you can have your TV and/or radio students whip up a really professional recording.

Once you have the list of who you want to be contacted and the recording completed, you are ready to go. With the programs I am familiar with, you simply upload the file and the recording, identify when you want the calls to be made, and forget about it. Literally, in a matter of minutes the calls are made and you can expect your online registration program to go wild! Organizations that have adopted this program have seen significant bumps in participation.

If alumni do not answer, the recording is left as a message. You'll receive full reports identifying how many alumni were reached. Services are also available to survey alumni.

Where can you use this concept?

- Promoting football, basketball, and other events.

- Special announcements regarding awards or successes on campus.

- Annual giving.

The great thing about this technique is there are no printing, postage, or special handling fees. Nor is there any graphic design or creative work. It's simple, cost effective, and it works!

 Interested in details? Visit www.internetstrategiesgroup .com and click "Phone Blast" in the Net Tips search box.

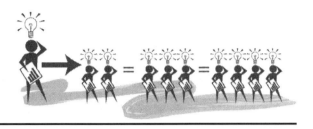

17 VIRAL MARKETING

The name has its roots in the way viruses spread rapidly. If an Internet site is growing quickly from users recommending the site to friends, it is benefiting from viral marketing. For example, when you find a great new website and you share it with your best friend, and she shares it with five friends, and her five friends share it with five friends, and their friends share it with five friends, you begin to understand how a website can grow swiftly. One person can, through their recommendations, drive hundreds of people in just one day. It's a powerful technique.

Tomi T. Ahonen and Alan Moore wrote a book, *Communities Dominate Brands*, which focuses on engagement marketing, also referred to as "participation marketing." The concept is based on consumers participating in the evolution of a brand. Instead of consumers being passive receivers of messages, engagement marketers stand on the belief that consumers should be actively involved in the production and creating of marketing programs. In their opinion, gone are the days when an organization controlled their brand. Brand in their opinion is in the hearts and minds of the users.

Well know websites like YouTube, MySpace, Facebook, and Flickr are good examples where the users/customers became involved in the production and creation of the marketing program and as a result rocketed these sites to stellar growth within a matter of a year or two.

Back in the early days of the Internet, Netscape, GeoCities, Tripod, and Hotmail were good examples of websites that grew to millions of users with zero marketing.

They grew by word of month only. While these sites had anywhere from 3 to 30 million members during that time, today's viral marketing is taking websites well past 100 million users!

In all of these examples, as the websites grew, they sold out to larger firms that would benefit from their new business model. In Skype's case, eBay realized free phone service would be a benefit for buyers and sellers of products and services.

One person can, through their recommendations, drive hundreds of people in just one day

When it comes to alumni online communities, from our experience, the value proposition is not so hot that others are compelled to invite their classmates to join. You will need to build into your website ideas and concepts that will encourage them to "spread the word" and share it with others.

So you ask, "How do I do that?"

In order for this to work effectively, a website needs to have something that is:

- New
- Free
- Fun
- Unique

Your members, like most people, love to share things that make them mad, laugh, or hit their shared hot button. With the web, it's easy for kindred spirits to pass along jokes, recipes, news, or items that interest them. If I see something that makes me laugh and I have some friends that share the same humor, I don't have to pick up a phone or lick an envelope and walk to the post office. If I want to share something, I simply click and send. We need to develop marketing programs that will take advantage of that kind of behavior!

You probably have a friend or two who you wonder if they do anything all day but scour the web to find political or humorous things to send to you. I bet you even found yourself forwarding some of the better material to your network of friends. **This is one of the things we can do to increase registrations and participation on your website.**

Think for a moment about what would get your members excited and engaged. What issues would cause them to forward and share the experience with others?

Mark Kingdon, in an article from the Clickz.com Network, offers some possibilities to keep in mind when you are crafting your viral marketing campaign.

A successful viral technique or campaign offers:

- Humor – It's got to be funny, provocative, irreverent, subversive, or deranged to get attention.

- Originality – It must be fresh; something the user hasn't seen before.

- Simplicity – The "payoff" must come quickly; time is at a premium. Most good viral campaigns aren't overly immersive. If they are immersive, the interface is very simple.

- Timeliness – Pop culture references must be timely; pop culture has a short life span.

- Subtlety – Great viral campaigns aren't overt product pitches. The association is subtle. If a reader feels they're shilling, they won't send it on.

Additional ways you could develop viral campaigns include:

- Create a fantastic eCard or YouTube video and encourage alumni to share it with others.

- Post a funny photograph of the President in a Halloween costume and set the stage for alumni to share it. Also, give alumni the ability to add comments and rate the photograph.

- Have some students "kidnap" the campus mascot and create a viral campaign that shows the mascot being taken across country.

- Post an opinion poll about a VERY controversial issue on campus or nationwide.

Really successful viral marketing campaigns are difficult to do and are as unpredictable as the next earthquake. You need to be thinking of creating viral marketing campaigns that will win small battles at a time. Taken over time, collectively, this technique will go a long way in helping you increase the number of registered users on your website.

18 PUSH/PULL TECHNIQUES

PUSH/Pull techniques are HOT. These techniques increase participation and the frequency that your alumni visit your online community for the least cost.

When you think about PUSH/Pull techniques, think about pushing information to alumni that pull them back to your website. The following are simple PUSH/Pull techniques:

- Sending a monthly eNewsletter that has links back to the website.

- A broadcast email that suggests alumni register online.

- A letter that asks them to complete a survey online.

PUSH/Pull techniques are designed to get more alumni participating on your website, but more importantly to INCREASE the frequency of return visits.

In developing your Internet strategy, you need to think about ways your online community can automatically provide PUSH/Pull techniques. Here are a few of the more common techniques built into online directories and communities:

1. Alerts

   Your alumni should be able to set alerts that notify them to come back to the alumni website when content that matches what they are interested in is posted. Examples of alerts could include:

   - Posting of new class notes of alumni who graduated the same year.

- Posting of jobs that match alumni's alert criteria.

- Posting of a sports or a specific category news story.

2. Hints and Reminder

Hints and Reminders can be used as a way to encourage your alumni to visit the different services you offer. Make hints and reminders smart! To make them smart, you will need to pull alumni to different parts of your online community they have not yet visited. For instance, if alumni have NOT registered for Homecoming or Reunion, a reminder will appear on their Private Profile pages reminding them to participate. This same tool can be used to encourage alumni to become a member of the alumni association.

> **PUSH/Pull techniques are designed to get more alumni participating on your website**

3. eMessage Center

All of us today are email challenged. We receive SO many emails that many are overlooked, even important emails. One thing to be cognizant of in building and expanding your online community is to not overload alumni with emails to drive them back to the website. This requires you to develop something along the lines of what I call the eMessage center. I would recommend that all community based PUSH/Pull techniques be delivered first to an eMessage center. The eMessage center collects the alerts and forwards them weekly, monthly, or when a certain number have accumulated. This technique protects the importance of the emails you send directly to them that you specifically want them to pay attention to.

4. Ask Alumni to Post Class Notes and Photos

I mentioned earlier that the Stanford Shyness Clinic has found that 60 percent of the general population consider themselves shy. That means 60 percent of your alumni will probably not post a class note or photo UNLESS they are nudged. That's where this service will help. Modify your online directory so your alumni can ask others to post class notes.

Who said building an online community was easy? It isn't, but when you think strategically and build in PUSH/Pull techniques to bring alumni back to your website, you will increase their participation and frequency of visits significantly.

Looking for proven ideas?
Visit www.wiredcommunities.com for
industry Best Practices!

19 INTEGRATED MARKETING

From my perspective, alumni professionals are true entrepreneurs. They are responsible for running their own business unit.

At smaller shops, the alumni director is in charge of marketing, communication, PR, membership, and customer service, PLUS they are responsible for creating services their customers will want. They truly are jacks of all trades.

Not only do they have to be jacks of all trades, they also have to generate revenue and control expenses. Who would want that job?!

With so many different responsibilities, it's hard to maintain a focus and do all of them effectively. One area that could benefit from increased attention and funding is the integration of the print and online marketing. If I was running your college, I'd give you a budget and the staffing to significantly increase marketing. I'd also expect to see numbers each year showing increases in:

- Online Registrations

- Data Acquisitions

- Participation At Events

- Contributions

- Communications

When you think about it, you have a great product and service, your customers already love you, and your only challenge is to get the message out. So how do we do that? A combination of print and online marketing techniques works.

When you promote your events and activities, create a minimum of five different ways to market the site to your alumni. Among these ideas I would suggest:

1. Mailing via letters and postcards.

2. Broadcast, animated, and multimedia emails.

> **From my perspective, alumni professionals are true entrepreneurs**

3. Alerts and reminders within your online community.

4. Automated Phone Calls.

5. Friend-inviting-friend campaigns.

In the past, you've been limited to marketing your events to one or maybe two mailings. Using these marketing tools, you can dramatically increase participation in events and activities.

Does this make CENTS?

As you begin to embrace the Internet you have to begin thinking outside of the box. Traditionally alumni, annual giving, and advancement professionals have used limited marketing to engage alumni. For the most part, limited budgets for printing, paper, and postage have kept organizations from sending multiple mailings. Now, however, you can smartly use virtually no-cost Internet marketing tools to market two, three, five times to your alumni. I spoke with a public TV marketing expert who provided proof that the multiple hits produced greater contributions, registrations, and participation. Stop leaving "cents" on the table and ramp up your marketing!

In 2006, there were more cell phones that accessed the Internet than computers that accessed the Internet

20 CELL PHONE STRATEGY

The cell phone is about to put computers out to pasture!

That may sound like a farfetched statement but we are rapidly moving toward a world where the computer is driven by our voice commands, and the need for keyboards will become less important. The sales of personal computers are already beginning to level off, while cell phones that have the power of the computer built into them are taking off. Currently, there are more cell phones in the world that can access the Internet than computers.

We've reached, as Malcolm Gladwell would say, a new "tipping point!" (Malcolm Gladwell is the author of the book *Tipping Point*).

Frankly, your online community is already dated if your alumni are not able to access the directory, the calendar, and their personal information from their phone, because every other online community is already providing this option to your alumni.

You may not be using your phone to access this information yet, but I guarantee within the next five years you will wonder how you survived without it. Already the youth of today have changed their behavior. My 17-year-old son, as an example, recently purchased a high-end cell phone with his summer job money that acts just like a computer. But this one fits in his pocket. Not only can he view Internet sites, but his three-inch touch screen makes it easier to make selections.

Tomi T. Ahonen and Alan Moore, in their book *Communities Dominate Brands*, have identified today's youth as Generation-C: the Community Generation. The defining and distinguishing characteristic for Gen-C is the continuous connection to and response to the digital communities. They see a present, not a future, where your students and young alumni are continually connected. Their phones are giving them yet another way to be connected 24/7/365.

As technology like this continues to enter the marketplace, your alumni's behavior will also continue to change. They will begin to think first about their phone as an information tool instead of their computer. They will begin to understand they can access this information anywhere, anytime, and anyplace they can access their carrier.

While I don't have as much time as teens and young adults to explore the capabilities of my phone, I have found myself standing in line at the airport, sitting in a taxi, or just stuck somewhere, where I pick up my phone and begin to check news, weather, and sports. It's only a mater of time before I become more comfortable

> **The cell phone is about to put computers out to pasture!**

with this technology. As your alumni's behavior changes and they spend more time on their cell phones, they will require more data, more information, and more content to consume.

This is a great thing! It means your organization can be one of the organizations that deliver information via your alumni channel. Later, we'll talk about creating a channel around your alumni association, so your alumni will have access to news information they can consume.

Cell phones are already allowing us to do more with our phones then we ever dreamed about. Think about what you can do on a cell phone now:

- Download and listen to music (goodbye iPod).

- Watch news, movies, sports, and TV programs.

- Access and participate at most commercial websites.

- Send and receive text messages (goodbye IM's).

With kids today receiving, as a "rite of passage," a cell phone by the time they hit their teens, it's no wonder they are viewing email as "the older generation's communication tool."

If your organization is not currently developing strategies to deliver your brand, your messages, and your services to your constituents by cell phone technology, you are missing out on their dramatically changing behaviors.

Need some tips on how to get started?

After talking to communication officers, enrollment management, and advancement officers, I've come to understand all are working 50-plus hours a week – just to keep up with their current responsibilities and tasks. Few have the time or the research to understand how to implement rapidly changing technology to stay relevant to their constituents. To help you start thinking about how to adopt cell phone technology in a few selected departments on your campus, here are nine ideas you could adopt:

Communication Office

- Give constituents the ability to choose the type of releases they are interested in, AND HOW they want to receive them (including by cell phone).

- Deliver famous/dignitaries' speeches via cell phone.

- Like American Idol, take votes and gain alumni support for educational legislation via their cell phone.

Alumni

- Modify your alumni website so they can access it via their cell phone.

- Adopt an online directory that can be searched via your alumni cell phone.

- Make it easy to register for events using their cell phone.

Advancement

- For interested annual giving participants send bar chart updates to their cell phone showing progress.

- For high-end givers, deliver a video statement from the President once a month.

- Create a series of videos on planned giving or estate giving that can be viewed on their cell phones while traveling on trains or as passengers in cars.

You can protect your organization's future by starting your research today. This includes budgeting for technology and implementing strategies to augment your campus-wide Internet strategy with a cell phone strategy too!

21 WHO'S ON?

A simple way to create community is to show who is on your website at any given time. Community is created when your website automatically brings people together who share common experiences.

Typically, this concept would show the name of the person, the class year, and their city and state, and would also provide a link to their profile page. In this way, if I landed on the front page of the alumni website, I might see alumni who are online at that moment who graduated the same year as me.

A click on their name would take me to their profile page, where I would be able to see they lived in the same residence hall and had the same minor as me. I could then elect to "page" the person and strike up a conversation with them.

When thinking about your web strategy, you should always think about creating points of interactions, points where people can accidentally connect with each other – all with the goal of giving them an opportunity to expand their career and personal contacts.

STRATEGY 22 PROOF OF GRADUATION

With today's technology, it's not too hard to make a copy of a diploma. Then using digital editing tools, it's simple to insert any name onto the copy of that diploma. You've probably heard the stories of professionals who have worked in a prestigious position for years, having claimed to have graduated from an Ivy League college, only to be exposed later.

A good way to control the authenticity of your college diploma is to provide an online website that provides businesses an opportunity to check the applicant's credentials. The site could include courses taken, as well as confirmation of majors, etc. For lack of a better term, let's call this a Graduate Curriculum Vitae.

How would this work?

Your IT department would need to create technology that would allow alumni to each have their own unique password-controlled page. This page would provide any or all of the following:

- Years Attended

- Major

- Minor

- Classes

- Organizations

- Year Graduated

- GPA

To protect the authenticity of your diplomas, students would be given their own Graduate Curriculum Vitae. Each graduate would be able to set up a unique URL that included their name and their year of graduation. They could put this unique URL on their résumé to share with prospective employers. Mine might look like this:

www.college.edu/2001/DonaldRobertPhilabaum

Remember, this is a tool to ensure your graduates get noticed by prospective employers to help in attaining that really great job. The version of a Graduate Curriculum Vitae that I envision would include the following:

- A cover page that has a diploma-style graphic along with the graduate's name.

- The next page would include a listing of courses the graduate took.

> **To protect the authenticity of your diplomas, students would be given their own Graduate Curriculum Vitae**

- Another section would highlight and focus on the groups and organizations of which the graduate was a part.

- An optional section would list testimonials from professors, administrators, family, and friends.

The testimonial concept could be interesting. Your graduates would have the option of filling in an online form that would send an email to specific people requesting a testimonial. When a testimonial is received, the graduate would then have the option of displaying it.

If you are considering adopting this, you are looking to provide these benefits:

- Giving your alumni a valuable career tool that will help them stand out.

- Protecting the integrity of your diploma.

As much as your students, their parents, and your college invest in the educational process, it would cost relatively little to create and provide such a service to your graduating seniors.

As we've talked about in previous chapters, it's important to be constantly reminding your graduates that the alumni online community is a valuable resource to help them get a job, find a mentor, or do business with others. A Graduate Curriculum Vitae is a nice way to show your graduates and your alumni that the college and the alumni association are interested in helping alumni advance their careers.

Interested in seeing an example?
Visit www.internetstrategiesgroup.com
and click "Vitae" in the Net-Tips search box.

It's a bit ironic that while most alumni associations are struggling to get young alumni to use their online directories and communities, at the same time 83 percent of their students are spending up to 79 minutes a day on commercial online communities

STRATEGY 23 | ENGAGE YOUNG ALUMNI

This is one of the biggest issues you face in your alumni association today!

Since 2000, I've suggested that if your alumni association did not develop an online strategy to engage and involve your young alumni, you could potentially lose out on the greatest opportunity to connect with young alumni that your organization would ever have. In that time, I've written blogs, articles, and white papers, and have focused my talks and presentations on a situation that is only getting worse with every graduation class.

A survey we did in 2005 of student orientation leaders proved I was right. The survey showed that the average student orientation leader was spending 79 minutes on Facebook and MySpace each day. Think about that. Your incoming freshmen register on Facebook the minute you give them their .edu address. Over the next four years, assuming that students are in college only eight months of the year, extrapolating the figures we discovered in our survey show that **your students will have spent 17,696 hours on Facebook and MySpace!**

This creates issues for your emerging Internet strategy.

- Every minute, every hour, every day, your students are updating data and information about themselves, their friends, their classes, faculty, and events and activities.

- At a time when many colleges are abandoning the production of the college yearbook, Facebook is rapidly becoming your students' online yearbook. Facebook is capturing the experience of their college years.

- When your students graduate, they are maintaining their relationship with Facebook, and in many cases, especially in state colleges, they are not bothering to sign up in their alumni online community.

All of the data and information students update in commercial online communities is unavailable to your alumni and advancement office. When I talk to advancement professionals about this issue, they remind me how they would use this data. Those I've spoken to have suggested that they would query students who, for example, had Professor Smith, and invite them to his retirement party, while at the same time asking them to contribute to a scholarship in his name. Alumni professionals have shared with me that they would love to be able to send an email to all students who lived in a specific residence hall/dorm and invite them to homecoming.

In an effort to help bring this issue to the industry, we held a series of Webinars, "Facing UP to the Facebook/MySpace Generation," that were built around my report of the same name. Over 750 alumni professionals attended these online Webinars to learn how their organizations could develop strategies to engage and involve young alumni.

At times, I felt a bit like Paul Revere might have as I jumped on my horse (in this case the Internet) and yelled as loud as I could, "The social networks are coming to take your young alumni away!" And they have!

My point then, as it is now, is that commercial social networking websites are stealing your brand and your data. Sites like Facebook, YouTube, and others required your students to show their affiliation with your college by using their .edu email address to enter. Once admitted, they assemble all of your students under your organization's name and then collect mountains of data about your graduates. (At the time of this publication, they have relaxed this requirement, allowing anyone to access Facebook).

What is even worse is their sites are addicting to students. Students create a set of behaviors that find them continuing to use the site and increasing the amount of data.

The more students use their websites, the more loyal they will become, and the harder it will be for them to break away from it. They will have spent far too much time building buddy lists, updating information, photos, etc., to want to switch to another online community, like YOURS.

The biggest risk I saw for your organization was, if you failed to engage and involve your young alumni in YOUR online community, you would never be able to get them registered in it after they graduated. Our fear then, which has been substantiated by graduating classes after 2005, is that graduated young alumni will continue to use Facebook/MySpace after they graduate.

And they are! Our research is showing this to be worse for state universities. A survey we conducted showed the average state university was registering less than ten percent of their young alumni in their online directory. Private colleges were doing far better, with the average registering about 50 percent of their alumni.

So what's the big deal? If you fail to get every single graduating student registered in your online directory, you lose an opportunity to:

- Communicate more frequently at less cost.

- Gather data and business information from them.

- Begin to build their sense of stewardship.

One of the reasons your young alumni do not use your online directory is you have not communicated to them early enough about the value of your community. Students should be hearing from your office the day they arrive on campus that the alumni online community will help them get jobs, do business with others, and find mentors within their field. It is essential that you begin this acclimation process from day one.

Now that I've droned on regarding the issues and the problems you face in engaging your graduating seniors, they should be painfully clear to you. So let's move forward with solutions. Here are seven great ways you can begin to engage and involve your students while they are on campus to ensure they register in your alumni online community:

1. You need to be involved in orientation. Make a presentation to parents and students to show them how the alumni online community will help them get jobs, do business with others, and find a mentor.

2. Assemble a group of students within each class year. Meet with them

periodically to share with them why their class needs to get involved in the alumni online community, as well as to solicit their ideas on how to continue to engage students.

3. Open your online directory to students, and a couple of times a year hold a week-long promotion that reminds them to update the classes they took, the events they went to, the professors they have, etc.

4. Promote on your campus the adoption of Campus-Wide Online Communities. In order to create a behavior pattern, your students should have an opportunity to participate in online communities provided by the college. This includes Prospective Student Online Communities, Orientation Online Communities, Residence Hall Online Communities, and Student Online Communities.

5. Give your graduates their own Graduation Online Community their senior year. They have special needs you could help them with. You'll find details on this in the discussion titled "Graduation Online Community."

6. Before they leave campus, teach your graduates how to network in person and use the alumni online community to network.

7. Ask your Network Weavers to schedule career networking events of graduates with alumni across the country. These casual events will give graduates the ability to network with working professional alumni.

The most important thing you can do is to begin to plant in your graduates' minds that Facebook/MySpace are great places to meet others, but when it comes to developing and advancing their careers, they will want to be part of the alumni online community. This strategy made my Top Ten list!

24 REWARD POINTS

How do you keep alumni coming back to your website?

Take a tip from the commercial world. Commercial organizations from grocery stores to airlines to coffee shops reward their customers for their frequent participation and purchases. Andy Tiedemann, Communication Director, Alumni Affairs and Development at Harvard University, is working on a concept like this for Harvard alumni. His goal is to provide incentives that will increase alumni participation on their website.

Why not offer that to your alumni in the form of award points – for each and every thing they do on your website? Using this technique, it's conceivable that alumni could be rewarded for:

Any time they update data	100 points
Post a class note	500 points
Attend an event	10,000 points
Build a buddy list	5,000 points
Add individuals to their list	1,000 points
Mentor a student	5,000 points
Contribute online	5,000 points

Each time they access the site	500 points
Pay alumni dues	5,000 points

You get the idea!

Now, for those alumni who dig rewards (and believe me there is a sizable number of them or commercial organizations would not be in the rewards business), you have the ability to show the top 100 point awardees. Membership and marketing professionals would be able to use these as a way to reward the highest point awardees with tickets or memorabilia, or encourage alumni to be dues payers.

Don't worry – this doesn't represent more work for your staff! All you would initially have to do is identify how many points each of these activities on the website would earn for your participating alumni. The program will do the rest! It will automatically reward alumni for each activity, tabulate their results on their personal profile page, and display the highest participants to encourage others to participate more.

Additionally, when your alumni search for other alumni, the program could identify how many participation points the "found" alumni has. In fact, it could even show what the average alumni participation points are. Talk about encouragement to do more! If you decided to go this direction, you would be making public what each and every alumni's personal participation and contribution to the alma mater is.

Imagine the fun your development office would have dissecting, evaluating, and analyzing this kind of information gathered over the lifetime of your alumni. I would predict they would be able to find trends showing alumni with higher participation points will be more receptive to workshops and information related to estate planning and contributions.

STRATEGY 25 ANALYZE PARTICIPATION

Who's using your website?

While it is VERY important to have a written Internet strategy to identify where you are going, it's just as important to have a process to analyze if you are going in the right direction to reach your goals.

As a part of your written Internet strategy, you will want to set goals on the:

- Percent of new alumni registered per month.

- How frequently you want them to return to your website.

- Number of class notes, résumés, data updates you want posted.

- Number of alumni who are connecting/networking with each other.

- How long they stay on your website.

Most websites include tools to view the above information. If yours does not, consider signing your organization up for Google's Analytics website analysis tool. This free tool provides a powerful set of website analytic tools that you can access from any computer, at any place or time. From our analysis of this product, it has more capabilities than most moderately priced website analysis tools.

I encourage you to put on your calendar an hour at least every quarter where you can sit down and analyze what happened the previous month. Your primary objective is to see if you are on track and, if not, consider making adjustments in your comprehensive written Internet strategy.

To help you get started, here are a few things you should be doing with the data and stats you are reviewing.

- Review last quarter's goals.

- List marketing and projects completed to achieve those goals.

- Identify which of these worked and which didn't work.

- Review the statistics showing the results of your efforts.

- Create corrective action.

- Identify new goals and projects for the next quarter.

Few strategies are more important than this one. After all, if you don't have the right information, there is a good chance you and your staff will be investing time and money in areas that are not going to provide you a solid ROI.

Consider hiring outside consultants to help you coordinate this process. Outside experts can bring in non-biased opinions and knowledge and keep you and your team focused on what you need to do, not what others want to do.

Does this make CENTS?

As your organization begins to commit money and resources to the online community, it's important to set goals and analyze the result of all activities to determine if you are meeting your goals. It doesn't make sense to invest the time and resources but not look at the result or periodically determine what you should do to improve the results. By not giving staff the training to know what to track, how to analyze and effect changes, your organization will be wasting a lot of cents!

26 | SURVEYS

The Internet provides your organization with powerful tools to get the required feedback from alumni regarding campus needs and wants. Today, surveys are easy to create, yet powerful ways to get immediate responses from alumni at virtually no cost.

As easy as they are to do, I'm surprised more organizations are not using them to gain a better understanding of what their alumni are thinking regarding campus issues, what their needs are, and how you can better serve them. Additionally, surveys can be used to find alumni who would be willing to volunteer to be Network Weavers and mentors.

There are a number of free services you can adopt that provide technology you could be using within minutes. Some of these include:

- www.surveymonkey.com

- www.questionpro.com

- www.snapsurvey.com

- www.zoomerang.com

While most of us in the industry think about surveys related to our own department, consider offering to conduct surveys for other departments on campus.

For example, the:

- President's office may be interested in knowing if the time is right for a capital campaign.

- Athletic departments may be interested in fielding alumni opinions to see if they would support a new football stadium.

- Deans of colleges may be interested in getting feedback on new curriculum or departments being considered.

- Communication offices may want to field opinions on changing a building or mascot name.

You have a powerful tool that is not being used as frequently as it could – or should – be. While you are considering offering others an opportunity to do surveys, you'll have to develop strategies on how frequently alumni can be surveyed.

I'd like you to consider changing your registration page to give alumni the choice to opt in on surveys. Some people just love to give their opinion on anything! Besides getting their opinion, you should make sure to provide them the results of your survey. You can use this as another PUSH/Pull technique, by sending an email to them to pull them back to the website to see the survey results.

Another great way to use surveys is to find out who is for and against issues. Wouldn't it be valuable to know which alumni are for or against the building of a new ice arena?

When you require alumni to login to complete surveys, you prevent any energetic alumni from taking the survey multiple times. Plus, you will be able to know who provided the responses. Knowing how they responded to the questions, you'll know if you should be contacting them for contributions OR if you should be contacting them via phone or letters to offer additional reasons why they should support the building of the new ice arena.

Don't forget to give incentives for alumni to complete surveys. Offer game tickets or discounts, or provide them special offers they can't refuse. Simple incentives can significantly increase participation, providing you more alumni to target your communication to.

If you want to build community in your alumni online community, you have to give them an opportunity to share their opinions and become engaged in debates on the important issues that will continue to shape your college in the years ahead. Online surveys are excellent ways to accomplish this.

27 SPECIAL ATTENTION

What are you doing to give special contributors and/or volunteers a feeling that they are being rewarded for their participation?

People like to feel as if they are part of an exclusive club or group or given access to information first. With that in mind, consider developing a special club that provides password access to:

- Updates directly from the President and the Board of Trustees.

- News and information prior to others receiving it.

- The ability to provide their opinion.

The idea is to make those who have access to this area of your website feel very special. You can do this by building some type of criteria for participation. For example, total contributions, total consecutive years contributing, volunteer hours, number of events participated in, leadership positions, etc., are all types of criteria you could use.

The President, for example, might present to this group an issue the college is facing and request their feedback. Members would have an opportunity to review the same documents, research, and materials, and provide their comments and suggestions for the President and the board to review.

As a member, you might be asked to participate in an opinion poll/survey each month. You would receive an email outlining the issues and then be asked to share your opinion. One of the benefits of participating is you would be able to see your position in relation to your fellow alumni. Finally, you would be notified of the direction the President's council went on the issues. If properly done, as a summary at the end of one year, the members would be able to see each issue, what the "committee" voted for and the direction of the President.

It might be hard to get the President's ear and participation on this immediately, so consider starting with a smaller idea, like any of the above. Once everyone sees the value of recognizing alumni within their area of special significance, and the ease at gathering and displaying their opinions, I suspect other departments will want to use this idea.

Your launch strategy should include
a budget that will enable you to use
multiple marketing methods!

28 LAUNCHING CAMPAIGN

If you've heard me talk at conferences, you've probably heard me say, "If you build it, they will come," (in reference to Kevin Costner's 1989 movie "Field of Dreams").

In real life, when it comes to your website, "If you build it, they won't come!" It just doesn't happen.

I've seen hundreds of launches and none automatically attract alumni.

Launching your website requires you to develop marketing strategies to reach alumni from all walks of life. It will require you to invest substantially more than you are investing in your technology to market the website. It will require you to focus 100 percent of your resources for at least three months to build the buzz and get involvement.

Are you willing to do that?

Most organizations are not. However, those that do not develop launching strategies receive only limited registrations and participation by alumni. Launching OR re-launching your online community should be a BIG, really BIG deal.

Seth Godin has written at least ten books and is well known for his early opinion that advertising will move away from mass marketing/advertising to permission-based marketing and viral marketing. His books remind us that we don't have to have large budgets to increase participation in our websites, but we do have to have a product that people are going to recommend to their friends.

In his book *All Marketers are Liars,* Seth reminds us that:

> Marketing is about spreading ideas, and spreading ideas is the single most important output of our civilization.

One of your challenges will be to not only include the right kind of tools and services but to provide opportunities and encourage alumni to spread the word.

One way that can be done is through testimonials and endorsements. The average person today is flooded with thousands of ads per day. Few have the time to sift through the clutter and determine what the right product is for them. Your launch strategy should use examples on how the online community will benefit them. You should have alumni sharing why the online community is valuable for them to reconnect with friends. Another will suggest they see the online directory and community as a powerful new tool to expand their business by networking with alumni.

Before you even consider doing an online community in house or outsourcing to another firm, I would encourage you to create a marketing strategy that includes:

- A budget set aside for your online community that represents three to five times your investment in technology.

- Goals and objectives.

- Assigned responsibilities.

- Scheduled meetings to assess progress.

- Identifying how your site can be promoted virally.

Once your marketing strategy is decided upon, you can move on to the launching or re-launching of your website. Here are eight tools and techniques to assist you:

1. Use multimedia eCards, animated cards, and HTML emails to garner interest.

2. Create a press release and send it through media where your alumni are concentrated.

3. Use Automated Phone Calls to economically reach all alumni via phone.

4. Send short YouTube-type videos featuring popular campus faculty, athletes, or administrators.

5. Send broadcast emails to all known email addresses.

6. Send postcards to targeted groups of alumni.

7. Create competition between classes and make them compete for the "Class with the highest percent registered."

8. Introduce an "Invite a Friend" campaign by alumni.

Each of these techniques can be effective. Taken all together, you would have a powerful launch strategy.

You don't have ten years to grow and populate your community. It's now or never! If you really want to use this as a tool to engage and communicate and accept contributions, you need to invest today. Every day you delay, it will get more expensive to communicate with your alumni and you risk losing the chance to engage them.

29 VIDEO

Welcome to the YouTube era!

YouTube is revolutionizing the way your alumni are entertaining themselves. Set aside a good hour of your time to look around the YouTube site to gain an understanding of where personal entertainment is headed among the younger generation.

On YouTube, you will find your alumni among the participants who are posting blog-type videos recounting their day, their job, their hobbies, and/or their interests. You will also find corporations who are posting videos to promote their products and services. For the most part, it's cool to look "unprofessional." The vast majority of the videos being posted are done by individuals with their home cameras. Some are vastly better than others.

So how does that affect you?

Your alumni are wired into the web via broadband and they are using the web to receive news clips and watch movies. They are quickly learning new ways to interact and create media. Just three years ago, multimedia eCards were exciting and effective ways to increase participation in events and fundraising. Now, you can expand your marketing techniques by including YouTube-style videos.

Besides, it's really fun to create YouTube-style videos! First of all, they don't have to look like they were done by a Madison Avenue marketing shop. You can create a video with an amateur movie camera that will enable you to:

- Tell a story enhanced by audio, video, and photographs.

- Increase participation in registrations in your online community, events, annual giving, and other activities.

You don't have to have the vision, skills, and experience of Steven Spielberg to create a winning video. YouTube has lowered the expectations of consumers. Simple is hot! Less professional is in! To be accepted, in fact, it has to look "unprofessional."

I know you are thinking that you don't have time to pull something like this together, but keep in mind that YOU don't have to do it. That's what students are for! A quick call to your film and photography deans or faculty will result in a flood of students who would love to create a series of videos for your alumni association. Not only will it look great on their résumé, but it will provide them with incredible "real-world" experience.

Consider using video as a way to market an event or activity. You could quickly assemble a crew of students with all the skill sets AND equipment to create a short 30-second invitation to homecoming.

So how do you get started?

1. Create a script.

2. Grab a student who is studying film or photography.

3. Line up your talent.

4. Have the students edit it.

5. Publish it on YouTube.

6. Send a broadcast email to all alumni linking to the video.

Keep in mind that this is just one of many different marketing methods you can use. You probably wouldn't want to use this to announce your capital campaign, but it will work exceedingly well for homecoming, reunions, and annual giving.

If you are looking for a way to engage and involve young alumni, you have to adopt this strategy. Your alumni are experiencing this kind of marketing on a daily basis. The technique has even evolved to TV commercials!

A major car manufacturer is currently airing a series of YouTube-type "self documentaries" of a young man who just bought his car and decided to take up the salesman challenge that it was so spacious he could live in it. So the young man did. In a series of commercials designed to run the same night, viewers get to see him "break in" his car as he explores what it can do during his travels.

In a digital world, the cost limitations imposed on you to market your events and activities goes away. You need to be adopting the same techniques that commercial organizations use to build their customer base. Failure to do this could result in a gradual reduction in participation in events and activities.

Wire Tips

Looking for proven ideas?
Visit **www.wiredcommunities.com**
for industry Best Practices!

Everyone wants a piece of your alumni. Athletics, the deans of your colleges, alumni, advancement, and others will want to communicate with your alumni. Develop a plan to coordinate everyone's contact!

30 EMAIL USE POLICY

Good News and Bad News!

The good news is, as you continue to collect more email addresses of your alumni, you will be able to communicate more frequently at less cost. The bad news is other departments on campus will also want to communicate more frequently too!

As the total number of email addresses increases, there will be greater pressure by other departments on campus to reach their constituents. The law school, engineering school, health, communication, and other departments will quickly recognize the value of the email addresses you have collected. Or they will attempt to mimic your success and begin to develop an email address database containing the same information you are collecting. If this happens, your alumni will find their mail box overloaded with emails from their alma mater. With too much contact, you face the risk of alienating them.

If you haven't done it yet, now is the time to begin to create a campus-wide email use policy.

There are ten steps you'll need to take to create an effective email usage policy. These steps include:

1. Identify your goals.

2. Determine the number of times alumni can be contacted by email alumni each month.

3. Identify if your email usage strategy will include soliciting alumni for contributions.

4. Bring other departments together and use their input to draft your email use policy.

5. Decide what types of email marketing tools can be used by all departments.

6. Develop tools so departments can target their individual constituents.

7. Get other departments to help offset the cost to coordinate the email use policy.

8. Build a strategy into your plan to fix bad and undeliverable email addresses.

9. Develop guidelines on how to write an email.

10. Determine how often and what type of marketing your affinity partners are allowed to do.

An email use policy will help avert issues and problems I guarantee you will run into as more departments want to communicate with your alumni by email. When your department coordinates this, you are assured you can control the direction the discussions take, and as a result will have a greater ability to affect the outcome.

Does this make CENTS?

If you describe your college departments as a group of individual silos that are about as likely to agree on an issue as members of two different political parties, your college could be wasting a great deal of money in duplicating services. If you have individual departments/colleges who are collecting their own email databases you can rest assured a lot of labor time is being used to fix and improve the database. You can save everyone money by centralizing the collection of email addresses.

STRATEGY 31 PARTICIPATION AND FREQUENCY

Few organizations understand how much time, commitment, and investment is required to increase participation in online communities.

Most organizations launch a site and go about completing the 43 other things on their job description, including handling fires and attending meetings and conferences. Then, when they have a chance, they look over their shoulder and glance at what is happening in the online community.

The result? Few alumni have registered and even less are returning to the website on any sort of consistent basis – if at all.

To increase participation and frequency of visits, you need:

- A written marketing plan.

- Funding to promote and market your website using various promotional channels.

That being said, you also need to have an online community that provides practical tools and services for your alumni. Once your alumni conduct a search for old classmates, there is a good chance they won't be back to your website for a couple of years. Adding services like:

- Class Notes

- Event Registration

- Online Giving

- News

- Opinion Poll

- Class Home Pages

- Reunion Information

- Career Center with Résumé Posting and Job Listing Capability

- Business Card Exchange

...all help increase the likelihood that your alumni will come back to the website.

Your marketing plan should include using both of these concepts. There is no doubt in my mind that marketing your community is one of the most important strategies that you need to develop.

Take the extra time to commit your strategy in writing. Your plan should include:

- What you want to accomplish.

- What marketing tools to use.

- A mix of online and offline marketing tools.

- Deadlines and timelines.

Once you have your marketing plan in place, give yourself time to make corrections if you are not reaching your goals. As you analyze your results, consider adding or subtracting services. If alumni are not using a specific service, increase your marketing to see if you can increase participation. If you can't, then replace that service with another.

To determine if alumni are returning to your website, ask your IT team to give you a report that shows numbers of those who visited each month, as well as how many visited within the past year.

Just a little additional effort in this area will result in thousands of additional alumni registering in your online community.

Want to do it right?
Visit www.internetstrategiesgroup.com,
click on Courses, and sign up for
"Create a Comprehensive Internet Strategy."

STRATEGY 32 QUOTE OF THE DAY

This technique is a no brainer!

One of the cardinal rules of building community is to create a great deal of interesting content your members will want to consume. Another is to do whatever you can to recognize your alumni and put their names out to be seen by others. People like to be recognized and providing a quote of the day gives them a chance to share their wit, creativity, and humor.

Here's how you can do this.

First of all, you need to create an online form that captures quotes. To follow the KISS (Keep it Simple Stupid) philosophy, all you need to get this concept working is to create an online form that captures the following:

- Name

- Graduation Year

- Email Address

- Author of the Quote

- Quote Category

- Quote

- Who they'd like to see the quote

Once you create the form, you'll need to "prime the pump" to raise awareness of the service with conventional marketing techniques and tools. Your email should ask them to share their favorite quote from someone else OR one of their own. Depending on the resources you have available, I'd suggest you automate this process so their quote is immediately put in the queue and assigned a date to be displayed.

If you have the ability to customize a program, I would suggest you include the following functionalities:

1. A database for all submissions.

2. A search tool so alumni can find quotes by name, graduation year, or quote category.

3. Automatically notify alumni when their quote is posted.

4. Allow others to post a comment to the quote.

Depending on your institution, you may want to include an approval process.

Finally, when you develop enough content from alumni, start a quote-of-the-day program. Interested alumni will receive a daily quote that will identify all of the above. It's a great way to keep your alumni connected to you.

33 TESTIMONIALS AND ENDORSEMENTS

The commercial world uses endorsements all the time!

Tiger Woods and LeBron James are just a few of the hundreds of professional athletes who endorse lots of products and services. Companies and nonprofits use celebrities to increase participation and awareness of their needs because testimonials and endorsements sell a lot of their product!

Your alumni are more likely to be convinced to use your online community if a peer, a classmate, or celebrity alumni are endorsing it. However, astonishingly few in the alumni industry are using this simple marketing technique. In a quick review of 100 alumni websites, NONE were using testimonials and endorsements from alumni to promote their website.

Can you imagine the excitement that would build around your online community if a celebrity or famous alumni were endorsing it? Not only is their endorsement more trusted, it's usually repeated and shared with others. An endorsement by the President of the class of 1968 is one thing, but an endorsement by Bill Clinton is another. Regardless of one's political party preference, alumni will pay more attention to an endorsement by someone like Bill Clinton. Additionally, an endorsement like this will create a buzz among alumni. It induces a sense of excitement that can initiate a snowball effect. In this case, the more alumni that are talking about your website, the better!

Testimonials are also powerful, but for a slightly different reason. They offer assurance – others have already tried something and were satisfied. Alumni, like you, are time starved. They simply don't have the time to test things that, to them, are unproven. They will more likely try something if someone else already has and was satisfied. Testimonials take the risk out of testing the "untested."

Endorsements and testimonials usually include all, or some, of the following:

- Photos of the person endorsing or offering the testimonial.

- Comments on how the service has benefited them.

- Handwritten signature of the endorser.

You have the option of delivering endorsements and testimonials using any, or all, of the following:

- Audio

- Text

- Photos

- Video

To get you started, here are eight different ways you could utilize testimonials and endorsements:

1. When someone visits the Business Card Exchange/Yellow Pages section of your website, have a video pop open of famous alumni, encouraging them to register their business and to do business with other alumni.

2. Your career center should have photos and testimonials of alumni from all class years showing how they got jobs and were able to find others to do business with.

3. Your mentoring program should highlight alumni, both students and mentors, who have benefited from their relationships.

4. Your online community/directory should display alumni who are connecting with each other after many years and show the fun and excitement of reconnecting.

5. Your giving forms should give alumni an opportunity to show why they gave.

6. When alumni register for the first time, famous alumni could encourage them to become a mentor.

7. When someone visits the reunion page, a video could open displaying famous alumni who are encouraging the visitor to attend the reunion because, "they are going."

8. Create a form where any alumni can post their testimonial comments.

Testimonials are powerful techniques to increase traffic and participation, and can easily take your online community to the next level. In most cases it's free to do, yet it can be among the most effective techniques you use. If you want to increase participation in your online community use this method frequently.

Homework!

Take a moment, right now, and create a list of the famous alumni you have. Categorize them within their fields of expertise, such as entertainment, sports, business, government, etc. Then think about the campus "celebrities" you have. Football coaches, athletes, the President, etc. Now, pick ten from these lists, and develop a campaign to use each of them to promote your website.

You have thousands of creative alumni who love to share and publish their thoughts. Alumni group blogs will provide them a forum to be heard.

34 ALUMNI GROUP BLOG

David Kline and Dan Burstein wrote an excellent book on blogging, simply titled *Blog!* The authors, among other things, suggest blogging is an incredible tool for self expression and community building:

> Blogging, in addition to being a huge phenomenon in its own right, is the key metaphor for interactivity, community-building, and genuine conversation; one to one, one to many, many to one, many to many.

To their point, there are many different ways you can use blogs on your alumni website. We've already suggested that you consider linking alumni blogs within your alumni website, and now I'd like you to consider creating an alumni group blog.

What's that?

An alumni group blog would be a blog that would be run and updated by a group of alumni who are focusing on single issues. The benefits of a group blog are:

- They require less work.

- They build an affinity around the authors.

- They create more content to bring alumni back to the website.

To give you an idea of what a group blog could be built around, let's consider for a moment building a group blog around careers. You could send an email to your alumni asking if they would like to become part of an official alumni blog that provides career information and advice to alumni, particularly students. The goal is to find alumni who have expertise and an interest in helping others advance in their careers. Their responsibilities would be simple, to write ideas and comments on how to search for a job, how to network/build your network, how to follow up on job opportunities and how to use your online community to get a job.

Once you have your volunteers in place, your objective is to get out of the way and let them run the blog.

Another way to use an Alumni Group Blog is to build it around retirement years. Again, you invite alumni who are interested and provide them the technology to update it at any time or place. This particular blog might have sections and expertise built around:

- Travel

- Health

- Cost of Living

- Government Programs

- Learning

- Hobbies

- Grandparenting

- Investments

Another Alumni Group Blog could be built around families. Consider a group blog that has authors focused on different areas of specialties, such as:

- Parenting

- Special Needs Kids

- Sports

- Homework

- Friends

- Drugs

Remember, on any website, content is king. You need to have content for all members of your community. I don't need to remind you that you have alumni of all ages. Those in retirement years are not going to be interested in the job blog, nor will they be interested in the parenting blog.

This strategy fulfills your need to give your alumni a forum be seen and heard. The more opportunities you create where you can recognize them, the more they will recognize the site to others.

35 EVENT NETWORKING

Have you ever walked into an event and felt nervous and unsure of yourself?

If you have, you are not alone.

Think about the last events you attended. It was the events where you had engaging conversations that you remember as being fun and worth your while. Try to remember the events where you barely interacted with others. You know as well as I that attendees at events and meetings walk away with a better feeling about the event if they were recognized or if they met a number of interesting people.

I'd like you to consider developing an organized plan on mixing and matching your alumni at events. Consider creating a goal of having alumni meet at least three new people at each event they attend. If you make this a public goal, you set an expectation and requirement that encourages each person who attends your event to achieve.

Internet technology will help you accomplish this.

First of all, you need to have an online event registration software package. Assuming that you do, I'd like to suggest that you make some minor modifications in the software to enable attendees to indicate:

- Titles of people they'd like to meet.

- What their hobbies are.

- What residence halls and what professors they had.

As alumni register for the event, they would be given an opportunity to share any or all of the above information. A couple days prior to the event, alumni who have indicated they want to connect with others would then receive an email that suggests they check out the profiles of those with similar interests so they can email them ahead of time and introduce themselves.

This technique will likely increase participation and participant satisfaction. It's a good way to improve your alumni ratings of the events. Alumni who KNOW they are going to an event that includes people they know are more likely to:

- Show up.

- Consider the event worth their while.

Events are a strong suit of most alumni associations. When you adopt social networking techniques to engage, involve and network alumni at your events, you will begin to cater your events around what they want to take away from the event – which is an opportunity to meet interesting people that will make their lives more fulfilling.

Joseph Pine and James Gilmore wrote a compelling book, *The Experience Economy*. The premise of their book is that consumers today will PAY more for a positive experience. You are already investing a great deal of your time and money in holding events and activities. Adopting this simple and low-cost technique will enrich the experience for your alumni, which will provide you powerful paybacks.

36 VIRTUAL HOMECOMING AND REUNIONS

Who's going to come to a virtual homecoming or reunion?

It depends completely on how you market it. A virtual homecoming could be a fun activity for time-starved alumni that are looking for a quick "nostalgia fix." Today's alumni are pulled in more directions than alumni from any previous generation.

They have careers, religious responsibilities, and community and family commitments that literally occupy every waking moment. How then, can you get them to relate to "homecoming," a concept developed in a day and time when 500 channels didn't exist, the Internet wasn't invented, and cell phones for each family member were only found on the Jetsons TV programs?

A virtual homecoming might be the way to reconnect busy alumni.

But how?

There are a number of ways to get alumni to take part in your virtual homecomings and reunions:

- Send notifications to your alumni informing them that if they can't make it to campus, they are invited to participate online.

- Most of your alumni today have broadband, which makes it easier to deliver speeches, parades, and award ceremonies. Consider having students videotape events, and posting the video online immediately after the event, for alumni to consume.

- Consider putting laptop computers with webcams around at the various venues and encourage alumni to use them to visit with alumni who are at home watching the events.

> **A virtual homecoming could be a fun activity for time-starved alumni that are looking for a quick "nostalgia fix."**

- After the event, send an email to all alumni inviting them to view the videotaped highlights.

You don't have to spend a great deal of time and effort to make this happen. Choose one of the options to incorporate this year, and add another next year. Along the way, you will increase the professionalism of your production as well as the remote participation by your alumni.

37 AFFINITY PORTAL PAGES

Reunions traditionally focus on bringing alumni together for anniversary years. Alumni come back to campus for the fifth, tenth, fifteenth etc. This has been an effective way to build nostalgia and bring alumni back to campus over the years.

However many alumni professionals are recognizing that as alumni become more involved in other organizations and expand their interests, building nostalgia around class year becomes more difficult. Many are exploring new ways to connect and engage their alumni around affinity groups. Their target – the groups and organizations alumni were a part of.

I'm continually amazed at the huge number of groups and organizations available for students on campuses today. It's not unusual to find 150 to 500 groups and organizations active on a campus. Some of these include:

- Athletic Teams

- Club Sports

- Campus Groups and Organizations

In addition to these, alumni associations are beginning to build affinity groups around:

- Events

- Majors

- Residence Halls

- Classes

- Professors

- Activities

A popular theory in the media business today revolves around a book written by Chris Anderson called *The Long Tail*. Part of Mr. Anderson's theory suggests that if you offer more variety, you will increase demand. Alumni relations seem to understand this. By reaching out to alumni based on the groups and organizations that helped shape their campus experience, they are increasing participation. We have a number of clients who are aggressively adopting this concept and are seeing a majority of their participation now being driven in from the affinity groups.

If you want to move in this direction but would prefer to take smaller steps, consider building simple content management pages that leaders of your clubs would be able to update. It's a good way to get administrators to understand the value of giving alumni the power and tools to organize themselves.

This trend is becoming easier because of Internet technology. Technology is available today that enable alumni to create and join affinity groups around any of those mentioned above. In addition, they can also join groups based on their hobbies, interests, or even the company they work for. Similar to Yahoo Groups affinity group technology provides:

- Calendar

- Listing of Officers

- News

- Opinion Poll

- Photo Album

- Directory

- Event Registration

Your band, for example, could create their own affinity portal page. They could post their own photos, maintain their own calendar, post news, and elect officers.

Your wrestling team, football team, and other sporting groups could create their own affinity portal pages. These pages, similar to Yahoo! Groups, enable your members to assemble around and manage their own groups.

To be effective, these tools need to be integrated with the alumni online directory. For example:

- When your groups create events, they should have the option of appearing on your alumni calendar too.

- When members search their group's directory, the search should be conducted on only the members of their group.

- Groups should have the ability to register members for events, but run the registration fees through the alumni association credit card processing company.

The greatest benefit you receive from adopting this technology is that, once you get it set up and running, your groups will manage and promote it. I'm always supportive of technology and concepts that increase participation but require minimal time commitments from you and your staff. Spend some time developing your affinity portal pages, and you'll be amazed at the traffic it will create for you.

Traffic results in more registrations, data and information updates, and contributions!

Looking for proven ideas?
Visit **www.wiredcommunities.com**
for industry Best Practices!

38 GRADUATES BUSINESS NETWORKING CARDS

Your graduating seniors need your help!

As your alumni association moves forward to offer more relevant services to a new generation of alumni, one of the greatest services you can provide them is to help them get a job!

While we advocate that you develop mentoring opportunities, sponsor career days and connect alumni with students while they are in college, there are a number of very special things you can do to help students get jobs immediately after graduation.

Let's assume you are looking to hire a college grad. Now imagine a scenario where a new graduate walks into your office and hands you a business card. You look at the card and a smile comes over your face. The business card has the alumni association logo, the applicant's contact information, and the statement "An Alumni of" on the card. Nice touch.

In today's competitive employment environment, your graduating students need all the help they can get to be noticed in an extremely crowded marketplace. Providing graduating students with official alumni business cards has many benefits. The cards will:

- Help your graduates make a memorable impression.

- Position your alumni association as a career enhancement organization.

- Generate positive comments from parents and graduates.

For employers, the business card is really a "proof" of graduation tool. Small businesses comprise 90 percent of businesses today. Many do not ask for proof of graduation. When your graduates show their graduation business card, you'll put them one step closer to getting an offer from employers.

There are a number of ways you can offer this to your graduates:

- You could print a set number of graduation business cards to your graduates and distribute them at a special ceremony prior to graduation.

your graduating students need all the help they can get to be noticed in an extremely crowded marketplace

- Consider having a firm capture their information for them and print and mail them to the graduates.

- Offer the graduation business cards for only those that pay dues.

This can be a powerful low-cost strategy to show young alumni the value of participating in the alumni online community. Membership organizations can use this as a tool to increase membership, too. Bottom line, this technique will fulfill part of your comprehensive written Internet strategy to engage and involve young alumni.

If you do nothing else, consider adopting this concept today!

Does this make CENTS?

One of the greatest gifts you can give your graduates is not only a job, but a great-paying job. Think about what you are currently doing to help them get jobs. Some organizations provide key chains, others water bottles, yet others special paperweights. If you were a graduate, which would you prefer? Any of the items I just mentioned, or a tool to help them get a job? Your graduating seniors will clip their Graduate Business Networking Cards to their resumes and hand them out at interviews. These will make them stand out over their competition. When they get good jobs, you'll get good donations!

Interested in more details?
Visit **www.internetstrategiesgroup.com**
and enter "Graduation Cards" in the Net-Tips search box.

39 DATA CAPTURE

Your development office has had years of developing business processes to capture address and information changes from your alumni. Staff, software, training, and procedures have been carefully worked out to maintain the integrity of the data and information you have about your alumni.

The only problem with the old way of capturing data is that it is incredibly costly and time consuming. As you become a more NET-centered alumni office you will find many ways to automatically gather new data from alumni that do not require cost or effort on your part.

You can gather more data on alumni from:

- Online Surveys

- Online Opinion Polls

- Event Registration

- Their Posting of Class Notes

Technology is also available to automatically request data updates from alumni that have not been changed during some time period. For example, a program could run every night locating alumni who have not:

- Changed their business information within the last two years.

- Added a second email address.

- Changed their home address within the last four years.

- Updated a class note within the past three years.

You get the picture?

A properly designed HTML email would include the information that is currently on file and request that alumni make any necessary changes or fill in any empty fields. If done correctly, alumni will be able to save the updated information right from the opened email. Convenient, fast, and effortless!

Spend a few minutes thinking through what additional information you could gather automatically to improve the integrity and quantity of data you have on your alumni. I think you will have fun doing it!

Remember the more data you gather from alumni, the more you will be able to target market communication to them. Targeted communication is more personal will result in more click-throughs and increased registrations.

40 INVITE A FRIEND

Or better yet, you might call this Invite-a-Friend On Steroids!

One of the biggest challenges alumni online communities face is getting more of your alumni registered on your website.

"Invite a Friend" is a viral marketing tool that can steadily increase alumni participation. Many websites are doing this today, but few are doing it effectively. When I think about an Invite-a-Friend method, I'm not talking about having a simple email forwarding tool. What I want you to think about is how to get the alumni who are registered on your website to "actively" invite 10, 20 or 30 classmates to register.

Let's say you have 10,000 of your alumni currently registered on your website. If each invited only five of their classmates, you'd have the potential to add 50,000 new people to the website.

So how do you marshal 10,000 alumni to help you?

You create a campaign, complete with web pages and a thermometer to show progress, and then dig in your heels and do whatever it takes. You spend money on postage, phone calls, flyers, eCards, and video invitations. Right now, you and your staff are doing the best you can to grow your website by a few hundred alumni per week. Just imagine the results you'd achieve with an army of alumni helping you.

Getting started with this concept is relatively easy. First, select 1,000 alumni who have a history of giving and volunteering. Then, create a special postcard that includes the college logo along with an invitation to the recipient to register in the alumni online community. Send them ten postcards to each of the 1,000 alumni and ask them to search through the online directory for people they know who are NOT registered in the community.

> **"Invite a Friend" is a viral marketing tool that can steadily increase alumni participation**

When they find classmates they know are not registered, they would simply copy their address information onto the postcard and send a personal note like:

> Fred, I was on the alumni online community today and noticed you are not registered. Stop by and get registered.

If they prefer, and assuming the alumni phone numbers are displayed in the online directory, they could call their friend and personally ask them to register.

Give rewards, send emails to your 1,000 volunteers, and keep them pumped about your progress. After a 30-day campaign, do a wrap-up to see which of your volunteers made the most contacts and how many new registrations there are, and look for the next 1,000 volunteers to repeat the process again.

You have a great deal to gain by increasing the number of your registered alumni in your online directory and community. Increased communication at less cost, increased contributions, and more engaged alumni are just a few of the benefits. If you are operating on limited budgets, this technique is a must.

41 SEARCH ENGINE OPTIMIZING

Yahoo and Google are reinventing advertising. Many of your alumni are no longer thinking about the Yellow Pages when they are looking for a product, service, or provider. At an ever-increasing rate, alumni are thinking first of searching online.

On first thought, it probably didn't make sense to invest time and money into registering your alumni online community in search engines to help them find your website. After all, they should be able to figure out where you are.

However, there are a couple of areas where I think you can benefit from search engine optimization. Before I go further, let's make sure that we are all on the same page as to what search engine optimization (SEO) means. Essentially, SEO is the practice of putting keywords within your website for search engines to be able to identify who you are and what you offer, so they can share your information with others who might be looking for you.

When was the last time you searched for your name or that of a friend or family member? Increasingly, Americans use search engines to find out information about those they know or just met. As this behavior becomes ingrained in alumni, many will not find themselves coming to the alumni online directory to find classmates, but simply using their favorite search engines to find them.

Earlier I mentioned that commercial social networking websites are your new competitors, now I'm going to suggest that search engines are also your competitors. You want your alumni to think about using the alumni online directory to find their classmates, NOT search engines. There's a great book by David Yoffe and Mary Kwak called *Judo Strategy: Turning your competitors' strengths to your advantage*. In their book, David and Mary suggest you look for a way to use the strength of your competitors to your benefit.

Here's a great way you can take advantage of search engines to drive your alumni to your website. Ask your data staff to give you the full name, city, state, and graduation year for all of your alumni. Then copy this information to a series of pages on your website.

Here's how this will work. Let's say we do a search on Yahoo.com of Sally Godswalksiki who graduated in 1980. Yahoo will find all relevant possibilities and present the information. One of the options includes the college name in it. You assume you can find out more information about the person at that link, so you click on it. When you click on the link, it takes you to a page that says:

> "This person is an alumni of 'Your college name.' If you are an alum, you can find detailed information about this person by logging into the alumni online directory."

It's a good way to drive alumni back to the website.

You might also want to optimize the pages of your annual giving and capital campaign website. By increasing your exposure and by bringing it to the attention of your alumni and the friends of the college, you will increase contributions.

Finally, consider optimizing some of your events and activities. By including a few extra steps you can bring featured speakers, bands, and/or activities to the attention of your alumni via many different channels. Marketing is all about getting as much exposure as you can. Search engine optimization will help you accomplish this.

42 PHOTO POSTING REQUEST

Another way to increase participation in your online community is to give alumni the ability to request others to post their photo.

Let's say you are searching through the directory, and you run across someone who lived in your residence hall. This person had long hair and a beard, and you can't help but be curious about what they look like today.

A simple button next to where the photo would be on their public profile page might say, "Ask Jeff to post his photo." By clicking on the button, an email forward form pops up to allow you to enter your comments and send it off.

Anything you can think of to add to your online community that delivers additional content is a good thing. People like to participate in a thriving, information-rich community. This is another example of PUSH/Pull techniques to bring alumni back to the website.

Your overall strategy would be well served adopting this concept.

43 CLASS NOTE COMMENTS

Class notes provide a lot of information about your alumni.

Online class notes are easier for alumni to share because they can do it 24/7, and they don't have to find an envelope, lick a stamp and then mail the note to you. On your end, when class notes are entered online, you don't have to open the envelope and type in the information. Online class notes are easier for alumni, easier for you, and far more accurate as your staff can't mistype important information.

Class notes find their way into alumni magazines, and in some online directories, within the public profile page of the alumni. Now, I'd like you to think about giving your alumni the ability to post a comment about a class note. Here's an example of what I'm suggesting:

Let's say you just finished reading a class note about your friend Jane, who just had a baby. You could immediately click on the button that says, "Send a response!"

Because Jane had categorized this class note as a baby announcement, up pops the alumni mascot depicted as a stork. Within the image is a text box for you to enter your comments. You fill in your congratulatory notes, suggest she call you when she's ready to show off the baby, and then all you do is press submit.

Whoosh, off goes the mascot-looking stork eCard to your friend. This is a nice way to take your class notes to the next level.

44 GENERATING REVENUE

I f all you want to gain from your online directory and community is to improve the address information of your alumni and to be able to help network them, you are missing out on your site generating a great deal of revenue

Here are just a few ways your online directory/community should be generating revenue for you.

Sponsor Banners

Your alumni with businesses can pay for NPR-style banner ads to announce their business or events. Fifty alumni placing banner ads for $200 per year generates $10,000!

Photographs at Events

Alumni love to have their photos taken with friends, coaches, athletes, the President or visiting dignitaries at alumni events. With an electronic camera, your staff takes the photo, uploads it to a website where alumni can order it. One hundreds photos sold at ten dollars each will produce $1,000 at your event.

Online Contributions

I've seen examples where a college with one-third of their 30,000 alumni registered in their online community contributed more than one million dollars over a five-year period. Larger institutions are seeing over a million dollars in online contributions per year.

Dues/Membership Fees

Tools are available to make it easier to become a dues-paying organization. Alumni can be reminded when their dues are up, and you can have their payments automatically deposited into the association's bank account.

> **Every department on campus has to act more entrepreneurial**

Merchandise

Make it easier for alumni to buy sweatshirts and other memorabilia. Consider offering something for sale on each page of your website. As alumni are browsing the website, impulse shopping can take over!

Every department on campus has to act more entrepreneurial. The athletic department has for years collected sponsorship and advertising money. Why can't you? If you are going to create a comprehensive Internet strategy, you will need all the financial resources you can get your hands on. Clearly, none of these concepts should be ruled out until you are assured you can get adequate funding from other sources.

Does this make CENTS?

It doesn't have to be this hard. If you don't have enough funds to develop your online community and add additional staff, why not become more entrepreneurial and find the money through sponsorship, advertising, ecommerce, and other techniques? I've heard the arguments and frankly they are hard to buy. The athletic department will sell advertisements to anything that is not nailed down. The college will change the name of a building for any price. Your public radio station takes advertising (they just don't call it that). It just doesn't make "cents" to not generate revenue from a variety of sources.

Interested in learning how to monetize your online community? Visit www.internetstrategiesgroup.com and click on "Monetize" in the NET-Tips search box.

45 AMERICANS WITH DISABILITIES ACT

The Americans with Disabilities Act has given a great deal of freedom and newfound respect to your alumni with disabilities. Not only has it required cities, buildings, organizations, and even colleges to provide ramps, accessible bathrooms, and walkways – **it also requires that all computers, software, and even websites be accessible to your alumni.**

Section 508 of the Act outlines specific requirements your organization must comply with in order to provide an accessible website. Failure to do so will ultimately result in fines, but worse, will disenfranchise alumni who will not be able to connect with their friends or even your alumni association.

For example, your website:

- Must have text labels on all data input boxes and photographs.

- Should not use flashing images that could cause an epileptic seizure in alumni with epilepsy.

- Should not use colors to indicate required data in registration forms that blind reading programs can't read.

Staying in compliance is a never-ending job. To make sure you are ahead of the moving requirements of the ADA Section 508C, someone in your office should attend conventions and continue to read industry information on an ongoing basis.

Your online directory/community company has to keep you ahead of important issues.

Over the last decade, your facilities manager has been required by the federal government to modify, adapt, and in many cases rebuild facilities to make sure they are accessible to everyone, regardless of their handicap.

They had two good reasons to do this. One, they could better serve their constituents, and two, if they didn't, the federal government would either sue them to comply with the requirements of the Americans with Disabilities Act, or they'd withhold funds for other projects the campus wanted to do.

Now that much progress has been achieved in this area, government agencies are putting more time and emphasis on Section 508, which requires that computers, software, and websites also be accessible to everyone.

While this is a tremendous benefit for your alumni who are:

- Blind, Color Blind
- Epileptic
- Quadriplegic
- Deaf

...it will require a good deal of expertise and talent for alumni associations to modify their online directory, calendar, events registration, address update tools, and news pages to continually comply to the ever-changing requirements of Section 508.

46 MONTHLY eNEWSLETTER

Some alumni associations look at the eNewsletter to provide an update of events and activities of the alumni association. Others use it to provide an update of what is happening on campus. Regardless, it's an effective PUSH/Pull technique that can drive alumni back to the website for more information.

Producing the monthly eNewsletter is a great deal of work. This responsibility has fallen, in most cases, on alumni professionals who don't have a great deal of background and expertise in writing, NOR do they have the time to write the articles.

One of the first things I suggest to those who find copywriting added to their job description is that they immediately make phone calls to the journalism, communication, and public relations professors and offer their students an opportunity to participate in real-world experience by managing the alumni monthly eNewsletter.

You bring a lot to the table. Students will not only be able to write and edit articles, but on occasion, they'll be required to interview alumni and, perhaps, famous alumni. Students will be able to show off their writings to family members, friends, and classmates. Everybody wins!

A couple of things to keep in mind:

- When you set this program up, ascertain that the professor agrees to be the "heavy" and to oversee the students' work, make sure deadlines are met, review the quality of the work, etc.

- Give participating students some kind of title and credit on the website for their participation.

- Line up at least six students to work on this project. This way, the work can be evenly distributed. The average newsletter might have ten stories, which could easily be handled by this many students.

- Develop your storylines at least a month ahead of the deadline, so the students have plenty of time to research and complete them.

- Require the students to build the newsletter and send it out.

It really doesn't make sense for you to handle this responsibility. It's not your core competence and it will mean more to alumni if they know the alumni newsletter is a student-produced product.

Take a little load off your work and help advance your students' careers at the same time.

Does this make CENTS?

How many eNewsletters are you sending out each year? My suggestion would be 24. Ouch, yes, 24. You should be sending out 12 eNewsletters from the alumni association and 12 from the college the students graduated from. Of course you would need to stagger the mailing. Not to belabor the point but you know the more you communicate with them the more they will feel connected and contribute. Invest in additional staff or student resources to make this happen so you can see increases in participation on your website and contributions.

47 CONTESTS

Everybody holds contests!

Radio, television, magazines, schools, companies, churches, and organizations are just a few that do. Contests are a proven way to engage and involve people. They build a sense of anticipation and excitement, and they are a lot of fun!

I'd suggest you hold contests at least on a quarterly basis. The more you hold them, the more participation you will get. There are a number of different types of contests you could hold. Some of these include:

- Giveaways

- Raffles

- Recognition for Creative Work

- Participation

Giveaways are the most popular type of contests. My favorite NPR station, WKSU-FM, has a fantastic relationship with airlines and offers premium gifts of two free airline tickets to anywhere in the continental United States. Participants in most giveaways simply enter an email address, and then the administrators pick the winner. It might be the tenth caller, the caller that guesses what year a song was written, etc. This type of contest is easy to administrate. In fact, the hardest part is probably finding the firms willing to provide products and services.

Raffles are also simple to administrate, profitable, and fun for the winners. A simple web search will produce a number of companies who produce raffle tickets. This provides organizations an easy way to have a professional-looking raffle program with minimal effort. Although I wasn't able to find a firm that could provide it, I'd love to see someone offer an online raffle program. Participants would enter their credit card and contact information and print out their tickets on their printer. If they lose them, they could print them again.

> **Contests are an incredible PUSH/Pull AND Viral Marketing tool**

Most raffles will have great first, second, and third prizes, and then an assortment of additional prizes. Consider asking alumni to donate professional services, such as hair cuts, tax preparation, retirement study, etc. You can offer these as secondary prizes so you can keep MOST of the money for your projects, or scholarships, or to reinvest into your Internet strategy.

Most of us forget about holding contests to recognize others for their creative work. However, this is one that meets one of our most important criteria in building online community. This criterion is giving your alumni LOTS of 15-minutes-of-fame periods. This category can become quickly segmented as you begin to target your contest to specific talents. For example, you might want to consider holding contests for the alumni with the following abilities:

- Writing

- Music

- Artistry

I can easily see a contest coordinated by your journalism or writing faculty where alumni share their poems, scripts, stories, books, etc., and members of the alumni audience and faculty select the winners. A program that allows alumni to rate work not only brings them back to the website frequently, but gives them an opportunity to be recognized by their peers.

You can set up the same type of contest with your art and music department faculty. I'd rather see you gain the support of your departmental deans and their faculty, students, and alumni, rather than you doing all the work yourself. Your job is to break through the silos on campus and use this as a way to engage and involve each of your deans. When they buy into it, you gain from the increased registrations, email addresses and other personal information collected.

You can hold highbrow contests that might support scholarships, or you can take the opposite approach and hold wacky contests. Think of off-the-wall ideas that bring smiles to everyone's faces. Wacky contests can do that. A wacky contest at an event might involve pie eating without using hands, eating the most hot dogs, etc. Online, you might hold contests to guess the number of:

- Points your football or basketball team will score at the next game.

- Hot dogs served at the homecoming game.

- Volunteer hours of all students in the last year.

- A's earned in the last quarter.

- Gallons of water the university uses each day.

- Contributions made in the last year.

You get the picture! Contests are an incredible PUSH/Pull AND Viral Marketing tool. They push information to your users, pull those users back, and because they are fun, your alumni will share them with others. The more they share, the more visits you get. You can't get a better way to increase participation for such a low investment in time, money, and effort.

If you are going to adopt contests, go all the way. Don't adopt just one contest, develop a suite of contests as we've discussed here. Get other departments involved, and then get out of the way and let them have fun. You'll reap the rewards in increased visits and more registrations!

You have to invest in the people
you serve if you want them to invest
in your needs!

48 SEASONAL ECARDS

Everyone likes to be remembered – even better is when it's unexpected.

Colgate University, like many of IAC's clients, understand the results of research that, among other things, indicated alumni who receive periodic "good news" are more likely to contribute more and more frequently.

Capitalizing on this belief, Colgate University asked our staff to create a unique Valentines Day eCard and, boy did we really give our heart and soul to this project. (Pun intended!) Our design team created a gorgeous Valentine's Day eCard (a flash card) built around a dozen or so campus photographs that faded in and out, depicting life on campus during the snowy month of February. They included scenes of students trudging through the snow, frost on the trees above the campus pond, captivating winter sunsets, and the happy smiling faces of young graduates whose hearts and times are living the life that the alum once knew.

Talk about an emotionally driven, sentimental, "happy" greeting from the university. It doesn't get much better than this. You can almost see the donations flowing your way!

This is an easy idea to copy and complete yourself. But don't stop there! I highly suggest you develop a strategy to send eCards at least three times each year. Here are additional holidays you could be communicating with your alumni using eCards:

Holiday	Date
• New Year's Day	January 1st
• Birthday of Martin Luther King	Third Monday in January
• Inauguration Day	January 20th every four years
• Memorial Day	Last Monday in May
• Independence Day	July 4th
• Labor Day	First Monday in September
• Veterans Day	November 11th
• Thanksgiving Day	Fourth Thursday in November
• Christmas Day	December 25th
• Valentine's Day	February 14th
• St. Patrick's Day	March 17th
• April Fool's Day	April 1st
• Mother's Day	Second Sunday in May
• Father's Day	Third Sunday in June
• Grandparents' Day	Sunday after Labor Day)
• Halloween	October 31st

This list provides a huge opportunity for you to target individual groups without mailing to everyone at the same time. For example, you could send mothers, fathers, veterans, and grandparents separate greetings with messages that speak to their heart. This not only gives them the feeling you really know who they are, it will provide you an opportunity to communicate with them more frequently.

You have to invest in the people you serve if you want them to invest in you. Remembering them on these special days in their lives that "define" who they are is a wholesome, fun, and creative experience for all involved!

Does this make CENTS?

Studies have shown the more you communicate with alumni, the more they contribute and the more frequently they contribute. In the past, small budgets have prevented you from being able to use Madison Avenue marketing techniques and barrage your prospect with your message. However, today with Internet technology, you can communicate frequently to your alumni, building their sense of nostalgia and keeping them informed about the great things your faculty, students, and other alumni are doing. This continual communication will remind them of the value of their diploma. As they continue to feel good about their diploma, they'll make you feel good with more donations!

Interested in seeing samples?
Visit www.internetstrategiesgroup.com
and click "eCards" in the Net-Tips search box.

49 SYNCING DATA

If you have an online directory, don't forget to sync the data between it and your legacy systems.

One of the greatest benefits your online community provides is a steady source of address and business information changes. The Internet enables your alumni to update their information 24/7 without having to lick a stamp, call your office, or fax in a form. When you make it convenient for your alumni to provide you data updates, you'll find more of them doing so.

Keeping your online and offline data in sync comes in three flavors:

1. Manual

    In a manual system, your alumni will update their information and an email will be sent to someone on your staff. From what I've observed, in this situation, someone prints the changes out and manually updates them in your legacy database.

2. Semi-Automatic

    Semi-automatic techniques reduce the amount of typing required, which increases accuracy and speed. These systems capture the information changes in a database that you can copy. Using simple scripts, you can view the information and copy and paste the changes into your legacy system.

3. Automatic

Automatic data syncing is the place you want to end up. In this method, both systems send data back and forth on a daily basis. This ensures that changes made in the legacy system are also updated in the online database, and vice versa.

Your long-term strategy should be to ensure that your online directory and community is low maintenance for you and your organization. You have way too much to keep track of to have to schedule data updates.

50 INCREASE GRAD REGISTRATIONS

Having attended hundreds of graduation ceremonies over the years, I have noticed a large number of alumni associations do not make much of an appearance on graduation day. To me, this appeared to be a natural way for students to learn more about how the alumni association would be able to help their career, and be there to put them in contact with others when they relocate to new cities.

Today, I'm seeing more alumni associations using graduation day as an opportunity to make sure the graduates have registered in their online community.

Here's how others are doing it:

Check with your graduation committee to find out when graduates are required to arrive, where they line up, and how many there are in each different section. Graduates tend to show up to assigned areas. Some will have 100 graduates, and others might have 600. This will help you identify how many computers to put in each location.

Have large posters that say, "Graduates Register Here!" By the time they reach graduation day, graduates are basically on autopilot and follow directions pretty well. You and your team can have a table with PC's, where you will help them get registered. While they are waiting, your staff can explain to them how they can use the alumni online community to get jobs, find a mentor, or do business with others.

If you have an online community running, chances are you've realized it takes work to expand it. Adding this as one of your strategies to increase participation will greatly expand your presence among graduating alumni, and will get you more registrations. Not a bad return on your investment for the limited time it costs you and your staff.

Does this make CENTS?

You have a once-in-a-lifetime chance to get your graduates registered in your online community BEFORE they leave on graduation day. Over the last decade I've watched in amazement as colleges around the country present a diploma to a graduate and then cut off their email address. Most IT departments claim they can't afford to provide them to the alumni. At a time that you want to keep in contact with your graduating students, it doesn't make a lot of "cents" to cut off their email address.

51 PORTALS FOR COLLEGES

If you've spent some time in politics, you are familiar with the phrase, "All politics are local." Tip O'Neill, former Speaker of the House, immortalized these words in his book about politics starting at the local level.

What I'd like you to think about for a moment is, who do you think your alumni have more allegiance to? Your alumni association or the department they graduated from?

Chances are, you'd agree that alumni are more loyal to and interested in the college they graduated from than they are the alumni association. If you agree with that, I'd like you to consider building an affinity website for each of your colleges. For example, if I graduated in the College of Engineering, I should have the ability to visit a college of engineering portal page that includes:

- Comments from the Dean

- Blog by the Dean and/or faculty

- News and information from the department

- Opinion Poll

- Photo Album

- Interviews with alumni

The idea is to keep your alumni centered on the people and staff they spent the majority of their time with. Your alumni will be more interested in reading class notes if they come from people who think like them and are in the same career path as them. The technology part of this is easy. However, the tough part of this strategy will be to get all of your deans on board.

To kick-start this strategy, I recommend you provide a proposal to the President to show the value of building affinity around each of the departments and requiring them to update content. Your proposal should have suggestions on how the affinity alumni website can include updated content that will continue to draw alumni to the site.

To accomplish this, include in your proposal the suggestion that:

- Students from the journalism classes interview alumni and post stories (these can be written and phone interviews).

- Get help from the communications and/or magazine departments to provide content and stories.

- Technology that includes RSS feeds so news articles posted by the President will show up on each portal automatically.

Adopting affinity portal websites for each department will increase the number of alumni who will visit the website, update data, and read the news and information posted. If you get a chance, read Tip O'Neill's book, *All Politics is Local, and Other Rules of the Game*. It is a one-hour read, and it's funny. It's full of common sense we don't usually see in politics.

STRATEGY 52 EMAILS AND AFFINITY PARTNERS

You and your affinity partners have a lot in common!

You both spend a GREAT deal of money communicating with your alumni. While your communication focuses on providing the good news that is happening on campus, and inviting them to events and activities, your affinity partners are interested in selling their services to them.

With very little effort, both you and your affinity partners can develop techniques to:

- Gather more alumni email addresses.

- Increase the number of alumni who register in your alumni online community.

- Generate more revenue.

Your affinity partners will benefit too. By helping them migrate to an email marketing strategy, your partners will be able to:

1. Decrease paper, printing, and postage costs.

2. Increase the number of customers.

3. Increase their profits.

4. Pay you more royalties/commissions.

Here's why:

> Let's also assume it would cost your affinity partners 60 cents to
> send a letter to your alumni, and that your affinity partners send
> two offers to each. The cost to send two offers would be $1.20 per
> alumni. Let's assume you have 20,000 email addresses your affinity
> partners can send to. Because you are giving them the ability to
> contact them by email – instead of by regular mail, you could save
> them $24,000 in just the first year!

In this scenario, your affinity partners will not only save paper, print, and postage costs, but there is reason to suspect their acceptance rate will increase online because:

- Online offers and solicitations can be customized based on known data and information about the alumni. The offer could be directed to them based on their class year or major.

Your affinity partners will save you tens of thousands of dollars in marketing costs

- Using multimedia eCards including photos, sound, video, and multiple frames provides a better format for them to "tell their story."

- It's frankly more convenient for alumni to click and inquire, versus filling out a form and mailing it back to their organization.

- Affinity partners will be able to do multiple emailings because of the cost savings and increased participation rates.

One study displayed the benefits of multiple emailings in increasing participation. This information shows that 58 percent of the orders came from the first mailing, and that mailings two through six generated an astounding 42 percent of the orders.

- Mailing one   58%

- Mailing two   11%

- Mailing three   7 %

- Mailing four   7 %

- Mailing five   5%

- Mailing six   12%

While this would probably be cost prohibitive to do multiple mailings via postal mail, it makes a great deal of sense (or cents!) to conduct multiple mailings online. Can you imagine how much more in royalties and commissions you would receive if your affinity received 42 percent more orders?

The second way you can benefit from teaming with your affinity partners is by having them stuff an insert into their mailings to encourage alumni to visit the alumni online community to register or update data. There are a number of ways to increase the call to action:

- Offer University screen grabs   (Bonus, respond today and you will receive)

- Game tickets   (1,000th response wins the ticket)

- Hold contests   (Only 50 sweatshirts available)

- Ask for opinions or survey   (Tell us what you think of this product)

- Refer to a friend   (forward this to a friend that would benefit)

- Testimonials   (President, prominent alum, etc.)

- Find the hidden message   (Have person look for a hidden message)

Your affinity partners will save you tens of thousands of dollars in marketing costs when they include offers to help drive alumni back to your website to register or update personal and business information. Even more importantly, each new alumni who registers and provides their email address will offer savings in communications and increases in contributions.

Here's how:

> Let's assume that your affinity partners mail to 30,000 alumni, with a flyer from you included, that encourages alumni to visit the online community. Assume now that five percent of alumni respond to your contest, free ticket offer, or prizes to register in the alumni

online community. Now you have 1,500 new email addresses you can communicate with.

What I want you to see is that there is a huge value to each address. Look at it from this angle; if you were sending two eNewsletters, or broadcast emails, each month, and it cost you 60 cents per mailing, you'd save $900 per month in postage or $10,800 per year. If your partner did two mailings per year, your savings double. Another way to look at this is that each email address that they help you to acquire saves you $1.20 per month, or $14.40 per year.

You also benefit from unsolicited online contributions. We see clients receive anywhere from 10 to 20 dollars in unsolicited online contributions from registered users per year. If you averaged on the lower end of this scale, the 1,500 newly registered users would also provide $15,000 in unsolicited online contributions.

Are you excited yet?! You are entering a time when you and your affinity partners can work collaboratively to increase participation and recognition!

Does this make CENTS?

The times, they are a-changing. Most college-educated consumers today are becoming savvy Internet users. Internet marketing is rapidly becoming the vehicle that gets their attention. Internet marketing includes video, audio, text, and two-way communication, not to mention instant ordering. However, most alumni affinity partners are still sending costly letters to engage your alumni. The higher mailing costs and potentially lower response rate is costing you a lot of "cents." Get together with your affinity partner to find out how you can help each other.

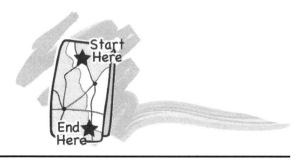

53 GOOGLE MAPS

I tried for months to come up with a workable way to use the "cool" Google maps technology to show where alumni are from.

My colleagues and I have had discussions at lunch, at the water cooler, over a few dozen beers, and bottles of glasses of wine, and each time we thought we discovered a way to use the technology, we ran into a road block. Our concern was that alumni may NOT want to have their actual locations disclosed to others via this technology.

Then, like a flash in the night, a colleague forwarded me an email, with the suggestion that I look at what Dickinson College has done with the Google Maps technology.

It was a breakthrough! I loved it.

Here's what they did, and the best part is, you can do it too!

A user is shown a page titled, "Where in the USA are Dickinson Alumni?" The user enters a five-digit zip code and then selects a 25-, a 50-, or a 75-mile radius to see alumni who live in the area.

A map is displayed that shows where alumni live, but only provides the zip code, the city name, and how many alumni live in that area. For example, it may show: Harrisburg, PA 17111, 42 alumni live in this area, No other identifying information is divulged.

Using Google's Satellite or Hybrid view, your alumni can see the block and house alumni live in, but they have no idea who they are. Taken to the next level, you could improve on this by allowing the user to click on the user's "balloon" to, assuming they have logged into the online directory and community, take them directly to that specific alumni's profile page.

Your alumni will find it a fun way to see if there are any fellow alumni in their neighborhood. You could use the tool to determine if it makes sense to invite a group of alumni from the general area to an impromptu breakfast meeting, for example. Think how easy it would be if you could simply click on their "balloon" to send out an invite.

54 NET-CENTERED ALUMNI ASSOCIATION

It's time!

Time to evaluate what kind of alumni association you want to become in this Internet centered age!

In a time when:

- It's increasingly difficult to get alumni to events and activities

- It's harder to get alumni to answer their phone

- The cost of communicating with alumni is increasing

...maybe it's time to rethink how you want to do business!

With over 70 percent of your alumni connected 24/7 to the Internet via broadband and increasing numbers participating in social networking communities, now is the time to build your relationship with your alumni online!

The rapid advance of technology and the fundamental shift in human behavior is presenting your alumni association with outstanding opportunities to stay connected with a greater number of alumni whenever it's convenient for them. By becoming more NET-Centered, you will be able to solve the above issues.

Organizations that recognize this change has occurred will be able to expand their relationships with alumni in many ways and connect with more alumni, more often - throughout their lives. To take advantage of this opportunity, organizations will need to pause, reflect on the way they are currently managing their relationships with their alumni and virtually reorganize the way they do business.

NET-Centered Alumni Association

We define a NET-Centered Alumni Association as one that recognizes that the Internet opens the opportunity to build relationships with a greater number of alumni than is possible with traditional alumni relations events and activities.

As a result of becoming a Net-Centered Alumni Association you will be able to shift resources to developing a written Internet strategy that is repeatable, measurable and predictable.

A NET-Centered Alumni Association:

- Evaluates how to effectively use Internet technology to reduce the cost of doing business

- Organizes job functions and responsibilities around the capabilities the Internet provides

- Provides Internet services that benefit students and alumni

- Teaches students and alumni how to network, both online and offline

- Reaches out to other departments on campus to create integrated solutions

While a NET-Centered Alumni Association looks to:

- Reduce their mailing costs

- Increase communicating to alumni

- Reduce labor cost by taking registrations online

- Receive unsolicited contributions by alumni who are visiting their online community

It also works to use Internet technology to help alumni to:

- Do business with each other

- Get jobs

- Reconnect

- Find help in transitioning

- Personalize their relationship with the alumni association

Internet Strategies Group

To learn more, if you want to become a NET-Centered Alumni Association, or to receive the white paper, go to

www.internetstrategiesgroup.com

and click "The NEXT – NET Things!" in the search box.

STRATEGY 55 TARGETED COMMUNICATION

A recent trend in alumni communications is connecting with, and building bridges to, alumni based on their campus affinities instead of the year they graduated. This trend suggests that alumni have more connection with, and nostalgia built around, the clubs, organizations, residence halls, and events they were a part of while they were on campus.

Engaging alumni around their affinities is problematic, because:

- You don't always know which affinity groups your alumni were involved or interested in.

- Even if you do know, it's difficult to gain access to the data from legacy systems.

While administrators know it's important to save this kind of information, it's only been recently that hard drive space and database systems have increased in the necessary power and flexibility to allow it. As a result, decades passed where comprehensive data about students and alumni was not collected.

Even if you did collect the information, with today's legacy systems, administrators have to make contact with a database person who enters your request into their queue of jobs. Chances are, they misunderstood what you wanted, and you ended up with a data set that was completely wrong. I've had countless conversations where administrators roll their eyes when relating the miscues they've had with getting the right data.

Bottom line, the process of getting access to the data you want becomes time consuming and full of extra steps, which get lost in your day-to-day responsibilities. After going back and forth trying to get the right data sets, it's easy to throw your hands up in the air and just give up!

One of the incredible benefits of developing your online community is that:

- You can ask alumni to update their online profile with information the legacy system may not have, such as residence hall(s) lived in and participation in groups, organizations, and sports teams. The goal is to develop a "360-degree view" of your alumni college experience.

- Tools are available today for non programmers to isolate information and use it to target specific communication to alumni. Using standard query tools, you can isolate the data you are looking for and continue to refine it until you are happy with what you get. The nice thing is, you don't have to write a memo or fill out a form – you can do it within your office.

Once you start down this path, you are well on your way to communicate and involve your alumni in the areas that most impacted them during their college years. For example, you could send targeted information to everyone who worked on the yearbook, all those who lived in Tri Towers, and all those who were in theatre in reference to the reunion for the current year.

If you adopt this concept, you will not only increase participation, you will begin to capture an increased amount of data and information about your alumni. Oh, do I need to remind your development officers of the value of this information?

Looking for proven ideas?
Visit **www.wiredcommunities.com**
for industry Best Practices!

PERSONALIZATION

Your Internet strategy should be built around personalizing the relationship and experience for your alumni. Your website should include technology that will not only recognize them, but also give them the ability to control what it provides them and how it presents itself to them.

As you build your Internet strategy, keep in mind how your users will want to engage with you and your organization, NOT only how YOU want to engage with your alumni.

Some things to keep in mind:

- Build your website to recognize your alumni when they return.

- Pre-fill data about your alumni when they return.

- Give alumni the ability to opt in and out of different services.

Here are seven ways you can accomplish some of the above:

1. When accessing your website, give alumni the option of being taken to their private profile page first.

2. Give users the option of being notified when class notes between specific class years or affinity groups are posted.

3. Provide the opportunity for users to change their username and password anytime without admin help.

4. Allow mentors to inactivate themselves at any time or to control the number of people accessing them.

5. Give alumni the ability to change the look of their private profile page (add and subtract services, change layout design, etc.).

6. Provide alumni the opportunity to post their own photo albums and provide the ability to "tag" the photos of the names of the alumni who are in the photos so alumni can easily find them.

7. Give users the flexibility to show who their friends are or to hide their information.

Spend some time with your team reviewing commercial social networking websites to find out how they let their users personalize their experience with their website. The bottom line! The more alumni who personalize their profile page and experience your website, the more ownership they will have of the site. You will increase participation and data collection as a result of this effort!

57 TELL USERS WHAT TO DO

I know! Nobody likes to be told what to do, but there are times, especially when we first experience something, that we like to be told what to do!

Your online community is really a brand new concept to your alumni. It doesn't have 50 years of tradition behind it. It wasn't something they used as students, and for the most part, the majority of your older alumni have not been active in online communities.

So like anything else that is new, you have to spend time educating them with what your online community can do for them.

How do you do that?

A VERY easy way is to develop a simple list that drives them to different services within your online community. For example, on the front page of your online community, you could include a fancy-looking graphic that lists the top five things for your visitors to do while they are there!

Try this list for an example:

Don't leave until you:

1. Read class notes.

2. Update your business profile.

3. Post a photo of yourself.

4.   Look for an old roommate.

5.   Register for an event.

To make it even more effective, allow the users to click on any of the above to be taken directly to that page.

People don't like to think!

You have to lay out your website so they can simply respond. In today's world, they have to make too many decisions. Build your web pages and strategy around eliminating decisions instead of adding to them!

58   FOCUS ON ALUMNI

What is the mission of your alumni association?

In my professional and casual conversations with alumni professionals around the world, I hear the following responses:

- Our job is to connect the alumni to the university.

- We provide a collective voice from the alumni to affect the direction of the university.

- We hold events and activities to connect alumni.

- Build relationships with alumni to benefit the development office.

- Friend raise!

- Fundraise.

Look at how your alumni office is organized. Is the alumni office organized to benefit the alumni or to benefit the above goals and missions?

I'd like you to consider building your core mission around providing these benefits to alumni:

- Assisting with job searches.

- Helping them do business with each other.

- Recognizing them for their achievements.

- Connecting them with people that will expand their interests.

- Giving them access to lifelong learning opportunities.

If you do, your web strategy will change to reflect tools and services that can deliver these benefits. We've talked at great length on how you can help them get jobs and do business with each other. When you adopt this philosophy, you will need to begin to adapt your online community to deliver these services. Your alumni will need to post job opportunities, identify what jobs they are looking for, be taught how to use your online directory to find alumni who can help them get a job, or to do business with someone.

I doubt there are many alumni who would turn down an opportunity to be recognized by your alumni association for their career, community, church, or other contributions. News stories, podcasts, and virtual award programs go a long way to building loyalty to the alumni association and the college.

While there are hundreds of organizations your alumni can join today, there will NEVER be an organization of people who walked the same campus paths, who invested time, money, and sacrificed to receive the same diploma. Your organization has a unique opportunity to bring together people who have similar goals, missions, and/or achievements to help expand their circle of friends. Your organization also has a unique opportunity to give your alumni access to others with resources that can take their ideas or projects to the next level. Again – NO ONE ELSE can fill this niche for your alumni.

Finally, one of the other things that can help your organization stand out from others is your ability to deliver lifelong learning opportunities to alumni. You already have tens of thousands of very happy customers who have enjoyed their learning experience and will, at various times in their lives, have the time and interest to "go back to the well" to quench their thirst for knowledge. Your organization should be thinking about delivering distance learning opportunities and offering a week, two-week, or one-month "on campus" learning experiences. We'll discuss this in more detail.

Much of what alumni relations are today has developed from a time and era when things were vastly different. Your customers' needs have changed. You have more competition for their time, so you need to rethink what your mission is and then develop your web tools and strategies around it.

59 ADOPT SPORTS SOCIAL NETWORKING

Sports social networking? What's that?

Actually, it's a fantastic way to connect your alumni based on their interest and love of sports. Sports social networking allows your alumni to find others who want to play football, golf, dodge ball, soccer, horseshoes, pool, and in fact, over 100 different games.

Here's how it works.

You enter basic registration information and then indicate what sports you are interested in playing. You can participate on two levels:

- Organizer of the games.

- Participant of the games.

As an organizer, you can schedule a game at any time or any place. When you schedule a game, all alumni who have indicated they would like to participate in the sport will receive an email asking them to "come out to play." As a participant, you have the option of accepting the invitation or ignoring it.

The service allows members to rate other players and leave comments about the games. It's interactive and fun, and when it focuses on your alumni, it's a powerful relationship building tool that YOU don't have to be involved in.

Everyone benefits:

- Your alumni find other alumni to organize "pick up games."

- You develop affinity groups around alumni's love of sports.

The nice thing about sports social networking is there is no need to load software, buy hardware, or even manage the process. Your only responsibility is to make it available to your alumni.

If one of your strategies is to increase the number of events and activities, but you don't have a lot of resources, consider promoting sports social networking.

At the end of the year, you'll receive reports showing the number of events alumni participated in and how many alumni are participating in them, and satisfaction surveys will help you determine the level of success that sports social networking has to your organization.

Interested in details?
Visit www.internetstrategiesgroup.com
and click Gamesnake in the Net-Tips search box.

STRATEGY 60 — OPINION POLL

Opinion polls are becoming more popular in online communities. Opinion polls not only provide your alumni a way to express their opinion, but they give them a way to see where their opinion sits with others.

Generally, your opinion polls should focus on known issues that require simple yes, no, or multiple choice answers.

Our experience has shown the more controversial the topic, the higher number of alumni that will participate. For example, if you sent an email to your alumni asking them to give their opinion on drinking on campus, or one that asked their opinion on abortion, I can guarantee you will have a higher percentage of alumni come back to give their opinion on abortion.

I'd like you to actively adopt opinion polls built around a number of categories. Because opinion polls are inexpensive, consider offering many of them built around:

- Predictions on how the teams will do.

- If the economy will increase or decrease.

- What should be done on important social issues.

- Support for congress/president, etc.

- Zany fun areas.

Depending on the type of poll, and the number of participants, your PR department could issue a series of press releases to be picked up by bloggers and news sources. The more opinion polls you offer, the more you and your administration will begin to understand who your alumni are and how to communicate your needs to them. Assuming you start this strategy today, over a period of 30 years, you'd have a complete history of what your alumni individually support. For example, you would know if I voted to support the building of a new ice arena on campus. If I did, you could target communication to me asking for support. If I didn't, you could offer more compelling reasons on why it is needed and why my support is still needed.

> **Our experience has shown the more controversial the topic, the higher number of alumni that will participate**

Most organizations are casually using opinion polls, but for those that are, they are missing out on a great deal of data their advancement office could be using. Adopt a more aggressive strategy to gather your alumni opinions through opinion polls.

Look Who's Recently Registered

1. Steve Zohn
2. Diana Schumacher
3. Fred Smith
4. Kyle Dick
5. Jonny Cage
6. Jim Donaldsson

61 LIST NEW USERS

One of the challenges you have in managing your alumni online community is the need to continually update content.

When you have 43 other things on your job description, it's increasingly difficult to find the time to continually change the content on your website. We've offered ideas on how you can use alumni blogs, student journalists, and options to display content via alumni posts as a way to show content is changing.

Now let's talk about an effortless way to show changing content that catches the eye of alumni when they return to your website.

Consider showing the last ten people who have either registered or visited the website. This tells your users that the site is active and, with a bit of good luck, the user will recognize someone.

Depending on the capabilities of your online community's IT staff, you could either just list the names of the last ten users on the website, OR you could include additional fields that tell the viewer more information about the user. This additional information will provide other connection points with the alumni. In the example below, you might have graduated from the School of Engineering. By including that information in the list, you are immediately attracted to Donna Jones, and may be curious to learn more.

Here are some of the fields we recommend you show:

Who's Been Here Recently!			
Name	**Year Grad**	**Degree**	**Visit**
Fred Smith	1990	Arts & Science	1st
Donna Jones	1945	Engineering	8th
Johann Iams	2000	Journalism	3rd
Jimmy Dena	1975	Art	4th

When you hotlink their name to their public profile, visitors can immediately check out the person who shares a commonality with them. Your web strategy has to include techniques to pique your alumni's curiosity and encourage them to look for additional information. Simple and well-executed tools like this will help you take your Internet strategy to the next level.

STRATEGY 62 FIX BAD/ UNDELIVERABLE EMAIL ADDRESSES

A few years ago, we did extensive surveys to determine how alumni associations were handling changes in bad/undeliverable email addresses for their alumni.

Our survey showed that 80 percent of alumni associations deleted bad email addresses and did not have a program to correct them. Historically, 17 percent of Americans move each year. Over the years, your alumni and advancement office has developed processes to track down alumni when they move.

Additional research conducted three years ago showed that as much as 39 percent of alumni email addresses were changing each year. While we suspect this has dropped over the last two years, your organization still has to have an effective strategy to stay ahead of this problem.

There are four primary situations that cause bad/undeliverable email addresses:

1. Changing email address to escape spam.

2. Starting a new job.

3. Switching to a new ISP provider.

4. Getting stuck in spam/junk email filters.

Your organization needs a policy that will deal with these, if not on a daily basis then, at the very least, on a weekly one. The same department that is handling the changes of physical addresses should be responsible for also tracking down email address changes.

I'd like you to consider the following:

- Ask alumni to provide you three email addresses, so when one is confirmed bad, you can switch to the next.

- Automatically send a postcard to alumni when the email address comes back undeliverable.

- Have alumni volunteers, students, or staff call all bad email addresses requesting an up-to-date version.

Sometimes it's better to gain an understanding of how much you are losing by not being able to reach your alumni by email. A common standard is to assume that it costs one dollar to send a letter or newsletter to your alumni. If you were communicating with your alumni twice a month (announcements of events, eNewsletters, annual giving promotions, etc.) you would save 24 dollars each year. If you have 1,000 bad addresses, you are losing $24,000 a year in savings. Viewing this situation from a monetary perspective should prove the need to invest the appropriate staff time to correcting bad email addresses.

If you have 1,000 bad addresses, you are losing $24,000 a year in savings

Does it make CENTS?

Most organizations have sophisticated business processes and budgets to identify when alumni change their physical addresses. However, many organizations have not set up similar business processes to fix bad/undeliverable email addresses. Emails have an enormous value to your organization. This includes hard savings from postage, printing, and paper costs. Each email also has a value as the more emails you have the more online contributions you will get. We can show you how each of your alumni email addresses could be worth $15 or more each year. That means each email that you don't correct, is costing you a LOT of money!

Interested in learning how you can determine the value of an email address? Take our course, "Triple Registrations in 9 months!" Visit www.internetstrategiesgroup.com and click on Courses for details.

63 LINK ALUMNI BLOGS

In the general chapter on blogs I briefly introduced the idea of linking alumni blogs, but lets take a moment to go into more detail.

You have some of the most creative alumni in the world.

Your alumni have been taught by some of the best faculty in the world and have expanded their vision and creativity. Many of your alumni are creating their own blogs based on their interests/hobbies, field of business, and/or expertise.

Bloggers benefit from their blog linked to many blogs. The more blogs that link to their blogs the better chance search engines will display their sites.

Search engines like Google have designed their software to recognize that a site that links to it from other sites must be an important site.

I'd like you to consider creating a blog that aggregates your alumni blogs. You might call it "'Mascot Name' Alumni Blogs" with the subtitle, "A premiere collection of alumni blogs."

Here are a couple of ideas to consider when building a blog that aggregates your alumni blog sites:

- Because blogs tend to focus on targeted, niche-oriented news and information areas, put alumni blogs under categories such as; art, politics, religion, etc.

- Have someone on your staff pick different alumni websites to highlight and drive traffic to their blog.

It doesn't even have to be a staff person! Consider having a couple of alumni or students handle this function for you. Many blogs are built around restating what someone says on another website and embellishing it to fit their message. Your alumni blog could highlight interesting items from other alumni blog postings, and in the process, drive traffic to them.

The benefits are obvious:

- You wind up with more content and, therefore, more reasons for alumni to visit your website.

- Alumni bloggers get another audience and possible distribution channel.

It really doesn't take that much effort. Here are some basic steps to get you started today:

- Send an email announcement to alumni telling them what you are doing.

- Collect all blog URL's.

- Create the blog and establish categories as stated above.

- Start your first blog entry with a reference to a couple of your alumni's latest posts.

You'll be surprised how easy this is and how excited your alumni will be to have this opportunity. Now that you know how to do it – JUST DO IT!

My Business

64 ALUMNI SPONSORSHIPS

I've always been a proponent of this concept, because it's a fairly effortless way for you to generate revenue to support your Internet initiative. Let's face it – money is ALWAYS going to be tight!

Presidents at most institutions are expecting your department to cut expenses or to become entrepreneurial and find a way to generate revenue. I'd like you to consider offering to your alumni an opportunity to promote their businesses and pay for it. You can use the proceeds to fund your online community. The advertising could be noncommercial, NPR-style advertising that compliments your web content and strategy.

I really think this is an idea whose time has come. Why? Most colleges are already selling sponsorships:

- Your college receives money every time your logo is used on clothing and projects.

- Your buildings draw huge fees from "naming" rights.

- Administrators strike deals to work exclusively with food and other vendors.

- You probably have affinity partners who pay you for the ability to market to your alumni.

- You have sponsors help offset the cost of events.

I originally introduced this idea in 1997 when we were building our Internet clientele and realized that alumni associations did not have the financial support to adopt online communities. I saw then, as I do now, that this can be a fantastic way to create the community, offer a service to alumni, provide benefits to the alumni association, and have it all paid for by advertising!

However, times were different then. Today, many alumni websites are receiving hundreds of thousands of hits per month. The businesses your alumni are working for will want to use this as a way to increase market share, to do surveys, or even to find new employees!

So why not let alumni advertise on your website?

As shown above, there is no philosophical reason why you shouldn't. There are countless precedents in every department on campus where advertising opportunities are used to offset costs on campus.

If you are going to do it, then do it wisely so you can generate a great deal of revenue!

It shouldn't be difficult to find alumni who are willing to advertise on your website. Let's assume you have over 10,000 alumni.

Most colleges are already selling sponsorships

Let's also assume that these 10,000 alumni work for a minimum of 4,000 different companies. Some of these companies are owned and operated by alumni. You have dentists, doctors, lawyers, and photographers who have their own businesses. You also have alumni with significant positions within the other companies.

All you have to do is send an email announcement to your alumni announcing the opportunity. I think you will be surprised by the results.

This program benefits the businesses your alumni founded or they wouldn't do it! Consider some of the following benefits:

- It builds their brand within a well-educated market.

- They can use it to attract quality candidates.

- It's an ego booster for management and alumni who work at their institution.

You can tiptoe into this market, or you can work with third-party providers who can handle the contact with your alumni, build banners to make sure they match your rules and regulations, handle billing, provide reports to customers, and handle customer service issues. You are sitting on a fantastic opportunity! What are you waiting for?

Not only will this generate revenue to enable you to continue investing in your online community, but you will find your alumni to be very pleased!

65 AUTO BIRTHDAY CARDS

Happy Birthday!

What are you doing to brighten the day of your alumni?

If you have alumni birthday information in your database, along with their email addresses, then you have a fantastic opportunity to send them a birthday card at virtually no cost.

According to the Greeting Card Association, 90 percent of all US households buy greeting cards, with American consumers purchasing approximately seven billion greeting cards each year. If you stretched these cards end to end, you could almost reach around the world 50 times! If you've considered this idea in the past, then the sheer cost of buying birthday cards, addressing them, and signing them everyday probably made you put it on the back burner fairly quickly.

However, electronic birthday cards that are automatically sent to alumni are proving to be an exceedingly popular and effective way to recognize alumni on their very special day.

Here's all you have to do.

Have your IT department create a program that runs every night, isolating alumni who have a birthday that day. The program should be capable of merging their contact information with an eBirthday card.

There are a number of options to consider adding to your program:

- Some institutions ask for a donation.

- You might provide links to websites where they can look up what happened on the day they were born.

- The program could list on your website that day's birthdays.

- The program could list other alumni that graduated near them who have the same birthday.

Birthdays are pretty special events for a lot of people. This is a great relationship-building technique. Adopting this strategy will keep you in your alumni's radar in a very effective way.

Not sure where to get started?
Visit **www.internetstrategiesgroup.com**
and click the word "Birthday" in the Net-Tips search box
to receive more information.

66 WIKIS

What's a wiki? Good Question!

According to www.wikipedia.org:

> A wiki is a type of website that allows visitors to easily add, remove, or otherwise edit and change some available content, sometimes without the need for registration. This ease of interaction and operation makes a wiki an effective tool for collaborative authoring. The term wiki can also refer to the collaborative software itself (wiki engine) that facilitates the operation of such a website, or to certain specific wiki sites, including the computer science site (an original wiki), WikiWikiWeb, and the online encyclopedias such as Wikipedia.

If you are like me, after reading the above definition, I was still confused! Let me try it again:

> A wiki is a free online software tool that will allow multiple people to post information in a collaborative manner, anytime, anyplace, as often as they wish, without one person controlling the process.

Is that any better? If not, read on. We'll look at examples of how you will be able to use wikis.

Content, Content, Content

Developing interesting and informative content is one of the key goals of any online community. For those involved in managing an online community, the key is to provide concepts, technologies, and ideas that will allow the members to participate in and then just get out of the way.

Wikis can help you do that.

The website www.wikipedia.org is a good place to start the discussion to help you understand how you can use this technology. Wikipedia is actually a volunteer online website where anyone can make modifications and changes in a collaborative online encyclopedia.

The website www.memoryarchive.org is an example of an idea you could adopt for your alumni. This website ask users to post their thoughts about places, times, and people. The idea is to let them

Create a wiki for each class and let alumni post their comments

share their thoughts about shared things. This website, for example, asks visitors to post their memories about 9/11. Individuals post where they were, who they were with, how they felt, etc. You might use this concept to give alumni the ability to post thoughts about campus life, events, activities, and classes.

The website http://www.everything2.com is a website where individuals can post material and/or information in a collaborative way to tell a bigger story. Consider doing something like this to engage your alumni to tell a story. You pick the story and alumni then continue to build on it.

Here are some other simple ways you could use wikis to engage and involve your alumni:

- Create a wiki for each class and let alumni post their comments. The wiki could include categories so they post their thoughts in "Organizations," "Events," "Sports," etc. In this example, alumni from the class of say, 1990, would see others' postings, which would give them ideas on what they wanted to share, and the site organically grows from there.

- Create a wiki for everyone who cannot attend homecoming or reunion and give them an opportunity to share their thoughts. Prior to a presentation, or during a dinner, use a data projector to project these comments for others to see.

- Create a wiki built around the football team. This might be your most popular application as fans will be able to post their thoughts in categories that might include "Referees," "Game Strategy," "Players Performance," etc.

- Wikis could also be used in this fashion by alumni who are attending your next event. You could provide them a wiki to share their memories about campus to spur discussion among them prior to coming to the event, as well as after the event has ended.

Need wiki software? There are many providers now! A Google search will give you more but here are a few to get you started:

- www.mediawiki.org

- www.wikidot.com

- www.atlassian.com

- www.snipsnap.org

Wikis may be a bit hard for you to put your arms around today, but in the future, as more examples become self evident, I'm certain you will find this technology a valuable tool in your online community.

Homecoming Networking
Reunion Football
Mentor

STRATEGY 67 FOLKSONOMY/TAGS

Ok, this one is a bit hard to understand, but bear with me and I'll make it as simple as possible.

Folksonomy is an Internet-based information retrieval technique of collaboratively produced, open-ended labels that categorize content on Internet websites. The labels are commonly known as tags and the process of labeling is called tagging.

Think of Folksonomy as a grassroots Dewey Decimal classification system for the web. It's really the "people's version" of the Dewey. Where the Dewey has rigid rules and categories, Folksonomy uses a loose, continually evolving definition of the rules that match society's current understandings and interpretation. Instead of the system following a controlled hierarchical process, it uses the collaboration of people worldwide, labeling things the way THEY think they should be labeled.

Tagging became wildly popular on sites like:

- Delicious

- Flickr

- YouTube

Within social networking communities, users can tag information so it can be associated with and readily found by others looking for the same thing. For example, in Flickr, a user may be interested in looking at all photographs with a William and Mary tag. There could be two or 10,000 photographs posted by three or thousands of alumni. You have to have some spare time when you start using tags, because you can get caught up in going everywhere and nowhere at the same time!

That's one of the attractive benefits of tags from my perspective. When added to your website, your alumni will begin to follow the tags and end up consuming the content presented, and before they know it, an hour goes by. One of the strategies I'd ask you to adopt is to find ways to not only keep alumni coming back to your website, but at the same time, to keep them on your website for longer periods of time.

Think of Folksonomy as a grassroots Dewey Decimal classification system for the web

Like Flickr, you could use tags to create more interest among your alumni in posting and viewing photographs. Let's assume you have given alumni the freedom to post photographs they had taken while they were on campus. Besides uploading the photos, you'd give them the ability to "tag" each photo. They might include the location where the photo was taken, the event where it was taken, the names of the people in the photograph, or even the state of mind they were in when it was taken!

Alumni can tag this information as they post it, or interact with it, so others will be able to find it. Click on a tag that says "Williamson Hall" and the viewer might see the hall from photos posted by ten different alumni, spanning decades. This technique also qualifies in our requirement that your website be FUN.

While your alumni will create their own labels, I'd like you to create labels to reflect the nostalgic feelings that have been felt by alumni for decades:

- We wore that?

- What a hair style!

- We had it tough!

- Instead of going to class, I…

- Extracurricular activities…

- These guys molded my mind?

Folksonomy is going to be a key ingredient in making your website fun for your alumni. It will be an important technique to keep them on your site, posting their comments, integrating their content, and searching through others.

Class of
70

CLASS PORTAL PAGE

Each graduating year is unique. Why not treat them that way?

As alumni associations move toward building affinities around the clubs, classes, majors, and interests of alumni, it still makes sense to continue building affinity around class years. The graduation year represents for many alumni a common thread that unites them all. Many colleges have developed and nurtured strong class year affinities, which show no sign of losing their appeal and potential to help the college.

Those who graduate the same year have shared experiences during their four years on campus that NO other alumni will be aware of. You need to capture these feelings early on so alumni have many years to reminisce and connect. The college of William and Mary does an excellent job of doing that. They provide a page dedicated to each graduating year that includes the events, music, movies, and other memorabilia that were unique to the years the graduates were on campus.

An easy way to do this is by creating a portal page for each graduating class. Instead of trying to do it all at once, start with a portal page for the upcoming graduation class and begin building them for the previous classes.

Some of the things you should include in your class portal pages are:

- Opinion Polls
- Photo Albums

- News

- Class Notes

- Featured alumni from that year

- Lost Alumni

- Projects the class is involved in

- Career Information

Your portal page can also include nostalgic information about the times they lived through while on campus:

- Significant movies

- Emerging actors of their day

- Bands

- Significant news and world events

- Most popular songs

Keep in mind my suggestion to build your brand around helping alumni advance their careers. Your class portal pages should continue that theme by providing an opportunity for alumni to share promotions and job opportunities, or assist in networking alumni with their firms' purchasing agents.

A portal page for each class year is helpful if you are asking class years to provide additional contributions. This is another tool that supplies unlimited quantities of content because it is your alumni who are posting the information.

While it might not make your short list, this technique is definitely something you want to adopt over time.

STRATEGY 69 ALUMNI CAMPUS PHOTOS

Earlier I shared with you the idea of scanning your old yearbooks and putting them online. Now let's consider giving your alumni the ability to post photographs they took while on campus.

It's another easy way for alumni to add content that is searchable, interactive, and visual.

Consider setting this up so alumni can add their photos by the year of their graduation. The assumption is that all photos that would be included in the 1980 photo album would be those taken that year and in the preceding three years. This would be a good application for TAGGING as we discussed in a previous chapter. Alumni could post their photo and enter tags to identify who was in the photo and where and when they were taken.

To gain maximum use and flexibility, your photo album should:

- Include the ability for alumni to upload photographs and label them.

- Provide capability for others to provide comments to the photos.

- Give users the ability to search for specific photographs.

- Include a process for viewers to rate photographs.

- Allow viewers to email specific photos to friends and classmates.

This new service will require you to spend a little time and effort marketing it to alumni, but once the message gets out, alumni will see this as a fun way to use old photographs to reminisce with each other.

This photo album should also have the ability to display the most frequently viewed photographs. Remember, users don't have a great deal of time and they want to get the best you have to offer in the least amount of time.

As we've talked about in the past, content is king. A website that only provides an online directory with tools that allow you to gather information from alumni will not be very active.

A real online community is one where users can interact with each other and the content they supply. This application is a really fun way to increase visits at your website and content at the same time.

MENTORING

Which is more valuable to you?

- The help and advice from a mentor in securing a job or handling a business issue.

  OR

- A discount on insurance, interest on your credit card, or hotels and rental cars.

If you are like most people, the help in getting a new job or advice on handling a business issue can, in the long run, have a more significant effect on your life than the discounts. However, if your organization is like most, you've had to shift priorities and adopt entrepreneurial tricks to generate money, which prevents you from focusing on programs and services that actually benefit your alumni.

I've discussed, in other parts of this book, the value of building your brand and the purpose around helping alumni advance their career and personal interests. I hope by now it's sinking in! The absolute greatest value your organization has to alumni is NOT providing a bridge to the university, or in holding events and activities, but in helping them do business with others, providing mentoring opportunities, and securing better jobs.

Mentoring is something that will benefit your students as well as your young alumni, and it will provide a sense of reward and satisfaction to your mentors.

To develop a successful mentoring program, you will need to:

1. Build a sense of responsibility to mentor within your alumni. You need to have a large pool of willing alumni to handle the anticipated needs of your students and young alumni.

2. Promote the opportunity to your students by showing them testimonials of other students who have had successful experiences at being mentored.

3. Provide easy-to-use technology that allows mentors and students to connect 24/7.

Take a moment to reflect on what resources, time, and commitment levels you are putting into a mentoring program. Does your team focus more on events, activities, membership, and marketing facets than mentoring? I'd like you to be thinking first about "what's in it for your alumni?" As you create more value in your online community for your alumni, everything you want will fall into place.

> **Mentoring is a key component of building your brand and differentiating your website**

Mentoring is a key component of building your brand and differentiating your website from third-party commercial social networking sites like MySpace, Facebook, LinkedIn, and others. You have a unique opportunity to mean something to your alumni by focusing on providing powerful and practical mentoring programs.

Looking for proven ideas?
Visit www.wiredcommunities.com
for industry Best Practices!

Raise $600,000 in less than a week
by engaging your alumni in athletic
activities worldwide!

71 SPORTS FUNDRAISING

In addition to using sports social networking software to connect and engage your alumni, you can also use it as a successful fundraising tool.

GameRaising is a sports social networking application that gives your organization the ability to bring your volunteers and supporters together to hold "mini" fundraisers based on their participation in up to 100 sporting events.

Supporters can choose the level they want to participate in (beginner, intermediate, or advanced), and they will be able to find high energy games like flag football to low/no contact sports such as golf, tennis, horse shoes, or bowling! You decide if it's a one-day, one-week, or year-long fundraising event! Your supporters could participate one day by playing golf, the next day by inline skating, and yet the next day by playing billiards.

It's easy to do!

Consider organizing an alumni sports fundraising day. All you need to do is create an integrated print and email marketing program to build excitement and participation. I would recommend that you develop a Phone Blast message with a famous sports alum and then follow up with a postcard featuring the same alumni in kind of an "Uncle Sam" look, that expresses "I want you," followed by a series of broadcast emails to build excitement and participation. Lastly, consider starting with a core of volunteers and then develop a friend-asking-friend campaign.

What's great about sports social networking is that everyone can play something! You might not be a candidate for flag football, but maybe you would be willing to play badminton. Others might not be interested in soccer but would be interested in playing pool. Got the idea? When you use sports social networking as a fundraising program, each host of a game becomes responsible for setting participation fees and collecting them from the members. Let's assume that 400 different alumni schedule sporting events around the world, and that the average number of participants was 30. If each charged 50 dollars, your alumni association would raise $600,000 for scholarships. Not bad!

The great thing about this fundraising program is alumni handle the scheduling, provide the venue, and feed their guests as part of their contribution. Plus you get alumni networking with each other in a fun and interesting way! It doesn't get much better than this!

Does this make CENTS?

This seems to be a no brainer! A sports program that results in contributions that you have limited participation in? Makes "cents" to me!

Interested in learning more?
Visit www.internetstrategiesgroup.com and click
"Sports Fundraising" in the NET-Tips search box.

72 ALUMNI BOOKS/ ARTICLES

You have many well established writers, artists, reporters, and poets.

Your website is a perfect vehicle to promote them. Search engines determine the relevancy of information by the number of references it finds on the Internet. Listing their accomplishments and samples of their work is another way to increase their Internet "exposure."

There are two primary benefits of helping to promote your alumni's work:

- They will receive more recognition.

- You get to effortlessly add their content to your website.

So how do you do this?

You'll need to have your IT team or Internet vendor create a series of tools that will enable your creative alumni to:

- Upload their poems, scripts, plays, songs, reports, photos, etc.

- Provide a summary.

- Provide links to additional information.

Additionally, you should consider giving your viewers the ability to interact with their information. Your viewers should be able to rate the information, email their friends to share it with them, and provide comments.

A theme I've tried to emphasize for the last decade is that your website has to be fun, interactive, and constantly changing. This simple tool does all that, plus it promotes and highlights the achievements of your creative alumni.

STRATEGY 73 FIFTEEN MINUTES OF FAME

You have thousands of alumni who have accomplished incredible things in their lifetimes. They have reached the pinnacle of corporate America, they have developed the stamina and physical capabilities to push the limits of the human body, and they have given generously of their time and money to help groups, organizations, and individuals in their communities.

The web provides you an easy and fun way to recognize your alumni for these accomplishments. This idea started to gel with me as I watched a college football game. College football games today are not only shown in high definition but they are also adapting the playbook of the pro games. While college football productions, in the past, have been sophomoric presentations with limited camera positions, today's college football games include the graphical glitz and glamour of professional football games. The graphics provided make the players look like they just descended from Zeus. Like professional athletes, they appear larger than life.

In the seconds between plays, graphics pop up on the screen that display the athletes like characters in well-known video games. As their image spins 360 degrees, the announcer provides details of the athlete's high school achievements, volunteerism, and usually a heartwarming story about how he helped his kid brother, stopped traffic for an elderly person, or read books at the local library.

In an effort to build more excitement and increase ratings, the networks are using technology to connect the audience to the players. This isn't just a football game anymore. This technology is enabling the viewer to bond with the players and to connect with and relate to them. It's engaging and involving the viewer, with the goal of increasing the number of overall viewers, which, in turn, increases advertising dollars.

You could do something similar with Internet technology and take your class notes to the next level. As a follow-up to my football analogy, it might sound more appropriate if I say, "This is like class notes on steroids!"

With technology, you could begin to make your alumni larger than life. Internet technology will also enable you to add sound, talk-back options, and links for more information. Here are a few ideas on how you can accomplish this:

> **One of the awardees was so taken with the experience that within 60 days, he contributed ten million dollars to the university**

- Create an online form that your alumni can fill in their achievements and attach their photograph.

- Include an opportunity for alumni to post email addresses of people and/or groups they would like notified when the story is posted.

- Design an administrative interface where volunteer alumni (or journalism/English students) can spice up and rewrite their entry so it has the excitement and presentation you are looking for.

- Create a graphic look that presents the photo and the edited story in a professional manner.

- Automate the process so the alumni and their contacts (friends, family, and colleagues) are notified of the posting of the story.

The idea is to create a system where your staff's only responsibility is to promote this as a resource for your alumni and to organize a group of volunteers who will edit and post the stories.

The benefits are powerful:

- You provide alumni with a potent recognition tool that they will share with others.

- You will see a significant increase in updates and news about other alumni achievements.

- Admissions will be able to show off successful alumni to prospective students.

I recently met with Gray Mounger, Alumni Director of California State University, Northridge. Gray holds an annual alumni awards dinner to publicly acknowledge successful alumni. One of the awardees was so taken with the experience that within 60 days, he contributed ten million dollars to the university.

You never know the effect recognition will have on others. What I do know is that this concept will give you an opportunity to recognize MANY alumni. Oh, and did I mention that they are the ones who are updating all of the content and data? You do nothing but provide them the forum to share their information!

A small investment of your time, resources, and money showing off the volunteer work, community contributions, and personal and business achievements of your alumni benefits both your organization and your alumni. I've suggested before that one of your primary goals should be to make heroes out of your alumni. By building the reputation and promoting your alumni for

one of your primary goals should be to make heroes out of your alumni

their achievements, you will help your admissions office increase the number of applications. People like to go to an institution that has produced a great many success stories.

You have thousands of admirable alumni who deserve this recognition. You'll never run out of talent to distinguish.

74 ALUMNI VIDEO CHANNEL

I can remember back in the heady dot-com days, a number of business ideas were built around creating channels of information. Companies were formed overnight using the concept of aggregating content and delivering it through niche channels. Because broadband Internet access was still years away, these organizations were delivering their content via text.

The concept of channels continued as organizations like AOL built powerful websites around interests and niches of the users. The term "channels," which is used in the broadcast world, was popular, but at a time when the Internet lexicon included "eyeballs," "sticky," and others, channels seemed to drop from press releases and daily newscasts.

However, fast forward to today and we are seeing TV, cable, and videos being distributed on the web. As more of this occurs, I am certain we'll hear entrepreneurs talking about their unique channels.

In fact, we are already seeing it. One of the more successful and popular new websites, YouTube, allows users to post videos in various channels within the site. While viewing some of the videos, it got me thinking about the benefits of creating an Alumni Channel.

What's that?

An Alumni Channel would be a web address that delivers news, information, interviews, and content built around alumni achievements, student and faculty accomplishments, and administrator news and information. While most information in the past decade has been built around text news, the Alumni Channel would still deliver interesting stories in print, but would also incorporate video and audio content.

The Alumni Channel should be promoted as the spot to gather news and information about the college, its people, and its athletic program. The Alumni Channel would have regularly scheduled programs and access to on-demand content for alumni OR friends of the college. It could even repurpose some of your faculty's videotaped lectures.

> **Your students will be thrilled to use their multimedia and interviewing skills and see their work published online**

The purpose of the channel would be twofold:

- Provide students real world experience.

- Deliver information via video and audio.

With the cost of producing video and audio so cheap, and with students who are moving into careers of broadcast and print journalism, you also have a ready-made source of talent to create the content. Three decades ago, you would have found me working on the campus radio station or getting limited time and exposure within the student TV studio. Your students will be thrilled to use their multimedia and interviewing skills and see their work published online.

There are two reasons why I recommend you create an Alumni Channel sooner rather than later:

- You need to build the behavior and start the habits now, before alumni develop loyalty and relationships with other channels.

- Broadband is opening up the opportunity to send video, not only via the Internet, but over your cell phones too. You need to be there!

Between 2005 and 2006, 25 million Americans switched from dialup Internet access to broadband. This rate is expected to increase in the coming years. By the end of 2006, broadband was expected to be adopted in 50 percent of homes across the country. As more video content is provided online, your alumni will spend an increasingly longer amount of time on the Internet. The point I'm making is that you need to communicate with your alumni the way they want to receive their communication, and you need to deliver your information where they are, which is on the Internet.

This is an exciting concept that enables your alumni to gain access to video-oriented news about the college. As time goes by, they may feel they never left campus.

It's a bit ironic that students who have embraced online communities more than others are not welcome in the alumni online community when they are students!

STRATEGY 75 "OFFICIAL" FACEBOOK & MYSPACE PAGES

Ten years ago, when I founded IAC, I spent 90 percent of my time convincing administrators they needed an online community for their alumni. A few years later, by 1998, I was suggesting they adopt online communities for prospective students, incoming freshmen, current students, and graduates. Surprisingly today, even with the success of MySpace and Facebook, nearly half of all alumni associations do not have a password-protected online community.

Alumni associations without online communities are losing a valuable opportunity to extend the campus experience to their alumni and to connect and network them with each other. What's worse is that these organizations are losing mountains of valuable data they could have about their alumni, as well as the ability to communicate more frequently with less time and effort.

MySpace and Facebook bring another set of challenges for alumni associations that do have online communities. Since 2000, I've been writing a series of reports about the negative effect of "unofficial" alumni online communities. It started with Classmates and became a significant issue as MySpace and Facebook continued to dominate the digital lives of students and alumni. It seemed to strike a cord, as over 250 alumni and admissions offices have attended our webinars that taught them the value of and how to create an "official" group page on MySpace and Facebook.

It's a bit ironic that students who have embraced online communities more than others are not welcome in the alumni online community when they are students!

You might think the word "not welcome" is a bit strong, but the fact of the matter is, for whatever campus policy, rule, or arcane argument, students are NOT allowed to participate in the alumni online community until they graduate. This exclusionary policy is forcing students to develop loyalties with third-party online communities. The end result for alumni associations is disastrous.

Since 2004, in surveys we've conducted, incoming freshman have pushed to get their .edu email address so they could register in Facebook! Focus groups we've conducted show students continue to use Facebook even after they graduate. It's not surprising. The survey we mentioned previously demonstrated that students are spending an average of 1,264 hours (or the equivalent of thirty-one 40-hour workweeks) during four years of college on Facebook!

> **Behavior – you need to think about that word long and hard.**

During that time, they are updating content that would have been extremely valuable to alumni and development offices. They are also building a strong loyalty to their site.

Behavior – you need to think about that word long and hard. If your students have not created any behaviors at updating their personal information and data in your alumni online community prior to graduation, you will have a VERY hard time getting them to do so after graduation. Ok, so I've reinforced the issues that third-party social networking sites have created for alumni associations several times now, so why in the world have I titled this section, "Build an official Facebook and MySpace page?"

It's because at this point, you have to do whatever it takes to get your recently graduated students and young alumni registered in your online community. One way you can do that is by creating an "official" alumni page on either MySpace and/or Facebook that will drive viewers to YOUR alumni online community.

Both organizations allow anyone to create a page on their site. Commercial companies are creating MySpace pages as a way to reach this highly targeted audience. Some organizations, like Apple Computer, have over 500,000 friends that connected to them via MySpace. This gives Apple the ability to send a message to their "friends" whenever they want.

You can do the same.

It's relatively simple to create an "official" alumni page on either Facebook or

MySpace. Neither should take you more than an hour to do. Once you have the page created, you will need to search on your college name and invite everyone who mentions it to be your friend. Once you get students and alumni to visit your Facebook or MySpace page, your goal will be to drive them to your alumni website.

This is a very inexpensive technique to expand your brand and use third-party websites to drive alumni to register and participate at your site. By all means – take advantage of it.

In addition, for those organizations that do have password-protected online communities, consider letting your students register in your alumni online community the day they arrive on campus. That way, you won't have to work SO hard later in getting them registered.

Not sure where to get started?
Visit www.internetstrategiesgroup.com and click on
"Facebook" in the NET-Tips search box.

Total the number of employees your college has committed to admissions, orientation, and enrollment management and then compare that to the number of employees you have committed to graduating seniors

STRATEGY 76 GRADUATION ONLINE COMMUNITY

What's so unique about your graduates?

Everything!

In his book 1996 book, *Growing Up Digital*, Don Tapscott, a noted futurist, identified that our youth would be embracing a digital lifestyle. If Don was predicting the stock market as well as he predicted today's youths' embracement of the Internet, I'd buy everything he told me. You judge for yourself from the following excerpt form his book:

> A new youth culture is emerging, one which involves much more then just pop culture of music, MTV, and the movies. This new culture in the broadest sense, defined as the socially transmitted and shared patterns of behavior, customs, attitudes and tacit codes, beliefs and values, arts, knowledge, and social forms. The new culture is rooted in the experience of being young and also being part of the biggest generation ever. But most importantly, it is a culture that is stemming from the N-Gen use of interactive digital media. We should pay attention because the culture which flows from their experience in cyberspace foreshadows the culture they will create as the leaders of tomorrow in the workplace and society.

The way you relate to your graduating students and young alumni has to be entirely different than the way you relate to older alumni. You have an incredible opportunity to develop a deeper relationship quicker with your Internet-savvy young alumni when you provide them with the communication and networking tools they are used to.

During their senior year, your graduates are getting ready to leave a place they have called home for four or more years. A place where professors have made an indelible mark on the direction these graduates are about to take. A place where new relationships were formed rapidly, and now just as rapidly are going to be left behind!

Graduating seniors have special needs. They are about to move to strange new cities and, in some cases, take the first "real" job they've ever had. Each will have to begin to figure out how to function as working professionals, when all they know is living the life of a student.

At every college and university in the world, an entire office is built around the needs of incoming freshman and transfer students. Orientation has become an entity that includes staffing and events. Administrators recognize the importance of getting students acclimated to the college and in helping them to build friends. Why? Retention! Every incoming freshman represents a pipeline of money.

Do me a favor. Total the number of employees your college has committed to admissions, orientation, and enrollment management. Now, compare that to the number of employees you have committed to graduating seniors.

When you start totaling the full- and part-time people committed to bring students to campus, and compare that number to those you have engaged in helping students in their senior year, it will probably show there is a serious lack of commitment to students in helping them get off and running in their business career. The point I'm going to drive at is that your organization spends a great deal to get your students' money, but in my opinion it is woefully underfunding supporting them as they move from students to working professionals. When prospective students and parents find this out, what signal does this send?

So what is your organization doing for graduates?

You probably have a career center for students, you definitely have a person who handles the commencement office, but what is your alumni association doing to help your graduates get through their senior year and ready for their rapidly approaching career? Have you ever surveyed your graduating seniors to see if you are doing an effective job in helping them move toward their professional career? Admissions, enrollment management, and student services survey students frequently; however, I have found few organizations that are actively learning how they can make the transition from career to business less stressful, more effective, and more rewarding financially.

In an effort to continue to build your message, your brand, to students and graduating students that the alumni office is there to help their career, I'd like you to consider creating a Graduation Online Community. Think of this as a special place that graduates can participate in during their senior year. Think of it as the bridge that leads them from the campus to their careers.

A Graduation Online Community should include practical and fun tools. Here are some of the things I'd like to see you include in your online community:

- Give graduates the ability to post comments on each other's profile page, similar to the "yearbook" signing of years ago.

- The Graduation Online Community would also deliver video presentations by experts on:

  - Networking to advance your career.

  - Tips on applying and getting a job.

  - How to use the alumni online directory and community.

- Provide relocation tools, such as where alumni can find established alumni in a community who are willing to help them get settled.

- Give them the ability to identify the kind of job they are looking for and in which states, as well as the ability to send a notice to all alumni in those areas.

- Include a page that details events, activities, photos, and blogs of their senior year.

- Include the graduation speeches and photos of graduation.

As we discussed earlier, your college has recognized the importance of providing incoming students an "orientation" toward the college experience. A vast amount of college resources are directed to them. You need to send a message to your graduates their senior year, that from the President's level down, the college will provide practical and successful tools to help them advance from job to job.

Adopting a GOC will also provide your admissions office with a powerful sales tool. Think about it. Admission counselors will be able to tell prospective students about the "special" community you create for graduates to help them during their transition year!

Your alumni association should own this space. You need to be the organization identified with helping advance their careers. The Graduation Online Community is one of the ways you can achieve this.

Does this make CENTS?

Your college invests a great deal of time and effort to provide an orientation program to your incoming freshman. You have dedicated staff and students whose sole focus is to make the transition for the students easier. Budgets provide enough money for speakers, mixers, and get-togethers and, in some cases, gifts like T-Shirts. While this was a unique time for your incoming students, fast forward to their senior year. As your seniors are breezing through their senior year, a whole new set of realities emerge. It's no longer, "Will I be liked? Will I find people like me?" Their new worries are, "Will I get a job? Where am I going to live?" You need to create an online environment that addresses their needs. Your value as an alumni association to your graduates starts before they walk across the stage on graduation day. Think a little out of the box and identify where your limited resources will best prepare your alumni for their future.

*Sure, your students know how to use
Facebook to procrastinate, poke others, and
in general look ridiculously unemployable,
but they don't know how to use online
communities to professionally network*

77 TEACH GRADS TO NETWORK

It's their senior year!

Your graduating students – soon to be alumni – are busy wrapping up their college experience and are beginning to stress out on what the future holds for them. They are among some of the brightest, most well-educated people in the world. They are experts in their areas of concentration, but the vast majorities are absolutely clueless on how to network in person and/or, for that matter, on using online communities.

As a result, they enter the workforce unaware of even the most basic networking skills such as how to:

- Introduce themselves.

- Remember the names of those who they were introduced to.

- Hand out business cards so people will remember them.

- Follow up on introductions with note cards.

When you think about it, it's really astounding that the average student leaving college has never read a book or attended a lecture on how to network. Dr. Ivan Miser is the President and founder of Business Network International, the world's largest referral organization with chapters in many countries around the globe. I was at his home one evening talking about the need for colleges to teach networking. This hit a hot button as Dr. Misner has long been an advocate that colleges should be doing more to teach students about networking BEFORE they leave college. In fact, in an article he wrote for *Entrepreneur Magazine*, he said:

> Don't hold your breath for the colleges and universities of the world to begin teaching networking and social capital. At this point, there are only two colleges anywhere that offer regular, core-curriculum college courses on networking and social capital. One is at Davis College in Ohio, and the other is at the University of Michigan. That's it.

> College systems are behemoths of bureaucracy that are so far behind the curve of small-business development that I'm beginning to despair that they'll ever catch on. Most professors have never had a real job in the business world, and they are completely out of touch with what's happening in real life, especially in **small business**.

At a recent industry conference in Singapore, I was reminded how simple networking tools, like business cards, can give your alumni an edge over competitors.

When I introduced myself to alumni and development professionals from all over Asia, I was continually impressed with how they handed their business card to me. Let me see if I can paint a picture for you.

> With both hands outstretched and their name and title facing me, they would "present" their business card to me.

This technique forced me to look at their card, read their name, and view their title. It was a simple but powerful way for me to connect a name with a face. On my 15-hour flight home, I reflected how much more effective that technique was compared to the customary "American" technique of:

- Sliding a business card across the table.

- Handing a business card with one hand.

Research has shown that business people who are continually working on building their network are much more successful than those who are not.

It's NOT what you know, it's WHO you know!

In a world where everyone agrees that "it's not what you know but who you know," you need to adopt Internet technology to help your alumni build networks of alumni who can help them get a job. Your investments in helping them learn how to build, and use, their network will also set the stage for your advancement benefiting from the contributions of successful alumni.

You can give your graduates an advantage that other graduates will not have. Teaching them the basic skills of networking complements your desire to get them registered in your online community. After all, your online directory and community is a powerful tool to assist them in networking with established alumni in addition to their peers.

> **Without these basic skills, they will never achieve the levels of success they dream about.**

Teaching graduates to network benefits everyone:

- Students become more confident and successful.

- You begin to show your graduates your commitment to help their careers.

So how do you accomplish this?

While I would prefer you adopt a more comprehensive strategy here, I realize time and resources are always an issue. Consider adopting any of the following:

1. Bring in noted networking experts prior to graduation that will teach basic networking skills.

2. Give your students any of the hundreds of networking books on the market as a graduation gift. (If you need help, I can share with you my favorites.)

3. Hold clinics on campus to show students how to network with alumni using the online directory.

4. Give your graduating students Alumni Business Networking Cards they can share with their classmates, family, and friends.

5. Provide your graduating seniors a Curriculum Vitae page they can share with employees.

Your graduating seniors are among the brightest you've ever graduated. However, without basic networking skills they will miss out on opportunities to take their career to the next level. Without these basic skills, they will never achieve the levels of success they dream about. The results are irreversible. They lose, you lose, and your development office will lose an opportunity to get a share of the wealth that could have been!

Make this a high priority as you build your Internet strategy! Adopt some basic network skill building techniques and help develop programs on your campus to give Dr. Misner some hope that American colleges are ready and willing to step up to the plate and teach their students how to network!

Not sure where to get started?
Visit **www.internetstrategiesgroup.com** and click on
"networking" in the NET-Tips search box.

INTERNET MARKETING

Marketing for alumni events and activities has been limited to whatever the budget is.

What would the effect on your events be if you had an unlimited marketing budget? You'd probably see a significant increase in participation at your events. If participation in events equates to increases in donations, then the additional cost to increase participation will pay off in the long run, right?

Yes, but you still have to get the increased budget, which is all but impossible at most alumni associations. However, using Internet technology and marketing techniques you can increase marketing without increasing your budget! The effectiveness of your Internet marketing increases significantly as you accumulate more email addresses of your alumni.

Sit down and watch TV some night and you will marvel at the number of times you see the same commercial within a two-hour period. The goal of the advertising agencies is to slam a message into your head as many times as they can. They realize they can't get their message across in 15 to 30 seconds, but giving multiple exposure to their message, and delivering it from a variety of different marketing channels, they have anecdotal evidence that supports the need to spend millions on advertising!

With Internet technology, you can adopt Madison Avenue techniques!

While your budget will prevent you from adopting all, or a combination of these marketing techniques, your steady embracement of Internet technology will give you an almost unlimited opportunity to market your large and small events.

> **Wouldn't it be amazing to have 10, 20 or even 50 more alumni attending an event?**

For most events, a postcard or flyer invitation is sent to alumni, followed by, in some cases, email reminders. I'd like you to be thinking about other email marketing opportunities.

For example, besides sending an email reminder or primary invitation, consider also:

- Using a video email message.

- Sending a Phone Blast.

- Emailing a multimedia eCard.

- Asking alumni to invite their friends via email.

- Sending animated eCards.

With the different email tools and services available today, you can develop powerful integrated marketing strategies that are guaranteed to increase participation. All it requires is a little more coordination and time involved in marketing your event. The upside is great. Wouldn't it be amazing to have 10, 20 or even 50 more alumni attending an event?

Need details on Automated Phone Calls and eCards?
Visit www.internetstrategiesgroup.com and click on
"phone" or "ecards" in the NET-Tips search box.

STRATEGY 79 BECOME A NET-CENTERED ALUMNI ASSOCIATION

Is your alumni association REALLY embracing Internet technology?

My book, *Create a NET-Centered Alumni Association* was written to provide a blueprint on how alumni associations could reorganize their alumni association around the Internet. The book provides ideas on how all departments can save money, work more efficiently, reach their goals, and work less when they adopt Internet technology.

I mentioned in Strategy 17, Viral Marketing, Tomi T. Ahonen and Alan Moore's book, *Communities Dominate Brands*, but would highly recommend you regularly read their website **http://www.communities-dominate.blogs.com** After reading their blog, you will begin to understand that a new revolution is occurring.

A statement from their book I think sets the stage for this strategy:

> If the last 10 years have caused disruption in your business, the next 10 years will cause much more so. Not driven by a controlled introduction of new technologies, but by an uncontrolled adoption of new, radical, unpredictable and even "unfair" methods by an emerging new element in consumption – the digitally empowered community.

If you are like most alumni associations then your programs, policies, and business processes have been built over the years and reflect your organization's core mission. The processes you inherited to do your job today are no longer relevant.

One area that I would love to see your board help you move your organization is toward a NET-Centered Alumni Association. What is that? It's simply an organization that focuses their organization on the application of Internet tools and services to reach the overall goals and strategies of the alumni association.

This really represents a philosophical switch as nearly every function in your office has to re-think how they do business and begin to look for ways to use Internet technology in order to be more efficient and better serve alumni.

Here's a couple of ways your organization will be thinking as a NET-Centered Alumni Association:

Marketing

A NET-Centered Alumni Association will adopt an integrated marketing strategy, utilizing best practices in mail and email marketing. Those responsible will focus more on email marketing techniques. For this person to be successful, the organization will have committed to adopt an Email Acquisition Campaign that will greatly increase the number of alumni that can be reached by email.

Events

Individuals responsible for events will look for ways that they can do their part in making the alumni association more NET-Centered. They will do this by adopting technology that will give alumni the ability to identify who they want to meet and network with at events. They will also adopt strategies to photograph alumni, post their photos, and give alumni the ability to write captions and/or comments on the photos.

Travel

Your travel team will adopt technology that will allow alumni to capture and share their trips with classmates, family, and friends back home. The technology will not only provide a permanent record of the trip for your alumni, it will provide a powerful marketing piece the alumni office can share with others to show them how much fun traveling with the alumni association can be!

Membership

To become a more NET-Centered Alumni Association, your membership team needs to adopt Internet technology that will establish members-only areas on your website. Those responsible will need to find ways to recognize members differently, and to give them advantages that others will not have. Maybe it's a more advanced career center and business networking tool. Perhaps it's number of free Alumni Business Networking Cards.

Online Community

Those responsible for your online directory will adopt the Network Weaving concept. They will utilize alumni volunteers in order to connect alumni who are not connected, as well as to connect those who want to be connected with others.

Alumni Magazine

Your alumni magazine should be integrated into your online community. If your alumni magazine is part of a different department, I would ask you to consider placing this staff under the direction of your alumni director.

Annual Giving

Your annual giving program will benefit from a strong and vibrant online community. Those involved with your annual giving program will benefit from the email addresses you collect. You will be able to add giving histories to their private profile page to increase their sense of stewardship and you will be able to show giving levels (President, Scholar, etc.). Both departments should be building strategies around your online community.

Becoming a NET-Centered Alumni Association requires everyone on your staff to focus on building your network, connecting alumni, and then showing others how alumni are benefiting from their expanding network. Becoming a NET-Centered Alumni Association means your team focuses less on what the alumni can do for the college today to, "what can we do to help our alumni in achieving their career goals?"

As a NET-Centered Alumni Association, your organization adopts a strategy that will help define to your students, your graduating students, and your alumni what you stand for. It will offset their impression that you exist solely for the benefit of the advancement of office solicitation efforts.

Interested in learning more about creating a NET-Centered alumni office? Visit www.internetstrategiesgroup.com and click "NET-CENTERED"in the Net-Tips search box.

300 online volunteers working just one hour per week will save you $300,000 in wages in just one year!

80 JOBS FOR VOLUNTEERS

At one point in the later part of the 1990's, AOL had over 10,000 volunteers who were moderating chat rooms and bulletin boards, and updating content on the website. These early pioneers and volunteers initially performed their duties out of love of the Net and interest in being a part of something really exciting and new. They were the early adopters.

To compensate and reward them for their volunteer efforts, AOL eventually gave them free Internet access. But as the saying goes, "All good things must come to an end." A group of volunteers eventually filed a class action suit claiming they were working long hours and not receiving commensurate compensation. The volunteer program eventually was discontinued.

You have thousands of alumni who could help you build and manage your online community. You have retired alumni, stay-at-home alumni, and others who may not be able to contribute money, but would love to contribute their expertise and time. You have a great many alumni who are not interested in taking an active role in running your alumni association, or in attending events or activities, but would love the opportunity to contribute/participate/volunteer on their own time, from anywhere and in an area that interests them.

So how do you begin to reach out to get volunteers and, once you have them, what do they do?

First of all, you have to identify where you need help in your online community. I've identified ten areas where volunteers can help. These include:

1. Welcome wagon greeters who show new registrants around.

2. Network Weavers to pull interested alumni together.

3. Chat and bulletin board managers.

4. Blog managers who encourage alumni to link in their blogs.

5. Alumni interested in mentoring students.

6. Alumni to help admissions recruit new students.

7. Marketing-oriented volunteers to help promote events and activities.

8. Alumni agreeing to post job opportunities within their firms.

9. Annual giving supporters.

10. Relocation advisors to help alumni settle into new cities.

Next, you have to create an online tool that will allow alumni to register for these activities, as well as tools that will enable you to manage them. You should consider including:

- Techniques that allow volunteers to report what they did.

- Capability to send targeted emails to groups of volunteers.

- Periodic communication thanking them for their help.

- Tools that will recognize volunteers.

- As alumni visit the page, show which alumni volunteers are online at that moment.

Once you've built your volunteer strategy and created the technology to engage, involve, and manage them, you are ready to get the message out and solicit volunteers. You can do that by sending broadcast emails and cards, and also by including articles in your alumni magazine and newsletters.

You already have a great deal of work on your plate and, I'm assuming, are working a 40-hour week, so if you want to create a really effective volunteer program, make sure it's maintenance free for you and your staff. One of your overall goals should be to automate your online community volunteer program so you don't have to spend the time managing volunteers.

When you consider the potential of having a couple hundred alumni volunteers doing things that you don't have time to do, I think we could do the math together that it would justify a full-time position.

Think about it this way, if you adopted ALL ten of my recommended volunteer positions and the average position attracted 30 volunteers, let's assume that each volunteer contributed only one hour per week. Do the math. Ten categories with 30 alumni each, with each putting in one hour of work per week – you end up with 300 hours of help building your community, each week, at no cost.

Now let's look at the economic value to you. Let's assume if you hired someone internally to handle these responsibilities it would cost your association approximately 20 dollars per hour. The net results! Your alumni would have contributed the equivalent of $6,000 in wages in just one week. Over the course of a year, that would amount to $300,000. If you worked for me and brought me a request to hire someone for $40,000 per year who would manage 300 volunteers who would save me $300,000, I'd approve the position right away. Wouldn't you?

Spending the time build a strong group of volunteers will enable you to accomplish more than you ever dreamed you could achieve with your web strategy. Think about how much you've accomplished as of today with the little money and the limited time you have had available to commit to your online community. Now, think about how much you could accomplish with 500 alumni volunteers!

I'd like you to focus on engaging your young alumni to volunteer. We've talked before about their frustration with not being able to contribute financially. Now you have an opportunity to give them a chance to support the needs of the alumni association by volunteering their time – by using technology that comes very naturally to them.

I guarantee that if you adopt this concept, you will reduce the stress you are feeling about having everything on your shoulders, plus you will become energized by the level of commitment and involvement of your alumni. I think this is such a critical area for you that I included this in my Top Ten Strategies.

STRATEGY 81 ONLINE VOTING

Online voting seems like a simple idea whose time has come.

If you are interested in becoming an organization that is driven by the popular vote of your alumni, then online voting is the way to go.

Online voting is:

- Instantaneous.

- Significantly less costly than paper ballots.

- Easier for the consumer.

It also gives alumni quick access to in-depth background information regarding the issue they are voting on. Online voting is also a fantastic PUSH/Pull technique that will drive alumni back to your website, and once you have them there, you can encourage them to:

- Sign up for an event.

- Update their personal information.

- Connect with friends.

Most online voting tools will only allow one vote per person and will provide documentation on who voted for what. Alumni associations we've talked with have used online voting to:

- Elect board members.

- Determine how to spend money.

A few have used online voting to help the organization determine if they should change their mascot. Controversial topics will significantly increase participation.

Does this make CENTS?

I'm continually surprised to hear alumni association who are hiring companies to create ballots and send them out to alumni. The costs are staggering. Not only are they paying for the postage, paper, printing, and management fee, there is no guarantee alumni will take the time to fill them out. Alumni are busy and for most, the ballot gets stuck in a "good intentions" file until it's too late to send it in. Your organization could save thousands of dollars by accepting only votes online. Alumni who want a paper ballot should be told to call and request one. I know that sounds cold, but it's a good way to force them to register and participate in your online community! Make "cents"?

82 ALUMNI BOARD TECHNOLOGY

As your board members become more Internet savvy, it only makes sense to help organize the information you provide them and the responsibilities you assign to them with Internet technology.

If you think back to prior to 2000, you had to send packets of information to board members via mail. Not only was it costly, but it was time consuming to send the documents by priority delivery. Gradually, the time and cost to do this decreased significantly when you, or others, started sending the information to everyone by email.

Now the natural evolutionary progression is to provide more sophisticated tools that automate the task of informing and managing your board. You could do that by adopting a password-protected board online community where your board member can:

- Read documents.

- Collaborate on documents at the same time.

- Vote for issues.

- Post their opinions and respond to others.

- Use online conferencing tools.

- Take part in surveys.

- Receive private information for board members only.

By including RSS technology, you can feed news stories from annual giving, the President's office, athletics, and other departments so your board page becomes the one-stop place for all news that will help them formulate their opinions.

Not only will this concept save you time and money, but in the long run it will:

- Result in more informed board members.

- Require less time of your board members and your staff.

Adopting Internet technology to better manage your board is another step in "working smarter, not harder." You deserve technology that will reduce the "details" that keep you from introducing ideas that will take your alumni association to the next level.

83 COMPREHENSIVE ALUMNI INTERNET STRATEGY

Ah, where do I begin with this?

Creating a comprehensive alumni Internet strategy is probably the FIRST thing you should do, even before you buy or create your online community. In the decade I've worked with alumni professionals, I've noticed the trend is to buy the online directory/community software without knowing what to do with it.

Committees who evaluate various vendors tend to focus on what the software does and how it works, but invest little time or discussion in developing a comprehensive written Internet strategy. It's not unusual to see a committee that includes IT, Public Relations, Advancement, Alumni Relations, and Annual Giving involved in evaluating the software necessary to create an online directory and community. Evaluating three different vendors could easily involve nine to twelve hours per person. It's necessary to do, but organizations should also be committing the same resources to create the strategy on what they want to do with the technology.

To develop a written Internet strategy, your team will need to hunker down and put an equal amount of time in determining what you want to accomplish. You need to collectively build answers to the following questions:

1.   Do you have a written Internet strategy?

2.   What percent of your alumni base is registered in your online directory?

COMPREHENSIVE ALUMNI INTERNET STRATEGY

3. What percent do you want to have registered in the online directory over the next three years?

4. Have you crafted a plan to increase the number of alumni registered in your online directory over the next three years?

5. Do you have a strategy to get your graduating seniors registered in your online directory?

6. What strategies have you developed to make students aware of the benefits of the alumni online directory?

7. Is your college considering adopting "Collegiate Student Online Communities"?

8. Do you place a value on each email address you collect, and if so, what is the value of an email address to your organization?

9. Have you developed an Email Use Policy for your campus?

10. What have you budgeted to spend in marketing your website to your alumni each year for the next three years?

11. How many staff hours/positions do you intend to commit to your Internet strategy over the next three years? Identify the names of the positions, the responsibilities, and the year you intend to fund the position(s).

12. What processes do you employ to fix bad/undeliverable email addresses?

13. From your perspective, what benefits do your alumni receive from your current online directory and community?

14. What do you think has been the most successful part of your current online directory?

15. What do you think has been the least successful part your current online directory?

You can see these questions are not simple things that can be answered quickly. They require the careful deliberation of your entire team. And these are not the only questions that need to be answered. Press me for more and I can give you another 100 questions that will help you define your comprehensive Internet strategy.

In order to create a comprehensive Internet strategy, a number of different departments should be included. My recommendations include:

- Alumni

- Advancement

- Annual Giving

- Admissions

- Athletics

- Student Services

In order to create an effective integrated strategy, I see four steps as necessary. The first step will be for the individual departments to get together to begin to craft their own Internet strategy. As a starting point, your groups will want to answer the following questions.

- What do we want to accomplish?

- What can we do to help other departments on campus reach their goals?

- What are our goals and benchmarks?

- When do we expect things to be accomplished?

- Who is responsible for each activity?

- What additional staffing and financial resources will be needed to reach the goals over the next three years?

The second step will require your department heads to meet with leaders of other departments in order to review their individual department's strategy, and to identify points of intersection where they can help each other reach their goals.

The third step involves each department reviewing how other departments want to integrate their strategies with their department's strategy.

In the fourth meeting, your department heads will finalize their strategy, create the benchmarks, finalize the responsibilities they have to each other, and set a time to meet in six months to see how the strategy is working.

Without a plan, your Internet strategy is barely moving forward. Yet this is a time when your alumni's expectations are expanding at a surreal rate because the companies, organizations, and industries that support them are moving fast to better serve them, while at the same time cutting costs and increasing revenues. They also understand that the more data they gather about your alumni, the better they will be able to serve them and retain their business.

You need to be there to match their expectations and their changing behaviors in order to reap the rewards of more communication at less cost, more data gathered, and more involvement overall.

While each department's strategies are going to be different, I highly recommend that your alumni strategy include the following:

1. Email Acquisition Campaign

2. Bad/Undeliverable Strategy

3. Website Registration Campaign

4. Career Development Strategies

Creating your Internet strategy takes some time and effort, but the time spent will not only be fun, it will provide significant payback in the coming years. You will never reach the level of ROI you should if you don't have a plan. This strategy is so important that I included it in my Top Ten Strategies.

Does this make CENTS?

Think about what your strategy is right now. Think about what you've accomplished without an Internet strategy. With a written Internet strategy your Internet site will deliver more contributions, more registrations, more participation with less hassle and stress by your staff. In my book, that makes a lot of "cents." You know the old saying, "Pay me now, or pay me later." Without a strategy, you will waste time and money and could make costly wrong decisions.

Want to do it right? Visit www.internetstrategiesgroup.com, click on Courses, and sign up for "Create a Comprehensive Internet Strategy."

84 RECOGNIZE COMMUNITY SERVICE

I've had the wonderful opportunity to visit hundreds of campuses around the world.

It's always exciting to see the facilities and physical environment that defines the campus. But equally exciting for me is to be able to see the moral, spiritual, and philosophical standards and goals that each college creates.

One that I hold dear to my heart is a college's focus on community volunteering. I've noticed some colleges offer suggestions on how much time students should commit to community volunteer projects, while others have set specific time requirements as a part of the graduation requirements.

Regardless of which category your organization falls into, you could be using Internet technology to:

- Increase participation in community service.

- Increase awareness of your college focus and commitment on volunteering.

- Provide recognition to students and alumni.

It's relatively easy to do.

Using Internet technology, you could bring together your students with those in the community who are in need. Think of it as kind of an auction. Your community members who need the volunteer time/help of your students post their opportunities, and your students who need to fulfill their requirements at community services offer to help them out. Once it's set up, you get out of the way and let everyone find each other.

Think of creating an online Community Service Online Community where:

- Individuals and organizations can post jobs/help they need.

- Students can identify areas they are interested in volunteering.

Properly configured, your online community will alert students when an individual or organization has a task that requires their skills. And on the flip side, when a student registers for the very first time, organizations and individuals are alerted to the student's availability.

The Community Service Online Community would, of course, maintain a record of all activities. Individuals and organizations that are identified as receiving a large amount of attention and time from the college campus might be able to help the college in other areas. Students who are putting in more time than most can be given recognition for their involvement.

Students could also use their record of involvement as another tool to show why they would be the right candidate for the company they would like to work for.

85 ONLINE DATING

You are in a perfect position to be a matchmaker! Why not take advantage of the opportunity?

Fifty percent of all marriages end up in divorce court. That means the majority of your alumni will find themselves single and looking for a significant other again. I'd like you to consider thinking about how you can help your alumni who are between relationships not only meet others, but also provide them tools on how to effectively date others. Scary thought?

The online dating industry is a billion-dollar industry. Most online matchmaking websites are mammoth online communities of people, many who represent themselves as something they are not.

The benefit you provide is that your alumni will know they are connecting with educated people who ARE who they say they are! Your online directory will only admit known alumni and graduates who have attended your institution. Because they have classmates who know who they are, your online community has a higher degree of "truth" built into it. If someone starts going overboard and putting information about themselves that pushes the edge, they risk the reprimand and ridicule of classmates who know of them that will bring them back to reality.

While your alumni online directory doesn't have to be a full-scale online dating tool, it can be designed for only those who want to opt in to it.

Here are a couple of ideas on how you can begin to take this need and provide a real service to your alumni.

Modify your directory so alumni can identify:

If your alumni marry, you have a better shot at getting their entire estate!

- Sexual Orientation

- Relationship Status

- What type of social relationship they are looking for.

Include additional tools that will enable alumni to link videos of themselves. Additionally you should:

- Develop an online affinity group built around singles.

- Use volunteers to organize singles-only alumni events locally.

I'm looking to:

- Develop business relationships.

- Find a compatible person.

Additionally, for those who are interested, consider offering a distance learning course on not only how to date, but the most effective way to use the online directory to date.

There are a couple steps you'll need to take to get this project off the ground:

- First, you'll need to make minor field modifications in your registration form to enable alumni interested in dating to find each other.

- Secondly, you'll need to find faculty who would be interested in developing podcasts and in holding webinars on dating and relationship techniques.

Internet dating sites are filling an important role in helping people find others with similar interests, hobbies, and career goals. You have a unique opportunity to bring together alumni who share similar experiences, education, and expectations – and they have an opportunity to develop new relationships. Your online directory offers a safe environment where your alumni have the confidence to know that the person they are talking to is a graduate of your institution.

Still not sure? Why not ask your alumni? Send a survey to get their opinion. You might be surprised on how enthusiastically they respond!

Does this make CENTS?

If your mission is to help network your alumni, helping them find a future mate is probably just as important as helping them find a better job. There is another benefit from helping your alumni connect with fellow alumni. If your alumni marry, you have a better shot at getting their entire estate! Your advancement office might have to compete with their kids or other nonprofits, but they won't have to compete with another college for a portion of the estate! Your institution ends up with more "cents" this way!

86 OPPORTUNITIES WITH YOUTUBE, FLICKR, MYSPACE, FACEBOOK, ETC.

Content is King!

The Internet is giving everyone an opportunity to be a publisher of whatever they want to publish. Your younger alumni and students are beginning to understand the power of sharing their content, and they have rapidly adopted this concept.

Some of the sites where they are sharing content include:

- www.flickr.com   Photographs

- www.youtube.com   Video

- www.myspace.com   Photographs and Video

- www.facebook.com   Photographs and Video

Younger alumni are changing their entertainment habits as a result of these websites. This normally "unprofessional" content, of which there is so much, is occupying some of the time they would have spent watching TV, reading, or other forms of traditional entertainment.

There are a number of ways to use commercial websites to build affinities around your alumni and continue to drive them to your website.

Flickr, for example, allows you to build a Flickr group photo album around your college or alumni association. Your alumni will be able to post their own photos, and you will be able to build interest among other Flickr users to post their own photos. Another nice feature of online websites like Flickr is users can tag photos with keywords like:

- Reunion 2003

- Class of 1995

- Tri Towers Hall

- "College Name" Yearbook Staff

A search will find all photos with the same tag. Flickr and other sites also provide slide shows of groups of photos, and alumni can post notes (comments on their photos), and others can leave comments about the photo. Once your alumni understand how to use something like this, they will continue to load in their photos, which will provide more content that others can view.

YouTube allows you to post any video of any length you are willing to upload. YouTube also would enable you to build a sense of community around your alumni and their videos. You can easily create YouTube groups for your college and invite your alumni to link their videos.

While I would prefer that you develop your own services that will capture the photos and keep your alumni on your website, third-party providers can be valuable tools to utilize until you have your own technology in place.

If ten of your incoming freshmen were recruited by alumni, assuming your tuition is $30,000 per year, your alumni association will have delivered $1,200,000 in tuition revenue over four years!

87 ALUMNI STUDENT RECRUITMENT

Your alumni are busy people.

Few have time to call or visit prospective students, but those who are tethered to their computers for work, information, and entertainment will find it easy to volunteer to recruit students for you. Even though they are busy, they, like you, have learned to multi-task. By providing them easy to use online recruitment tools, you'll find your alumni will not only locate the necessary time, but they will look forward to the task at hand.

With a son now looking for colleges, I'm getting a firsthand view of how colleges are marketing to youth today. Out of a dozen colleges who are sending letters, postcards, emails, and view books, only one college has had an organized program that sends personalized letters (testimonials) from their alumni. This midsize private college sent a series of letters over a couple months. It's a nice touch, but it had little influence on my son. First of all, the letters were too long. Students are not used to reading letters, and while the testimonials were well written and compelling, they didn't communicate in the medium in which teens listen today.

Broadband is rapidly changing the way this generation is using the web. Content in writing is getting less attention as video is becoming easier to produce and distribute. Instead of having alumni send a testimonial letter that gets two seconds of the prospective student's time, a video of the alumni, interviewed at their office, at a club, at a ball park, riding their bike, hiking, lecturing, or doing what they were educated to do, will go much further with this generation.

Let's look at some Internet techniques you can adopt that will make it easier and more effective for your alumni to recruit students.

- Use online submission forms for alumni to recommend to prospective students to receive information.

- Create a follow-up system that alerts the alumni when the material is sent.

- Provide a feedback system for the alumni to update the results of contact with the student.

- Have admission counselors use the information to set in motion a series of additional personalized points of contact.

- Use student talent to do a series of "YouTube" interviews with alumni about why they chose the college and the benefits received.

Your alumni are among the most powerful recruitment tools your organization has. Few admission offices are fully exploiting them. Prospective students today want to know what their education will do for them. Prospective students today are anxious to know what their future holds for them. Giving them more access to your alumni, who once had the same fears and worried about the same issues, to show them what they can be, is priceless.

Your admissions office is rapidly losing the ability to control their message. Today, they are faced with third-party blogs by students or individuals who are interested in dissing your college. Their comments from other students who are looking at colleges are sadly making a dent in how students make decisions.

My point is simply this: if you present this plan to your admissions office, they will GLADLY pay for it. In fact, paying $15,000 a year for you to drive students their way is nothing for the admissions office. If you deliver one extra student via your alumni recruitment program, they will have gotten their return on investment the very first year, and they will make money. Then they have the next three years to benefit from the yearly tuition the student pays.

At most private institutions, this could be $30,000 a year. Not to belabor the point, but the help your department provided to acquire that one student will result in over $120,000 in tuition over the life of the student. Imagine if you deliver ten students a year. Their combined value to your college in tuition payments would be 1.2 million dollars!

Don't forget to develop a way to recognize alumni for their help in recruiting students. Develop a list that shows who has interviewed the most prospective students, who has forwarded the most number of leads, and who has emailed students who were interested in learning from alumni what their experience was at the college. Make a big deal about the number of students your alumni recommended, who actually attend the college. Find a way to show the value of their help by using the tuition dollars that the student will pay over four years.

Let's assume John Q. Smith recommended ten prospective students to the college and five of them enrolled. In this example, with John Q. Smith delivering five new enrollees in just one year at $30,000 each, the value of the four years of tuition his students will deliver represents $600,000 in revenue to the college (based on a four-year college education). That's huge!

Recognition is a powerful way to keep alumni engaged and involved in this. For alumni who want to give back to the college, but may not have a big wallet, this is a great way to thank them.

Be a hero with your admissions office and work together to develop alumni and Internet technology to ensure a steady supply of freshmen students. Use this approach to get additional funding from admissions to help you continue to improve your online community for your alumni.

Everybody benefits! The more alumni you get registered and participating in your online community, the more prospective students they will recommend.

Does this make CENTS?

Your admissions office is spending anywhere from $500 to $2,000 to acquire each incoming freshman. Your alumni should be part of the student acquisition team. Properly set up, your alumni can get everything they need from online and the support they need from your admissions office. If you move in this direction, you should have your admissions office "pay" you for your help.

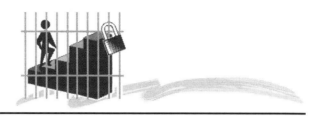

88 MULTILEVEL SECURITY

When you build your online community, you need to think about controlling access to specific areas.

In building hundreds of online communities, IAC has encouraged clients to keep much of their community open to friends of the university, parents of prospective students, parents of currently enrolled students, and community members. This is vital, because you want the general public to be able to see you have vibrant and active alumni association. As you are building your online community, you should be thinking of the different layers of security that your site may need. Here is a list of typical "roles" or layers of security you should consider adopting.

- Public

- Parents

- Students

- Alumni

- Dues Payers

- Board Members

- Chapter Administrators

- Office Administrators

- Super Administrators

Areas of your website like events, class notes, photo albums, alumni blogs, books, websites, and news should be available the public. You want prospective students and parents to see that things are happening, that your college has a vibrant and supportive alumni association.

You might have a Parent Online Community only parents have access to, and if you are a dues-paying organization, you might have provided areas ONLY for your dues payers. For example, dues payers may be the only ones who can send eCards or download screen savers.

Another important note:

Put all of your alumni data behind secure servers!

To further protect your alumni data and information, consider putting your alumni personal data behind secure servers. When they enter the online directory area, for example, the web address will change from: http:// to https://. This is similar to what you see when you enter your credit card number at a secure online site. This extra level of security will encourage alumni to share more data and additional information.

Looking for proven ideas?
Visit www.wiredcommunities.com
for industry Best Practices!

MERGING YOUR MAGAZINE INTO YOUR COMMUNITY

Does anyone read the alumni magazine?

It depends on who you ask. Some will tell you that their alumni consider it one of the more valuable services provided by the alumni association. Others will shrug their shoulders and admit they just don't know. From my perspective, if the alumni magazine is the most important service your alumni association provides, then your alumni association is losing touch with reality!

Over the last 50 years, alumni associations have developed sophisticated alumni magazines to keep alumni informed about accomplishments and needs, and to nurture a nostalgic feeling. Along the way, the budgets grew, the number of editions grew, and at the same time, it became increasingly difficult to identify the return on investment of the magazines.

If the trends that are now occurring in the commercial newspaper and magazine industry are any indication, today is a good time to re-evaluate your alumni magazine strategy.

Here are a few of the things my research is showing:

- Newspapers are continuing to cut staff because advertisers are switching their investments to online advertising opportunities.

- Young alumni prefer to get their news online.

- Magazines are losing subscribers who are getting their news online.

- Readers prefer shorter stories. They don't have time to read long and in-depth articles.

While most of us in the alumni industry would have thought those with college degrees would be more likely to read newspapers and magazines, research is proving a growing majority of college educated people PREFER digital news and information. You don't have to do a lot of research to see and understand the trends.

I'm a big proponent of immediately beginning to integrate your magazine content online and in beginning to reduce the number of magazines you print and mail. When you integrate your alumni magazine with your online community, you can also add technology that will enable alumni to:

- Rate the story.

- Forward it to a friend.

- Add personal comments.

- Email the author directly.

Plus, because of the web you can:

- Post longer versions of the story.

- Add sound and video.

- Include more photographs.

Integrating your alumni magazine into your online community will save you money and it will give your alumni many more ways to interact with the content. This is always a good thing!

Does this make CENTS?

Tens of thousands of dollars, if not hundreds of thousands of dollars are being invested in the alumni magazine. Yet the commercial news industry is facing record falloff in readership and advertising and as a result they are cutting expenses and migrating their publications online.

Take the total you invest in your alumni magazine per year/divided by the number of your alumni. Now do the same for your investment in your alumni online community.

Not sure where to get started?
Visit www.internetstrategiesgroup.com and click on
"magazine" in the NET-Tips search box.

STRATEGY 90 PROMOTE CREATIVE ALUMNI

One of the strategies I'd like you to integrate into your online community is recognizing alumni for their creative achievements.

Too often, we only take the time to recognize "significant" achievers. We recognize the politicians, CEOs, and significant volunteers. We tend to overlook the hundreds, if not thousands, of truly creative alumni who labor at their art to display an outward expression of their vision.

If you are like most colleges, you have an departments in art, theatre, architecture, and other creative divisions. Each of these have produced an enormous number of alumni who have produced incredible works of art, have written songs, poetry, books, scripts, and plays. These truly talented alumni have created amazing products of art, without the satisfaction of being recognized or having the receipt of feedback from others.

You can deliver a worldwide audience to your artistic alumni and, at the same time, provide them additional recognition when you adopt an Alumni Creative Works Gallery. An Alumni Creative Works Gallery is an online gallery where alumni can:

- Create a profile page providing background information about themselves.

- Post their work within specific categories.

- Upload photos of their work and provide written and audio comments about it.

- Identify if the work is for sale and what the cost would be.

Viewers should be able to:

- Search for specific types of art or artists.

- Post comments.

- Rate each piece.

- Purchase the work.

- Send an ePostcard to friends showing the artist's work.

- Communicate with the artist.

- Personalize the site to alert them when new postings are made.

Your Alumni Creative Works Gallery should also include an Artist of the Week feature. This could be done by simply linking to the profile page of the artist or by a blog article. I would strongly recommend you build a blog in your site that can be updated by a series of volunteers. These volunteers will be responsible for reviewing the artist's work, lifting their awareness, and suggesting alumni take a look at them.

You have to RECOGNIZE in order to receive!

Depending on the time the faculty are willing to put into this project, technology is available where they could do podcast interviews with alumni. These interviews could range from reminiscing, to serious discussions about art, and to the influence of others on the work by the alumni.

Part of your job as an alumni professional is to give alumni as many "15 minutes of fame" as you can possible create. Alumni who feel good about themselves, who recognize the alumni association as an organization who is helping them become more known and recognized for their achievements, will be more willing to support the needs of the college. You have to RECOGNIZE in order to receive!

This is another area you should not have ownership of. Your role is to reach out to your deans and get their buy-in. Once you get it, it should be their responsibility to promote to their alumni, populate the area, and then manage it. You might suggest that the deans locate students who would be responsible for managing and maintaining the website.

Not only will they get "real world" experience as curators of the online museum, but they will also have an opportunity to meet other artists who have already made their way in life, but, at one point, walked the same paths on campus that the students presently are.

Your job as an alumni professional is to connect alumni and to recognize them for the valuable contributions they have made. Providing an Alumni Creative Works Gallery will go a long way toward accomplishing that.

91 PROMOTE MERCHANDISE

Want to sell more merchandise?

You can't sell a lot of merchandise when your alumni have to click five times to find the merchandise page. Retail sales are all about convenience and impulse. Think for a moment on how stores strategically place items in the check out area. Their experience shows that while you are standing in line, you will be tempted to pick up a few more items.

You have to think about your online merchandise strategy the same way. Merchandise has to be front and center on every possible page of your website, not just in a special section titled "merchandise." Your website needs to capture the attention of your alumni as they are wandering around so they are driven to see more products.

Here are a couple of ways you can do that.

On the front page of your website, consider putting a small 1 x 2-inch column that shows a couple of the leading selling products. Let's assume they are water bottles and baseball hats. A typical viewer may see the brightly colored items on the front page but may not order them.

On the next page they click to, in the same area of the page, they see a T-Shirt and duffle bag. Then on the next page of the website, again in the same corner of the page, they see a book and a pen set with the college logo on it. As they say in the industry, "The third time is the charm." It might take a series of enticements to get your alumni into the buying mood, but when you do, they will click on the items and end up in your online storefront.

Not only will it brighten up your website, but it will produce more spur-of-the-moment sales. This technique will capture compulsive shoppers, plus it will make your alumni more aware of the different merchandise available to them.

If you are not sure, consider modifying, at the very least, five main pages on your website with this concept for holidays, especially at the end of the year. I guarantee you will sell more merchandise! When you do, don't forget to send me a check for helping you out!

If you want to market effectively on the Internet, you will have to produce as many contributions as you can.

Marketing on the Internet,
Michael Mathiesen

STRATEGY 92 — EPHILANTHROPY TOOLS

Your alumni are giving online at record rates.

Nonprofits are leading the way in this area after experiencing the public embracing that occurred online in the giving to support relief efforts for natural disasters in 2005 and 2006.

Giving online is easier and faster for contributors. For nonprofits, it's significantly less costly to acquire and process an online gift. But more importantly, studies are showing that online contributors tend to give more. Annual Giving programs are not yet aligned around this strategy. They question I need to ask you is, "Why not?"

For the most part, this is because there has not been a great deal of experience within the industry. Most are just beginning to understand the benefits of adopting ePhilanthropy tools. For example, alumni tend to give more when they donate online, and in addition, collecting the money is faster and cheaper. When alumni enter their credit card online, the money shows up immediately in the bank! That means it will end up costing less time and money tracking down the pledges.

It wasn't that long ago that administrators and the general public debated about accepting credit cards online. Today, industry professionals are trying to figure out how to take advantage of contributors' changing behavior.

We've recommended to clients over the last decade that both online giving and the online community need to be tightly and carefully integrated. The online community has to FIRST deliver unique services and benefits to alumni and SECONDLY serve your organization. Screaming DONATE HERE buttons send the WRONG signal to members of your community. You have to include subtle, unique ways to build their sense of stewardship.

Plus, you have to work closely with your annual giving and advancement office to develop an integrated online giving strategy. Both of these departments need to have a full understanding of the power and the potential of the web in order for them to recognize why they should be partnering with you. Each needs to understand that you can integrate their requirements with alumni, and that they can do so with relatively little effort.

So, how can your online community do this subtly? Let me show you ten ways:

1. Include your alumni's giving history within their private profile page.

2. Show your alumni giving "category/level" on search results pages.

3. Give alumni the opportunity to tell "why" they gave.

4. Let alumni challenge their friends to give.

5. Create class gift pages to show who in a class gave.

6. Give alumni the opportunity to identify what categories they would give to.

7. Automatically remind alumni when it's annual giving time again.

8. Give alumni the ability to thank other alumni who have contributed.

9. Use Google maps to show who is giving in your area.

10. Show videos of students who have benefited from giving.

Build your own strategy on how to integrate your online community and your giving strategy. You can adopt one, two, or all ten ideas. Take the first step to create a strategy. Show your advancement staff how you can benefit them. One of my firm's smaller private college clients, for example, has received over $200,000 a year in unsolicited online contributions. Even if your online community resulted in $30,000 in unsolicited online contributions for your advancement office, a percentage of those were a result of compulsive reaction to the opportunity presented and would not have contributed through the traditional channels.

You should consider negotiating with your annual giving and advancement team to pitch in and pay at least $10,000 to $30,000 of the costs to maintain, market, and improve your online community. Again, everyone benefits from this process. The more alumni who register and sign up, the more contributions the annual giving and advancement will receive.

Interested in learning how you an introduce Internet tools
and strategies into your annual giving program?
Visit www.internetstrategiesgroup.com
and click "Giving" in the Net-Tips search box.

93 ATHLETIC AFFINITY

I've talked about strategies to involve faculty, students, administrators, alumni and other departments like admissions, but we've not talked about strategies to involve your athletic department.

When you think about it, a good portion of your alumni have either participated in athletic teams, or they have attended athletic events as spectators. So we have to find ways to use Internet technology to give this group an opportunity to reminisce and share nostalgic memories.

Here are a few ideas to kick around:

- Create a photo album and ask alumni athletes to post photos they took while on campus.

- Build affinity "club" pages around each sport.

- Have your students interview past athletes.

- Invite alumni to have photographs taken at events with past star athletes.

The photo album might be a good first step as it's one of the easiest technologies to add to your website. Once you add the photo album, your next step is to invite alumni to dig up their old photographs and upload them for others to see. Make sure you add a photo album that will allow alumni to post comments.

Your goal should be to enable viewers to interact with the photos and with each other.

Building an affinity club page around football, soccer, wrestling, and other sports is a fantastic way to engage alumni around the friends, relationships, and sports they participated in or supported. The affinity page should include a personal photo album, opinion polls, news, and other community-building tools. This is a powerful affinity group that will enjoy having their own "corner" of the website to connect with each other.

I always look for ways to give your students real-world experience while, at the same time, recognize the creativity, achievements, and talents of your alumni. Think about how you can use students who are studying journalism, public relations, and related professions to interview past athletes and produce video, audio, and/or text content to share with others. When you do things like this, everyone wins! Not only do you get content on your website without doing anything, but your students get "real-world experience" and your alumni receive recognition that will leave them blushing with pride.

Having grown up in the photography industry, I've learned the power of photographs and I love the opportunities that digital photography provides. Consider, at the next football game, inviting back a well-known alumni who starred in the sport to take a digital photograph of them with anyone who is interested. This is a neat PUSH/pull technique that will bring people back to your website to look at their photograph. You should set this up so they can print the photograph to their printer. Value-added benefits like this will impress your alumni and provide them with "positive" feelings about the college.

Because this benefits their career, charge
30 dollars to participate. Assuming you have
20 participants per session and you have 100
sessions per year, this program could deliver
$600,000 in revenue!

STRATEGY 94 FAST NETWORKING

One of the ways you can differentiate your alumni online community from the hundreds of others available to your alumni is to focus around helping them do business with each other.

Adopting Fast Networking techniques would help you show your alumni that you are doing just that. This is an interesting new technique that helps business people to network with others quickly. Built somewhat on the framework of "Speed Dating," where you have about five minutes to meet and interview prospective dates, Fast Networking techniques allow business people to share what they are looking for, or what they have to offer, to groups of people with little effort.

Think about the time and effort that is required to get someone to an event or activity. If you've worked in sales and marketing, you know it takes hundreds of phone calls to find a prospect, and then it takes another 20 calls to bring the customer on board.

Fast business networking is a way you can help your alumni:

- Find a product, service, investor, and/or investment.

- Cut down on the time and expense of acquiring customers.

So how does this work?

Your alumni would simply fill in an online form that would provide detailed profile information about themselves, what products they offer, what products they need, etc.

- They would be invited to a session with about 20 others.

- Each would be given two minutes to explain what they do and to indicate how they can help others.

- The software will let them submit questions to each presenter.

- They can elect to do business or to share leads with each other.

Because this benefits your alumni's careers, you could charge 20 to 30 dollars for each participant. Assuming the software is automated, this program could develop as much as $600 per session held.

I've suggested that part of your mission as a NET-Centered alumni association is to help alumni do business with each other. This technique goes a long way in sending the message that you are working on their behalf to help them advance their careers. It should be no surprise that the more you help them, the more they will help you when you have needs!

95 USE ONLINE AUCTIONS

Online auctions can be a great deal of fun for you and your alumni.

If your organization already has an auction on campus, consider adding an online version for alumni who are not able to come to campus. Online auctions have become so easy to use that millions of people of all ages are using eBay on a regular basis. eBay users understand that auctions provide them an opportunity to save money, make money, and to develop a "niche" collection of "whatever," or just simply to have fun. Even my 13-year-old daughter uses eBay to sell clothes she's grown out of. It makes me wonder if Goodwill has much of a future!

A number of online auction tools are on the market for you to choose from. A simple search on "online auctions" will give you plenty of research information to sort through. You will find providers who will:

- Host your auction.

- Allow you to be a part of their auction.

eBay has an option where your group can set up your own online auction. You can use their infrastructure, software, and payment system and collect the vast majority of the money. It's a great deal.

Auctions can be pretty easy to set up. If alumni are donating content, you can have them upload photographs, enter the information, and set minimum bids. Auctions are good PUSH/Pull techniques. Most software will alert your alumni when someone has bid higher than your bid. The alert pulls you back to the website.

Your major responsibility will be to update both the content and the information for the auction. Some tools allow your alumni to describe the item they are offering to auction and to upload the photographs. These same tools will remind the alumni to whom to ship the item.

This is another area where you don't have to take on this responsibility. I'd suggest you run a couple of articles on your website and send out a broadcast email looking for a volunteer who is familiar with online auctions and who can coordinate your upcoming auction.

In reviewing the tools that are available, I'd advise you to find one that requires the least amount of time and effort by you.

96 BEHAVIOR ANALYSIS

While it's important to analyze which parts of your website are getting the most use, or how long alumni are staying on a page before they exit it, or simply to see how many visitors you are getting each month, I hope I can convince you that it also makes sense to examine what your visitors are NOT doing.

Depending on the type of software you are using, you may have the opportunity to isolate alumni who have, for example, read a class note but have NOT posted a class note. By examining their behaviors, you will begin to learn how to engage and involve them.

In an example like the one we just shared, you know the alum is interested in hearing what others are doing. However, they either felt they had nothing to share or they were intimidated to share it. Knowing who viewed class notes gives you the ability to craft a targeted email that coaxes them to post a class note. By using simple data mining techniques like this, you can also find everyone who viewed the homecoming page, but failed to register. A carefully written email, or even a phone call invitation from a volunteer, may be all that is needed to encourage them to attend.

You could use this technique for everyone who has looked at a profile page, but has not posted a photograph. Or consider identifying everyone who has read information about annual giving but has not contributed.

Other areas include:

- Those who have looked at job posting but have not posted their resume.

- Alumni who have viewed the "Be a Mentor" area but did not sign up.

- Alumni who have updated their information but did not post a photograph.

You can also use this technique to find others who are heavy users of your site so you can:

- Thank them for their participation.

- Ask their opinion on how to improve the site.

- Ask them to be volunteers.

Some of the ways you will find out if they are "heavy users" include:

- Identifying alumni who have performed the most directory searches.

- Alumni who have posted the most class notes and/or photos.

- User who have sent the most eCards.

Taking the time to get to know who your users are, what they are doing on your website, and then thanking them, will help you continue to improve the experience for your users.

As your online community strategy continues to focus on what your alumni are doing, you will continue to find unique ways to personally engage them.

Looking for proven ideas?
Visit **www.wiredcommunities.com**
for industry Best Practices!

97 BANNERS

A re you using conventional marketing techniques to promote the services within your online community and events?

One easy and powerful technique to achieve this is to adopt banner advertising. Banner ads can be easily created to:

- Increase participation at events.

- Increase registration in the online directory.

- Remind alumni to update their personal information.

- Drive alumni to different parts of your website.

- Increase participation in annual giving.

I'm not talking about screaming ads offering ten percent off, but highly professional ads that compliment the design of the website. Take a cue from public TV and radio ads – low key and noncommercial.

The nice thing about using banner ads on your website is that you will be able to track how many times your alumni clicked through them. Over time, you'll begin to see a trend on what wording, colors, and styles get the highest click-throughs.

98 LIFETIME EMAIL

During the four years your students are at your college you provide them with a personalized email address. In order to participate with online classroom tools, many colleges require the students to continue to use their assigned college email address. Ironically, nearly all colleges begin the process of cutting students off from their email address soon after they walk across the stage on graduation day.

There are a couple of options available to you. You could provide mail forwarding only or web-based email. The email forwarding is the easiest for your college to do as it does not involve storing the emails. A software program requires your alumni to identify what their current email address is and anytime they use their college email address, it will show up in their current email address. The only risk is that the alum changes their email address and doesn't update the college website. Not updating will prevent people from reaching the alumni via the college email address.

The other option is to offer web-based email for your alumni. Web-based email is like gmail, yahoo and hotmail. Today they are fully functioning email tools that enable your alumni to check their email from any computer in the world. With the popularity of gmail, web-based email has increased in popularity.

Providing your graduates with an college email address they can use for the rest of their lives has a number of advantages.

- Alumni have to reach a portal page to pick up their email.

- A portion of your alumni will love the "vanity" of having their college email address.

- Alumni will be able to use the email address when searching for jobs.

The portal page that provides them an entry point into their emails can include daily news and information about your alumni association. The more they use their lifetime emails the more news you can deliver to them.

Having a college email address is like having a vanity license plate. Not only does it identify who you are but it shows where you've been. Alumni proud of their college and their degree will recognize this small gift as one that just keeps on giving.

One of the best reasons to provide alumni a lifetime email address is to help them get a job. Think about it. When your alumni are out of work all they have is a personal email address. Quite frequently personal email addresses are a funky combination of information that, well frankly at the time it might have been humorous to the alumni but when using it for business purposes it might not be the right idea.

If you are not currently providing your alumni lifetime email addresses, you should consider it. Not all alumni will use the service but those who use it will be reminded of your college every day.

STRATEGY 99 GRADUATION PHOTOGRAPHS

My biggest fear is that your graduates and young alumni will be so locked into using social networking sites like MySpace and Facebook, that they will not register in your alumni online community.

In a day and time when your graduates are more preoccupied with Facebook and MySpace, you have to find a hook or technique to get them to register in your online community. Once such hook could be as simple as importing the photo taken of them as they receive their diploma on graduation day into their profile page.

More than likely, your college has a photographer that is utilizing digital cameras to photograph your graduates when they receive their diplomas.

I strongly suggest that you approach the department responsible for hiring the graduation photography company PRIOR to the signing of the NEXT contract. Discuss with them how important it is to negotiate a deal where the photographer will provide your institution with a copy of the digital photograph of each graduate. In this way, you can upload the photo into the graduate's private profile page for a reasonable price. The photography company will probably want to wait until they receive their initial orders from students before allowing the photographs to be posted online.

Not only is this a fun way to get your graduates back to the website to see the photos, but you'll benefit from the required change of postal and email address information they'll have to input in order to view the photo. Additionally, you will have the ability to print name tags using their graduation photograph for future reunions.

Before you try this, make sure your IT team has the expertise to match the right photograph with the right person! The last thing you want to have happen is to mismatch the graduates' photographs.

If you are looking for a way to bring your graduates back to your website immediately after the graduation to network with each other, or simply to stay connected to the university, this is an idea you will want to emulate.

Your core competence is alumni relations, not creating online communities. You and your staff would benefit from bringing in outside experts to provide consulting, training, and guidance to prevent you from making costly mistakes.

STRATEGY 100 TRAINING FOR YOU AND YOUR STAFF

There are four specific reasons that alumni online communities are failing today. Most do not have:

1. Enough staff & resources.

2. A comprehensive written Internet strategy.

3. Educated staff on what to do.

4. Training for their alumni on how to use the community.

By now you have realized that you can't develop a comprehensive Internet strategy without a better understanding of what you want to do, or more to the point, what you CAN do. The Internet, for the most part, is a relatively new phenomenon that few organizations have any expertise with, or for that matter, any understanding of what to do with it. If I asked you what your core competence is, what would you say?

I would assume that you would identify your core competence as engaging, involving, connecting, and communicating with your alumni. Not developing online communities. I've spoken to at least 100 organizations that have developed online communities with the help of their IT departments. Nearly all of them felt that the online community they offered was not matching their alumni's expectations. They felt this way because participation rates were ridiculously low. All were struggling with what they needed to do to increase participation. Because the online community was developed in-house, the changes and modifications to the community, such as those I've identified in this book, take a back seat behind 80 other departments who need the IT department to make urgent fixes or improvements to their software.

However, there are a number of ways that they, and your organization, can increase participation and registrations in your online community. Each center on providing expertise and training that is not found within your department.

Let's take a look at the five areas you can effectively train yourself and your staff:

Consulting

Over the years, those involved in annual giving and capital campaigns have partnered with consultants to provide expertise they didn't have internally. Not that they should, but at many organizations the alumni director is also in charge of annual giving. As this person is stretched to the legal limits of their capacity, a lot of money remains on the table because they have not been able to introduce proven best practices adopted by their peers.

Courses and Training

Courses are now available through a variety of organizations to help your team gain a better understanding of what they could be achieving with their Internet strategy. The Internet Strategies Group, as an example, provides a series of courses that individuals can take whenever they want, to give them the expertise and understanding of what others are doing, of what works, what doesn't work, and to mold this knowledge into an Internet strategy that will benefit your organization.

Discussion Groups

Your team needs to belong to bulletin boards and discussion groups focused on providing online communities. This includes commercial online communities too! If your alumni association is going to be a player in the online community business, you need to have staff that will 1) have the time, and 2) have the interest to participate with these groups. They need to join online communities centered on things that interest them, as well as communities like Facebook, MySpace, and YouTube, just so they can be aware of what services their alumni are being offered.

Read Blogs, Reports, and Books

Your team also needs to use RSS feeds to stay alerted to industry blogs like www.wiredcommunities.com that feature three different organizations each week who are innovators in using Internet technology to better serve their alumni.

Conferences

Conferences are another great place to get institutional knowledge developed by colleagues in the industry and/or outside experts. In the course of a few days, a few of your team will be able to pick up a number of great ideas. However, I caution you to not put all of your resources to conferences. Think back to the last conference you attended. Within two days, you probably attended at least eight break-out sessions, three that had really great ideas you wanted to implement. Unfortunately, by the time you got back to your office, the realities of deadlines, meetings, and emergencies quickly displaced the fire you had in your belly to adopt the ideas you learned at the conference. As the days turned into weeks, the ideas, the how to's, and your plans faded into a distant memory…until the next conference reminds you.

If you are serious about developing a comprehensive Internet strategy, you need to outline a process to train and educate your staff. You should also determine, and set aside, a budget for over three years that will enable you to bring in consultants that will help you and your team stay on track. The payoff and the rewards will be tremendous! A three-year commitment will not only get you where you want to be faster, but you will put less stress on your staff and generate a higher return on investment.

You and your staff deserve to know more and to have access to industry training. This is so important that I included it as one of my Top Ten Strategies.

Does this make CENTS?

What's your core competence? Where did you and your colleagues pick up your knowledge and expertise on developing and managing your alumni online community? As an organization that represents an educational institution I know you believe in education and training. However, have you stopped to think what kind of training your institution has offered you to help you manage and develop the most important alumni technology in the history of your organization? I can assure you the IT department and others are spending massively to train their staff. You and your colleagues deserve more training. Not only will it take the mystery out of developing and managing your online community, it will save you "cents" and your senses in the long run!

WEBINAR
LECTURE SERIES

What if you had a chance to go back to college and listen to your favorite subjects again?

As time and distance moves you further away from campus, the desire to learn and explore new subjects doesn't diminish. In spite of billions of facts and information now available to us via the Internet, your alumni are showing they are interested in participating in the traditional lectures on subjects ranging from law to outer space!

I'd like you to consider adopting an online lecture series that delivers lectures to your alumni in a variety of subjects and topics. The program could be designed so alumni would be able to listen to the lectures on their computers. These live sessions may also be recorded and archived for future use or to have posted on your website.

By adopting a lecture series, you will not only generate a revenue stream by charging for participation if you choose, but you will provide a unique "virtual bridge" back to campus to reconnect alumni, satisfy a thirst for learning and reignite their sense of nostalgia.

There are many benefits to adopting your own online lecture series. Your faculty will enjoy having the opportunity to spread their wings and offer to their former students' refresher courses or updates on research they are doing.

There are four benefits of adopting a lecture series:

1. You connect alumni to YOUR college as well as others with similar interest

2. The series will generate additional revenue for your alumni office

3. Your faculty will receive additional recognition on campus and afar

4. A more connected alumni - is a contributing alumni!

There are four distinct ways to offer this:

1. Provide general interest lectures

2. Offer lectures focused in individual disciplines like art, business, law, engineering

3. Provide interviews of successful alumni

4. Offer interviews of campus professionals, athletes, coaches etc

You will be hard pressed to find a more cost effective way to gain all of these benefits!

> To learn more about online lecture series,
> visit www.internetstrategiesgroup.com,
> and click on "Back to Campus Lecture Series"
> in the NET-Tips search box

SUMMARY

Overwhelmed yet?

I hope so! If you aren't, I haven't accomplished my goal of proving to you that your investment in online community software represents only ten percent of what you should be investing in your Internet strategy.

To gain the full value of your online community, you must:

- Create a written Internet strategy.

- Bring on additional staff in the form of volunteers AND paid staff.

- Commit more resources to market your website.

- Continue to expand services within your community.

I've offered many arguments on why your college should be providing you more resources to build your online community. I've shown you how to create a written Internet strategy so you can request more funding and staffing to execute your plan. You've read how to develop a beautiful plan that shows a remarkable ROI. And, I've shown you 101 proven strategies that have worked for others.

We've discussed at length that NOW is the time to act. Your alumni are savvy Internet users and are joining many different online communities. If you don't move today, you will lose a once-in-a-lifetime opportunity to engage your alumni in your online community – so this means you should act now!

Under your leadership, your alumni association can become an increasingly relevant association to your alumni that will have a powerful effect in future annual giving and capital campaigns.

Thank you for taking the time to read this book. I encourage you to continue to expand your knowledge, and that of your colleagues, through online training, webinars, conferences, and by visiting www.internetstrategiesgroup.com!

TEN CATEGORIES TO FOCUS ON!

By now, you have a better understanding of what you need to do to create your own comprehensive Internet strategy. You can pick and choose the strategies you want, or you can engage in an aggressive campaign to adopt strategies that will help you achieve your goals in specific categories. For example, you may want to focus this year on communication. The chart below will give you all of the 101 strategies that will help you do that.

You will find some strategies will be listed in multiple categories:

Category	Chapters
Fun	1,6,11,13,15,24,32,42,47,48,59,65,73,85,90
Registrations	2,8,14,19,25,28,41,50,62,87
Participation	5,17,18,31,37,40,46,83,97
Career Networking	4,10,13,35,38,59,77,80,94
Data Collection	14,39,43,49,62
Content	5,6,7,9,11,15,26,29,32,33,34,73,74,75,99
Communication	16,17,19,29,46,52,55,75,78,89
Networking	4,10,13,23,35,38,59,77,94
Young Alumni	10,23,24,29,38,47,50,59,76,77,85
Strategy	2,3,4,8,19,25,26,44,58,78,83,100

Write down what you want to accomplish, when and who is responsible!

Your comprehensive Internet strategy will take time to develop. That's no excuse for going slow, but a statement to remind you to create implementation phases that give you, your staff, and your alumni the time to absorb the new services and innovations. Use this form to organize your thoughts.

Phase One   From ___/___/___ to ___/___/___

	Strategy	Who's Responsible	Goals
1.	_____	_____	_____
2.	_____	_____	_____
3.	_____	_____	_____
4.	_____	_____	_____

Phase Two   From ___/___/___ to ___/___/___

	Strategy	Who's Responsible	Goals
1.	_____	_____	_____
2.	_____	_____	_____
3.	_____	_____	_____
4.	_____	_____	_____

Phase Three   From ___/___/___ to ___/___/___

	Strategy	Who's Responsible	Goals
1.	_____	_____	_____
2.	_____	_____	_____
3.	_____	_____	_____
4.	_____	_____	_____

Phase Three   From ___/___/___ to ___/___/___

	Strategy	Who's Responsible	Goals
1.	_____	_____	_____
2.	_____	_____	_____
3.	_____	_____	_____
4.	_____	_____	_____

ACKNOWLEDGEMENTS

In the past decade and perhaps longer the following people have been a part in helping develop the information you are reading or played a key part in helping along my journey to become more "NET-Centered. My thanks to all!

Allison Garcia	Christine Curry	Edward Cain
Angie Moneypenny	Cindy Filler	Elizabeth Williams
Anne O'Donnell	Cindy McClanahan	Emma Conway
Annette Levitt	Coralee Holm Zizza	Eric Tammes
Ashlee Ilg	Curtis Rodgers	Erin Hovey
Aziz Raad	Dabney Philabaum	Evon English
Barbara Burke	Dan Johnson	Gae Philabaum
Becky Dostie	Daniel Saevig	Gail Dancer
Becky Smith	Dave Daywalt	Gary Overmoyer
Ben Chalot	David Roloff	Geoff Harrington
Bernie Schneier	Dean Hart	Gregory Kozick
Bill Outhouse	Debbi Eckroad	Hoyt Smith
Brad Luczywo	Deborah Corasio	Isabella Cota
Brenda Hartman	Diana Schumacher	Ivan Archer
Brenda Narducci	Dianne O'Connor	Jacqueline Manser
Carolyn Young	Dodd Snow	Jane Findling Burton
Catherine Cala	Donna Chase	Janice Corbett
Cathy Fresch	Donna Worley	Jean Wilczynski
Chris Austin	Doug Hubert	Jeff Rhodes
Chris Weaver	Doug Smith	Jen Renallo
Christine Bradbury	Duane Wiles	Jennifer Patton

Jennifer Smith
Jeremy Keas
Jeremy Rufener
Jeri Allphin
Jessica Litwin
Jill Keogh
Jim Coll
Jim Davis
Jim O'Hare
Jim Porterfield
Joanne Courville
Jodi Swartz
Joe Smith
John Erstling
John Hatton
John Kane
John McCreery
John Narducci
John Rose
John Skeriotis
Jose Gonzalez
Joy Wagman
Julie Bressor
Julie Morgan
Julie Mullin
Julie Purcell
Karen Fitzgerald
Karen Galentine
Karen Zuchowski
Kate Cipriano
Kate McClintock
Kathryn Meyer
Kayla Price
Kelly Brennan
Ken Arrant
Kier Selinsky
Kirsten Philabaum-
  Barrett
Kris Smith
Kris Lensmeyer
Kyle Dick
Larry Arps

Larry Powell
Laura Chaney
Laura Hanes
Laura Hooper
Laurie Schaibly
Len Gruver
Lewis Denbaum
Linda Oliver
Lisa Kolb
Lisa Miller
Lisa Mrazik
Liz Zupher
Lohit Vijaya Renu
Lois Goblet
Luisa Tam
Lynsey Flage
Mae Suramek
Mandy Ferrington
Margaret Pomfret
Mark Shardlow
Marla Partrias
Mary Moore Morgan
MaryKay Maclver
Melisa Parkerson
Melissa Mourer
Melissa Nederostek
Melissa Williams
Michele Potter
Michelle Pilak
Michelle Suarez
Mike
Monica Woods
Natasa Pajic
Nick Moulakis
Nick Nazarian
Nicole Ryan
Nicole Totans
Pam Driscoll
Paul Koonsman
Paula Lee
Peter Poulsen
Phyllis Rodgers

Rachel Puckett
Rachel Ronning
Reveremd Andrew
  Newberry
Rita Gullion
Rita Kroeber
Robert Paczula
Robin Summers
Russ Figueira
Sam Bennett
Samantha Church
Scott Erskine
Scott Lange
Sharon Howard
Shellie Hadvina
Sheryl Sheatzley
Stefan Davis
Stephen DeSalvo
Steve Spry
Steve Stomer
Steve Zohn
Steven Diguiseppe
Sue Hatos
Sue Owen
Sue Warren
Susan Hopkins
Susanne Starck
Suzanne Clark
Suzanne Sullivan
Sylvia DeValut
Ted Randall
Tenneil Moody
Thomas Enalfarb
Todd Taylor
Tom Cassidy
Tom Costigan
Tracey Duncan
Tyler Bowen
Vanessa Fiery
Wanda Rutledge
William Gross

ABOUT THE AUTHOR

Don Philabaum

Don Philabaum founded IAC (www.iaccorp.com) in 1995 to provide online communities to groups and organizations. Today, his firm provides password-protected online communities and ePhilanthropy tools to 200 organizations around the globe. Don has written three books, *Create a NET-Centered College Campus*, *Alumni Online Engagement*, and *Create a NET-Centered Alumni Office*. He has also written numerous reports and white papers about social networking communities such as Facebook and MySpace.

Don created www.wiredcommunities.com to recognize alumni and development professionals who have implemented successful Internet ideas and strategies. His talks, books, reports, and white papers suggest that alumni and advancement professionals need more staff and resources to develop an Internet strategy that matches the expectations of their alumni. In 2006, Don founded www.internetstrategiesgroup.com, a consulting division of IAC, to help alumni and advancement professionals develop achievable Internet strategies for their organizations.

Don also authors the blog www.onlinecommunities.com to provide business and organizations ideas on how they can use new media tools to better serve customers and increase profits. Don enjoys sharing this information at industry conferences by providing keynote or session presentations. You can reach him directly at dphilabaum@gmail.com.

Made in the USA
Lexington, KY
13 December 2016